Jesus of History, Christ of Faith

Saint Mary's Press
Christian Brothers Publications
Winona, Minnesota

Jesus of History,

Christ of Faith

by Thomas Zanzig

Revised Edition

Large cover photo:
The Judaean wilderness
Front cover, inset photo:
The upper Jordan River

Imprimatur:
† Most Rev. John G. Vlazny, DD
Bishop of Winona
19 November 1991

The publishing team included Julia Ahlers and Barbara Allaire, development editors; Stephan Nagel, consulting editor; Susan Baranczyk, copy editor; Amy Schlumpf Manion, editorial assistant; Barbara Bartelson, production editor and typesetter; Mary Duerson Kraemer, indexer; Penny Koehler, photo researcher; Evy Abrahamson, page designer and illustrator; Ken Call, illustrator; Mapping Specialists, Ltd., mapmakers; and McCormick Creative, cover designer.

The acknowledgments continue on page 301.

Printed in the United States of America
Printing: 6 5 4 3
Year: 1998 97 96 95 94
ISBN 0-88489-273-5

Contents

1

The Search for Jesus:
Sources in the Christian Testament and Beyond

ONCE when Jesus was praying in solitude, and the disciples were with him, he asked them, "Who do the crowds say that I am?" They said in reply, "[Some say] John the Baptist; others, Elijah; still others, 'One of the ancient prophets has arisen.'" Then he said to them, "But who do you say that I am?" Peter said in reply, "The Messiah of God." [Jesus] rebuked them and directed them not to tell this to anyone. (Luke 9:18–21)

"Who Do You Say that I Am?"

His Early Years

Nearly two thousand years ago he was born in poverty. The magnificent paintings of his birth by countless artists, the inspiring sound of Christmas carols sung by choirs, and brightly wrapped presents under decorated trees tend to mask the fact that his real "birth-day" was very humble.

He was raised in the obscure Galilean village called Nazareth, in Palestine, a country no bigger than Massachusetts. The names—*Nazareth, Galilee, Palestine*—sound remote, strange, distant, as do the names of so many towns and villages that have become famous chiefly because of their association with him: *Bethlehem, Cana, Bethany, Capernaum.*

He was the son of a carpenter, and he trained to be a carpenter himself. Today, TV commercials proclaiming the glories of new power tools and the helpful services of the local hardware store make it difficult for us to understand and appreciate the particular joys and challenges of carpentry two thousand years ago. How much we think we know of him; how little we really do.

We know very little about his early life. Most of what we claim to know is drawn from our understanding of his Jewish roots, from our knowledge of the historical circumstances of his time, and from the recollections of people upon whom he made a powerful and lasting impact. We can only speculate on what he looked like, the types of people he associated with as he grew, the kind of education he attained.

Nevertheless, our strong impression is that we know him well. His face is, after all, recognizable in literally thousands of paintings, films, and statues. All of the images of him are different, yet all of them look vaguely similar. The stories surrounding him have become as familiar as reruns of old favorites on television.

Many people think that his profound ideas came easily to him—certainly without a need for formal education. Somehow his having to go to school strikes us as almost humorous, even ridiculous. How much we think we know of him; how little we really do.

His Public Life

We have only a brief and somewhat confusing record of what is called his *public life,* which started when he was about thirty years old. He almost seems to have come out of nowhere, taking the people of his time by surprise. His people, the Jews, had waited a long time for someone to claim what he would claim—that he was "the One sent by God," who was to free them from their oppression. Yet when he was among them, many of the Jews rejected him. He was so unlike what they had hoped for and expected.

In some respects, his public life seems to be as cloudy and vague as his early life. For instance, he may have been a public figure for as little as six months or for as long as three years. The few written records we have of his life and work—what we

Most of Jesus' public life was spent in Galilee, and in the towns around the Sea of Galilee.
Photo, facing page: The sun sets on the Sea of Galilee.

call **Gospels**—seem so often to conflict with each other on the details of his actions and words that some people choose to reject them as unreliable, even as fables and fairy tales.

In his own time he was most often regarded as simply a teacher, yet his "classroom" varied from the formal setting of Jewish houses of prayer and worship to crowded and dusty streets, from peaceful lakeshores to rolling hillsides. His basic message as he delivered it might well fill only a small pamphlet. Yet library shelves today groan under the weight of thousands of books that have attempted to "simplify" and to explain that message. He felt his message was so simple that even children—perhaps *only* children—could quickly understand it. It was a message about a good God and a proclamation of unlimited love, of generosity, of a world of peace, of brotherhood and sisterhood. It was a message of hope in the midst of despair, of joy beneath the tears and hunger, of freedom from the chains of oppression, of life in the face of death.

The man who preached that message of unbounded hope, of unquenchable joy, of profound liberation and abundant life, was savagely executed on a cross by people he had somehow frightened. The glorious vision he offered had become for some people a horror show. His words of love and joy and peace had become for some a threat, even a curse. How could this happen? How much we think we know of him; how little we really do.

No Time to Mourn

Like so many great leaders throughout history, he was fully appreciated and understood only *after* his brutal death. That in itself is not unusual. We humans often seem to appreciate wonderful gifts only when they have been taken from us, to experience deep love when the ones we love are absent,

to recognize great people when death snatches them from us. John F. Kennedy, Martin Luther King, Jr., and John Lennon were all relatively young when assassins' bullets brought them down. Our human inclination in such cases is not only to mourn the loss of what once was, but also to ache for what might have been—the promise that might have been fulfilled, the wisdom that might have been shared, the talent that could have been tapped, the songs that could have been sung.

But with *this* young person, this man from Nazareth nearly two thousand years ago, the response was strangely, mysteriously different. Following his death there was barely time for grief and no time to write an obituary. All the talk of "what might have been" had just begun when a shocking message rang out across the land: "The one whom you have crucified has been raised by God and is now alive!" That proclamation changed the course of history, shook the world at its foundations.

And yet, in cathedrals and churches across the world today, that message of joy, which has transformed the lives of so many people throughout the past twenty centuries, is often received with a yawn, with boredom, with apathy. We have, after all, heard it before. How much we think we know of him; how little we really do.

Who Is This Man?

Nearly two thousand years have passed since the days when "the carpenter's son" walked the roads of Palestine, and still we must ask, Who is this man? He was given many titles during his earthly life—*teacher, rabbi, prophet*—and still we must ask, Who is this man? We need to constantly seek out new answers to that question, primarily because of what people claimed about him *after* his death: that he was raised from the dead!

Illustration: **How much we think
we know of him; how little we
really do.**

the world as **the Christ,** the Anointed One sent by God to redeem the world from sin. Many people are very familiar with stories about Jesus and with explanations of his message that the *church*—the whole community of believers gathered in his name—has developed through the years. Some of these people, certainly, find deep joy in their faith and consider Jesus and his message the very center of their life. But for many others, matters of faith and religion have become routine and boring; these people have lost the sense of joyous surprise that can be a part of their experience of Jesus and his message. Why is this so? Perhaps the name *Jesus* and the title *Christ* are *too* familiar.

Perhaps we do not know as much as we think we do.

Jesus and You

In the scriptural passage that begins this chapter, Jesus asks two questions of his disciples. His first question is, "Who do the *crowds* say that I am?" The disciples tell him that they have heard many answers: John the Baptist, Elijah, or one of the ancient prophets. Then Jesus makes the question more personal, more direct: "All right, that's what everyone else has been telling you, but now what about you—you as a free individual, you as an adult who must think for yourself? Who do *you* say that I am?" This question posed by the historical Jesus years ago is the same one that Jesus, now recognized by Christians as the Christ of Faith, sets before each new generation.

And what about you? Upon what foundation or basis are you to make judgments or decisions about Jesus? For perhaps fifteen or more years, you have been hearing what the "crowds" have to say about Jesus—from your parents, from the pulpit in your

The titles he then received—*Lord, Redeemer, Savior, Son of God, the Christ*—come so easily to us now that we have lost touch with what they mean. We fail to realize how haltingly these titles must have been uttered by those who first spoke them. We forget that many people throughout history have endured torture and execution with these words on their lips and joy in their hearts. How many throughout history have fallen to their knees with the overwhelming realization, "My God . . . he's God!"? Yet how many "put on" their faith in him with the same sense of routine they have when putting on a well-worn shirt? How much we think we know of him; how little we really do.

Not as Much as We Think

This is a course about a man from long ago, the son of a carpenter from Nazareth, the one called simply Jesus in his own time but who is now recognized by more than a quarter of all the people in

---

Illustration: **The resurrection of Jesus gave his followers hope that they too could be transformed to a new life.**

parish, from teachers. You may have been expected, largely because of your age, to accept their conclusions without explanation of how they had arrived at them. When you asked, "Who is Jesus?" you may have been given a number of answers: the Son of God, who died for our sins; a great miracle worker and healer; a teacher of marvelous truths.

When you were a child, such responses may have been adequate. But that may no longer be the case. As you have grown, you have likely had new questions to ask and new answers to find about Jesus. There comes a time in everybody's life when they must freely choose the values, ideals, and beliefs upon which they will base their life. If you are going to make a mature decision about your own response to Jesus, you will most likely need more information. The purpose of this course is to provide information, so that you can discover for yourself an honest, mature answer to the question, "Who do you say that I am?" **1**

A Look Ahead

In General

This course is an attempt to offer you sound information about Jesus, as clearly and directly as possible. However, it does not begin with the conclusions about Jesus that the Christian church has reached over the process of two thousand years of study, reflection, prayer, and historical experience. Rather, this course begins at the beginning, starting with the earliest sources we have for understanding Jesus: the Christian Scriptures—and more specifically, the four Gospels of the Christian Testament.

By exploring these basic sources, three main questions can be addressed:

1. Who was the historical Jesus, the man who lived nearly two thousand years ago in a place called Palestine?
2. Why did this man, Jesus, come to be recognized as the Christ of Faith?
3. And perhaps most important of all, what does it mean to call Jesus by this title, *Christ of Faith?*

Only through the perspective of the Christian Scriptures can we begin to get a clearer, fuller picture of Jesus. Only in this light can we understand the early church's teachings about Jesus the Christ, as well as understand how the church's current teachings about Jesus have developed from the early foundations.

More Specifically

The early part of this course will focus on the historical, cultural, and religious background of Jesus, which can make his story and the impact of his message in his own day more interesting and

---

1
Imagine that right now Jesus confronts you with the question, "Who do you say that I am?" Write your honest response to that question.

Photo: **Up to this point in your life, many of your ideas about Jesus have probably come from the preaching you have heard in church.**

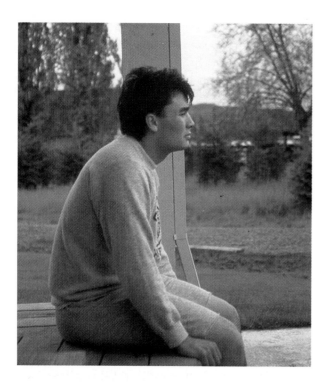

understandable for us today. This early material will also include an overview of *how* to understand the Christian Scriptures, and specifically the four Gospels, as sources of information about Jesus.

After providing this background information, the discussion will move on to the life, ministry, and message of Jesus as they are described in the pages of the Gospels. The middle chapters of this course will highlight the core of Jesus' message, his proclamation of what he called the *Kingdom of God*. Also, these chapters will look at his sometimes confusing stories and his even more challenging actions, including his miracles. Finally, this material will explore the most emotionally charged parts of Jesus' story: his brutal execution by crucifixion and his wondrous resurrection—the event that caused the earliest Christians to recognize Jesus as "the One sent by God."

In the last three chapters of this course, the focus will shift to some of the earliest teachings about the meaning of the proclamation that Jesus was "the One sent by God." Chapters 11 and 12 will cover what Saint Paul, one of the most influential people in the history of the entire church, taught about Jesus, especially in his letters to early Christian communities. The course will conclude with a chapter that briefly reviews the church's evolving understanding of Jesus through its long history of some two thousand years.

No Need to Make Up Your Mind

One thing to be clear about from the start of this course is this: Even after the whole discussion of Jesus and his message, you need not come to some definite conclusion about your response to him. The intent of this course is *not* to convince you that you must believe in or accept Jesus. That is a deeply personal decision that only you can make, and you may need years to come to some conclusion. What is hoped is that this course can be a valuable aid for you as you work toward that conclusion.

For Review

- What sentence is repeated several times throughout pages 7–10? What point is the author trying to make by repeating the sentence?
- Jesus' followers responded to his death differently than people have responded to the deaths of other great leaders throughout history. Why was this so?
- What three main questions will be addressed in this course?

Photo: **Belief in, or acceptance of, Jesus is a deeply personal decision. You may need years to find your own response to Jesus' question, "Who do you say that I am?"**

How Do We Learn About Jesus?

At first the question, How do we learn about Jesus? may seem like a fairly easy one, with an obvious answer. But in fact, in the search for a mature understanding of Jesus, this initial question is about as critical a one as we can encounter. If the sources that provide the foundation of our understanding are shaky and questionable, then everything we build upon that foundation will be uncertain and easily disproved or uprooted. If our foundation is solidly and clearly constructed, however, we can pursue the search for Jesus with confidence and conviction. 2

Faith Sources

How do we, today, come to understand Jesus? A logical response might flow like this:

Many of us, first of all, learn about Jesus from our parents and others close to us. But how did those people learn about Jesus, and what makes their understanding acceptable and trustworthy?

They probably learned about Jesus from their own parents, of course, and also from parish communities and their leaders—from pastors and other priests, from teachers, from other laypeople, and so on. But this answer again leads to another question: Where did all those parish communities and all those teachers and others get their information?

A little reflection turns up a good answer: Those parishes and their leaders received their information from the bishops and the pope. But the full answer still eludes us. Where did the bishops and the popes over the last two thousand years or so get all their information, and how do we know

that all the things they have taught about Jesus are reliable and worthy of our acceptance as truth?

The questions seem to be getting tougher, but we can come up with another answer: Church leaders commonly look for guidance from men and women who have devoted their life to the study of church history, the Bible, and other sources of information about Jesus. Those who concentrate on studying the Bible are often referred to as *biblical scholars;* those who study the history, beliefs, and teachings of the church are called *theologians.* But do these people just come up with their own opinions about matters of faith? How do we know they can be trusted?

Well, throughout the years, the scholars and theologians have based their understandings of Jesus on the teachings of the Apostles and the experiences of the early followers of Jesus.

Clearly, we are getting close to the roots of the matter. But some final questions still confront us:

- How did the Apostles and those who walked with, listened to, and learned directly from Jesus pass on information and insights about him to the members of the early church?

Before reading further, write a brief response to the following question: *How can we be sure that what we are taught about Jesus is true and not just made up?*

Photo: **Many of us first learned about Jesus from our parents.**

- How have the information and insights been accurately preserved over the last two thousand years?
- How can we, *today,* get in touch with those very early teachings about Jesus and compare our own understanding with them?

In other words, on what solid information can we reasonably build an understanding of Jesus, so that we can make a mature and solidly based decision about him?

There is, it seems, only one real answer: We must turn to the same foundation upon which all of the popes, bishops, scholars, and other believers through the years have ultimately based their own teachings about Jesus and their faith in him: the Christian Scriptures.

The Christian Scriptures

The Hebrew Scriptures: When Christians refer to "the Bible" or "the Christian Scriptures," they mean a whole collection of sacred writings that includes what has commonly been called "the Old Testament." This testament is central to the Jewish faith. Out of sensitivity to our Jewish sisters and brothers, the term *Old Testament* is not used in this course. (We tend to regard things that are old as being out of date or of less value.) Instead, the writings are referred to as the *Hebrew Scriptures* (because they were originally written in the Hebrew language). As will become evident in the next several chapters, a full Christian understanding of Jesus cannot be had without the Hebrew Scriptures as a source.

The Christian Testament: For reasons similar to those given above, this course uses the term *Christian Testament* rather than *New Testament* to refer to the section of the Christian Scriptures that

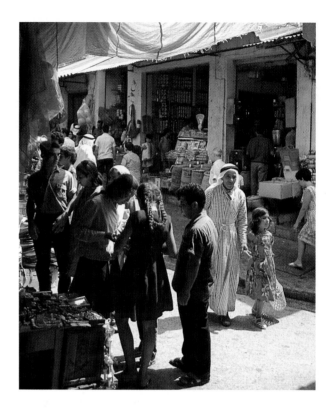

pertains specifically to Christian faith. The Christian Testament tells the story of Jesus and the earliest Christian communities.

Ultimately, the Gospels

When it comes to understanding Jesus' ministry and life, we must rely primarily on four short books included in the Christian Testament: the Gospels of Matthew, Mark, Luke, and John.

Just about everything the Christian church teaches about Jesus comes through the Gospels. The Gospels, in turn, serve as the scale or test of truth and authenticity for everything the church teaches about Jesus. The Gospels are *the* link between Jesus of Nazareth and the people of every age throughout history who have claimed to be his followers. **3**

■
Photo: **On a market street in Jerusalem, the old blends with the new.**

3
Using any complete Bible, compare the size of the Hebrew Scriptures with the size of the Christian Testament. Then locate the Gospels and note what percentage of the entire Bible these

readings take up. Write down any insights or questions that come to mind in light of these comparisons.

Not the Only Sources

Seen together as the **Christian Scriptures**, the Hebrew Scriptures and the Christian Testament provide what can be called **faith sources** of information about Jesus. They are faith sources because they came out of believing communities, communities that saw the work of God in all aspects of life. The Christian Testament, for example, was written specifically to announce God's redeeming, transforming love to all the world. The scriptural accounts about Jesus and the early church are therefore different from the objective kind of reports we might expect to find, say, in the newspaper, on television, or in a history textbook.

How can we be sure that the writers of the Christian Testament did not just create Jesus out of their own imagination? How can we be sure that he actually existed? Fortunately, the faith sources are not the only sources of information about Jesus. (Chapter 2 will take a closer look at how we are to understand the faith sources and their relationship to the following historical sources.)

Historical Sources

Several nonbiblical and non-Christian sources are available to help substantiate that Jesus actually did exist as a historical person.

Josephus, a Jewish Historian

Josephus, a Jewish historian, mentioned Jesus in his writings toward the end of the first century C.E., roughly sixty years after Jesus' death. As a non-Christian, Josephus would have had no reason to accept the historical reality of Jesus unless there was some sound basis for it.

In one of his works, Josephus discusses disturbances that were caused by the Jews during the

Just a Matter of Time

Notice that the dates in this course are identified with the letters B.C.E. and C.E. rather than the more familiar B.C. and A.D. This is becoming more popular in educational publications. The abbreviations B.C. and A.D. refer to the periods before and after the birth of Jesus (B.C. stands for "before Christ," and A.D. stands for *anno Domini* "in the year of our Lord"). Understandably, some non-Christians find that frame of reference offensive. The new abbreviations use the *common era*—the calendar system used in most parts of the world—as a frame of reference. So dates are referred to as either before the common era (B.C.E.) or during the common era (C.E.). If a date is not accompanied by an abbreviation, one can assume that the year is during the common era.

Though perhaps somewhat confusing at first, the change in abbreviations—like this course's use of the terms *Hebrew Scriptures* and *Christian Testament*—is an attempt to show respect for traditions different from our own.

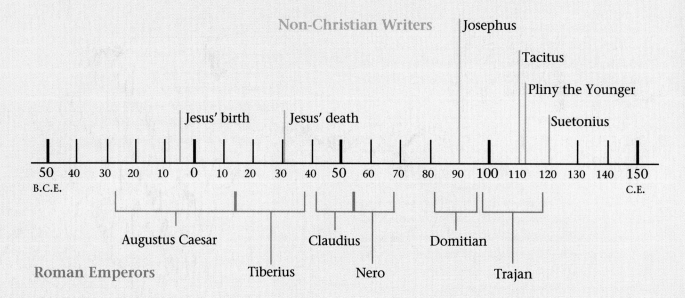

time Pontius Pilate was governor of the region of Judaea (26–36 C.E.). These disturbances centered around a man named Jesus and his followers. Josephus identifies Jesus as "a wise man . . . a doer of wonderful works, a teacher of men who receive the truth with pleasure," and he notes that Jesus was later condemned by Pilate to crucifixion. While this mention of Jesus does not suggest that Josephus himself accepted Jesus or the claims made about Jesus by his followers, it does seem clear that Josephus recognized Jesus to be a historical person who had a profound impact upon the people he encountered.

Roman Writers

Tacitus: The Roman historian Tacitus referred to Jesus in his account of a fire that burned Rome in the year 64 C.E., for which the emperor Nero supposedly blamed the Christians. Tacitus himself obviously had no great love for that strange group of people called Christians:

Christus, the founder of the name, had undergone the death penalty in the reign of Tiberius, by sentence of . . . Pontius Pilate, and the pernicious [or wicked] superstition [Christianity] was checked for a moment, only to break out once more, not merely in Judaea, the home of the disease, but in the capital [Rome] itself, where all things horrible or shameful in the world collect and find a vogue.

Nero's hideous torture of the Christians, as described below, reflects not only Nero's sick mind but also the extent to which many early followers of Jesus would go rather than deny their faith:

. . . [Christians] were covered with wild beasts' skins and torn to death by dogs; or they were fastened on crosses, and, when daylight failed were burned to serve as lamps by night.

Some historians doubt Tacitus's claim that Nero was responsible for the persecution of many Christians.

Pliny the Younger: Another Roman source, a man named Pliny the Younger, was governor of one of the Roman provinces in Asia Minor about the year 110 C.E. He wrote to the emperor Trajan for advice on what to do about the Christians. The Roman officials were always concerned about the growth of any political or religious sect, and the Christian communities baffled them. Although Pliny's letter mentions Jesus, it offers no new information about him.

Suetonius: Around 120 C.E., the Roman historian and lawyer Suetonius compiled biographies of several Roman emperors. In a discussion of the emperor Claudius, Suetonius says that Claudius expelled the Jews from Rome because of the riots they were constantly causing, "on the instigation of Chrestus." Though there is some debate over the word *Chrestus,* scholars generally agree that it refers to Christ.

Note that at the time of Suetonius, Christians were still commonly regarded by the Romans as a Jewish sect. That is why Suetonius's account says that Claudius expelled the *Jews* from Rome. (The connections between the Christians and the Jews will become clearer later in this course.)

Though these historical sources do not give us more information about Jesus than we find in the biblical sources, they do support the historical existence of Jesus, and they show **Christianity**—the movement based on Jesus' life and teachings—as worthy of at least brief mention. The fact remains,

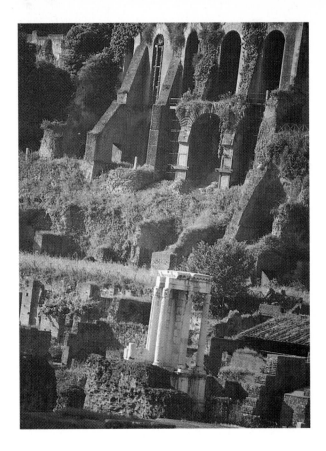

however, that if we want to know about Jesus to any reasonable degree, we must turn to the Christian Scriptures and, more specifically, to the Gospels, which proclaim Jesus and the Good News he shared.

For Review

- Provide a one-sentence definition of each of these terms: *Christian Scriptures, Hebrew Scriptures, Christian Testament.*
- What role do the Gospels play in the church's teaching about Jesus?
- Identify each of the following persons and summarize what they, as a group, contribute to a study of Jesus: *Josephus, Tacitus, Pliny the Younger, Suetonius.*

Accounts by non-Christian, Roman sources provide evidence that Jesus actually lived and that after his death, he had many dedicated followers.

Photo: **The hillside ruins of the Forum, a center of political and civil life in ancient Rome. Early Christians faced fierce persecution in Rome.**

The Christian Testament

A Collection of "Books"

The Christian Testament is composed of twenty-seven separate works, representing not only different authors but also different types of writing. There are personal letters; homilies, or sermons, from early liturgical or worship services; some highly symbolic and imaginative writings; and of course, the Gospels. These various works are often called the *books* of the Christian Testament, even though none of them fit the description of a book in the usual sense. **4**

The twenty-seven books of the Christian Testament developed from roughly twenty years after the death of Jesus (that is, from about 50 C.E.) to about 100 C.E. This period of some fifty years of development may seem quite long, but consider that the development of the Hebrew Scriptures spanned over one thousand years!

One principal theme unifies the writings of the Christian Testament: they all deal in some way with the life and ministry of Jesus and the impact he had on the community of those who believed in him—what we now know as the church. Only the four Gospels deal directly with Jesus—his life, his preaching, his wonderful works, and very importantly, his death and resurrection. The other writings—the letters of Saint Paul, for example—offer us little information about the historical life of Jesus. They concentrate instead on the happenings within the early community of faith; the meaning of Jesus' life, death, and resurrection for the individual believer; various difficulties encountered by the first Christians as they moved out into the world; and so on. In that sense, the writings other than the Gospels are about the lives of the Christian community and the individual Christian more than they are about the life of Jesus himself. In the Christian Testament, only the Gospels offer us anything like a historical portrait of Jesus.

Writings with Special Authority

As noted earlier, it took some fifty years for the writings of the Christian Testament to develop. However, it took even longer for the church to officially recognize these writings as having special importance and authority in the life of the Christian community. Prior to the development of the Christian Testament, the earliest Christians—many of whom were very devout Jews—had the Hebrew Scriptures as their only sacred writings. The Christians commonly used these writings, for example, during community prayer and worship.

The new writings that emerged from the community of Jesus' followers initially came about to meet the specific needs of that growing, worshiping community. These new writings included short sermons, collections of the sayings of Jesus, hymns to be used during worship, collected stories of Jesus' wondrous works, and so on. Many of these writings were eventually lost, while some were combined into the works we now recognize as the individual books of the Christian Testament.

By the end of the second century—that is, more than 150 years after the death of Jesus—the church had come to some general agreement about accepting the Gospels of Matthew, Mark, Luke, and John as particularly special and authoritative. Debate continued about many of the other writings that had developed within the community. It was not until the end of the fourth century that the church finally and formally approved the collection of twenty-seven books that we now know as

---

4
Write down the titles of any twenty-seven books you find on any bookshelf in a library, in the classroom, or at home. Then look at the collection of books in the Christian Testament (see the list on page 20). Write a short paragraph discussing the different meaning the word *book* has for each collection.

the Christian Testament. This collection of special and authoritative writings is often referred to as the Christian **canon.** (The word *canon* comes from the Greek word for "rule" or "standard.")

The Canon of the Christian Testament

The twenty-seven books that developed out of the faith experiences of the early Christian community can be classified or organized in a variety of ways. The books are summarized below according to the way they appear in most Bibles today.

The Gospels of Matthew, Mark, Luke, and John

The four Gospels include information about the life, works, message, death, and resurrection of Jesus. All of the Gospels are organized chronologically, which suggests that they are something like biographies of Jesus.

The Acts of the Apostles

The **Acts of the Apostles** is Luke's account of the early days of the Christian community under the leadership of Saint Peter. Though Luke does record the initial development of the church in Jerusalem, his main focus in Acts is the spread of the Good News throughout the Roman Empire after the death and resurrection of Jesus. In a special way, Acts gives attention to the missionary work of one of the church's most famous personalities: Saint Paul. The Acts of the Apostles is commonly seen as a companion to Luke's Gospel, and many scholars suggest that the two should be read together as one major work.

Thirteen Pauline Epistles

The Acts of the Apostles is followed by a collection of thirteen **Pauline epistles** (*epistle* means "letter"), either written by or attributed to Saint Paul. Most scholars today agree that only seven of these were actually written by Paul. The other six are thought to have been composed by writers who wanted to honor Paul or who sought special authority in the community by claiming Paul as the author of their letters. The primary purpose of all the Pauline letters was to support and further educate either individual Christians or small communities that had been brought to believe in Jesus through the missionary work of Paul and others.

The Letter to the Hebrews

The **Letter to the Hebrews** is another work often attributed to Paul, but scholars generally believe it was written by an unknown author. Though commonly referred to as a letter, Hebrews does not take the form of a normal letter of the time. Rather, it is a kind of extended sermon to a group of Christians who are in danger of falling away from their belief in Jesus.

The Catholic Epistles

After the Letter to the Hebrews comes a collection of seven epistles attributed to other personalities: James, Peter (two letters), John (three letters),

Jesus was raised in Nazareth, a village in Galilee.
Photo: **Nazareth today**

*Broadly, yes. Life, ministry, passion, death, resurrection.
Within, no. – no chrono ordering*

The Books of the Christian Testament

Here is a list of the books of the Christian Testament in the order in which they appear in the Bible:

Gospels	Matthew
	Mark
	Luke
	John
Acts	Acts of the Apostles
Pauline Epistles	Romans
	1 Corinthians
	2 Corinthians
	Galatians
	Ephesians
	Philippians
	Colossians
	1 Thessalonians
	2 Thessalonians
	1 Timothy
	2 Timothy
	Titus
	Philemon
Letter to the Hebrews	Hebrews
Catholic Epistles	James
	1 Peter
	2 Peter
	1 John
	2 John
	3 John
	Jude
Book of Revelation	Revelation

and Jude. Some or all of these are often referred to as **catholic** (meaning "universal") or **general epistles**, because they are addressed to believing Christians as a general audience rather than to specific individuals or communities.

The Book of Revelation

The Christian Testament concludes with a very strange and complex work: the **Book of Revelation.** Some Bibles refer to this book as the *Apocalypse,* based on the Greek word for "revelation." Its highly symbolic and mysterious language reflects a kind of writing that had been popular among the Jews since about two hundred years before Jesus. Most contemporary scholars agree that the Book of Revelation was written for the late-first-century Christians, who were suffering persecution at the hands of the Romans for their beliefs. The book encourages them to remain faithful to Christ. It also deals with their expectation that Jesus will return again in glory at the end of time to fulfill God's work on earth.

Keep in mind throughout this course that the twenty-seven books of the Christian Testament did not actually develop in the order in which they appear in the Bible. Because the Gospels come first, it might seem that they were written first; however, this was not the case. The fact is that Paul did his missionary work, wrote his profound letters, and likely died before the first Gospel took the form we now recognize. Paul's first letter to the Thessalonians is generally considered the first book of the Christian Testament to be written, roughly around the year 50 C.E. The Gospels were written approximately between the years 70 and 95. The last book written is generally believed to be the second letter of Peter, written about the year 100.

The present organization of the Christian Testament developed for a variety of reasons: the relative popularity of each of the Gospels within the early community of faith, the length of Paul's letters (they are organized from the longest to the shortest), and so on.

For Review

- How many books are in the Christian Testament? During what years was the Christian Testament written?
- What is the principal theme that unifies the writings of the Christian Testament?
- What are the main concerns of the non-Gospel writings of the Christian Testament?
- Provide a one-sentence description of each of the following: *the Gospels, the Acts of the Apostles, the Pauline epistles, the Letter to the Hebrews, the catholic epistles, the Book of Revelation.*

Turning to the Gospels

This course on Jesus will largely focus on the portraits of Jesus found in the Gospels. Brief consideration will be given to the understanding of Jesus that emerges from Paul's ministry as it is recorded in the Acts of the Apostles and in Paul's letters. Only periodically will a few of the other books, for example, the letters of John, be mentioned. And some of the books of the Christian Testament will be passed over, only because they tell us very little specifically about Jesus and his message. If this were a course on the Christian Testament itself, the approach would be quite different. However, the constant concern in this course is, Who is Jesus, and what are we to make of his ministry, message, death, and resurrection?

With a basic background on the whole Christian Testament now laid out, the discussion can turn to a more thorough treatment of the biblical writings that will serve as the main sources in this study of Jesus—the Gospels.

Photo: **The Hebron Hills, near Jerusalem**

2

The Gospels:
Central Sources
for Understanding Jesus

It is this disciple who testifies to these things and has written them, and we know that his testimony is true. There are also many other things that Jesus did, but if these were to be described individually, I do not think the whole world would contain the books that would be written. (John 21:24–25)

Searching for the "Jesus of History" in the Gospels

The previous chapter listed the Gospels as part of the faith sources of information about Jesus, meaning that what we learn about Jesus from the Gospels is revealed through the eyes of people who believed him to be the Christ. Before taking a general look at the origins, development, and key characteristics of the four Gospel accounts of Jesus' life, it may be helpful to take a fuller look at what it means to call the Gospels "faith sources" rather than "historical sources." 1

Objectivity: The Only Test of Truth?

Some people have the mistaken notion that because the Gospels were written by believers in the Risen Jesus, the accounts are unreliable sources of historical information about Jesus. These skeptics think that in order to be acceptable as true, the information that comes to us about Jesus has to be totally accurate and objective. But as will be seen shortly, objectivity is not the only test of the truthfulness of a story. A clearer understanding of what is meant by the term *history* will help to show why this is so.

What Do We Mean by "History"?

History can be viewed as the simple recording of observable facts and events, as if these facts and events were captured accurately by movie cameras and tape recorders or transcribed into words by reporters. This is a simplistic and naive understanding of history, however, because life is too complex for this kind of objective description.

To demonstrate this point, think of one event that happened in the world today and compare the reports of that event as given by two television stations and two newspapers. Obviously there will be some basic similarities between all these news stories, but some of the differences in reporting and understanding may be truly startling. Discrepancies might appear in the basic details of the reports, and various understandings and opinions on the meaning of the event are likely to be presented as well.

In other words, what we normally call "history" is not simply the objective recording of facts and events. Rather, it usually involves an interpretation of those facts and events. The information comes to us through the eyes and perspective of the person doing the recording. And no one's perspective is totally objective, because this would require one to be without a point of view, which is impossible!

A key point to remember when studying the Gospels, then, is this: Most information or knowledge that comes to us is, in some way, an *interpretation of reality*. This applies to writings such as the Gospels, which are clearly a unique kind of historical writing, as well as to other kinds of information. Even the firsthand knowledge we gain through our own experiences is interpreted by us. We see it from a certain perspective, which is influenced by our past experiences, our family and community, the culture we live in, and so forth.

Photo, facing page: **The old city of Jerusalem and the Kidron Valley, as seen from the Mount of Olives**

1

Choose any public figure—for example, an athlete, a musician, or a politician—and list at least ten items of information you would expect to find in a thorough biography of that person.

Keep your notion of a biography in mind while reading about the nature of the Gospels.

The Truth Requires More than One Perspective

As stated above, in telling any part of history, no one person is able to see the whole picture. Consider this example:

- Each student in your classroom is asked to draw a picture of the room from his or her usual or assigned seat. The teacher does the same from his or her desk. In looking at the finished drawings, it very quickly becomes obvious that things look different when seen from different points of view. Though each person's picture is a truthful representation of what that person could see from his or her place in the room, a much fuller, more accurate representation of the room can be gained only when everyone's pictures are brought together.

From this example it is easy to see the importance of reading more than one newspaper or watching more than one news program. Doing so enables one to gain a more balanced, fuller, and truer understanding of the events in the world. 2

The Good News, Not the Daily News

Undeniably, the Gospels lack a great deal of the kind of information one would expect to find in a historical account of a person's life. The Gospels do not provide precise dates of Jesus' birth and death, a description of what he looked like, or any detailed information about his childhood and adolescence, his education, or his parents. As chapter 1 made quite clear, there is a lot we do not know about Jesus. The Gospels are definitely not biographies of Jesus. However, as the preceding sections on history and judging truth have shown, the fact that the Gospels are not historical biographies does not automatically make them untruthful.

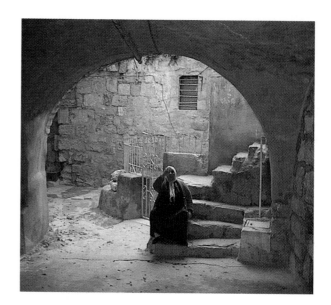

But if the Gospels are not biographies of Jesus, then what are they? Chapter 1 categorized the Gospels as faith sources, writings that came out of the community of Jesus' followers. The word *gospel* itself clues us in further about what it means to call the Gospels "faith sources." *Gospel* is derived from the very old English word *godspell,* which means "good news" or "glad tidings." That word, in turn, is a translation of the Greek word *evangelion,* meaning "the proclamation or announcement of good news." (Note also that we call the authors of the Gospels the **Evangelists,** based on the Greek word, *evangelion.* The authors of the Gospels are, literally, proclaimers of the Good News.)

So from the origins of the word *gospel* we learn that the purpose of the Gospels is to proclaim a message of faith in Jesus. The Gospels are, in other words, **testimonies of faith.** As such, their primary purpose is not to provide accurate historical accounts of the day-to-day life of Jesus. Rather, they are attempts by the early followers of Christ to share their experiences of Jesus with the world.

2

Pick a photograph of a room or a landscape and briefly describe everything that you can see in it. Next, list the things that you cannot see clearly, or at all, because of the point of view from which the photo was taken. For example, if you can see one side of a tree, you most likely cannot see its other side. What are two ways that you might learn about the things you cannot see?

Photo: **An alley beside the Church of the Nativity, in Bethlehem. This church is on the site traditionally held as the birthplace of Jesus.**

What was done by the early Christians in sharing the Good News is not much different from what we do in telling others about a significant happening in our life. Sharing precisely every last detail is often not our main concern. Instead, we want to give whatever information will best help us convey the meaning and significance of the event in our life. Leaving out many of the details does not lessen the truth of our story. 3

Having the Gospels as our main sources of information about Jesus does not eliminate the need for at least some sort of nonbiblical and non-Christian evidence of his existence. The nonbiblical and non-Christian evidence presented in chapter 1 affirms the historical truth that Jesus actually walked the earth, and thus that evidence helps to affirm the validity of the Gospels.

What Does It All Mean?

The Meaning of Religious Truth

Overall, understanding the Jesus of the Gospels involves looking for the historical truth about Jesus and finding what is called religious truth. For Christians, religious truth is the deeper meaning that God intends to reveal to people through historical events. Seekers of religious truth believe that God is actively present in the world, working with all of creation—but especially human beings—to bring about peace and justice for all of life.

It is religious truth that the Scriptures—both the Hebrew Scriptures and the Christian Testament—are primarily filled with. The authors of the biblical literature were, in a sense, attempting to reveal reality through the eyes of God. They were far less concerned with the historical facts, or what an event might have *appeared* to be on the surface. In other words, the biblical writers set out to do precisely what modern reporters supposedly try to avoid: they interpreted events in light of their own faith convictions or the faith convictions of their community.

But just as historical truth cannot be found in isolation, religious truth cannot be dependent upon the interpretations of one person, or even one group of persons, from a particular time. Figuring out religious truth is the task of the whole community of believers, a task that spans every time and place.

The Stories of a Community

Obviously, a totally objective and fully detailed understanding of Jesus as he lived and preached

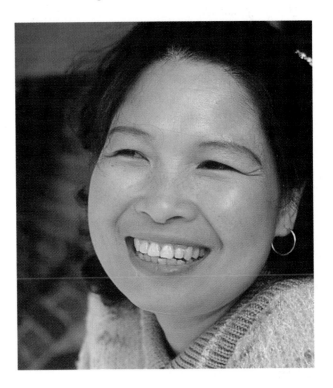

3
In a short paper, briefly summarize a favorite story that has been told over and over by one of your relatives. Then respond to the following questions: *To what degree do you think the story has* *been changed or exaggerated over the years? If the story has been changed, does that lessen or cancel out the value or meaning of the story itself? Why or why not?*

Photo: **The Gospels are meant to be "good news" or "glad tidings" for us.**

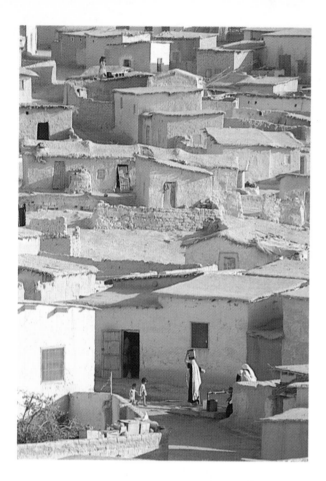

words firsthand is valuable, but understanding the meaning of those words is far more important. Witnessing an event in person may be exciting, but understanding the meaning of the event is far more significant.

The ongoing task of the Christian church is to reassess the significance of Jesus' life and message for each new age and culture. Jesus lived and preached in a time and culture very different from our own. A personal and prayerful reading of the entire Christian Scriptures is encouraged for all Christians. But it is important as well for them to look to biblical scholars and others in the church for guidance in properly understanding the meaning of the Scriptures for today. Even this course, for instance, is not based solely or even mostly on the personal opinions of one person. Its information and insights come from a whole host of sources from within the Christian community, including the work of respected biblical scholars and theologians and the official teachings of the Roman Catholic church.

some two thousand years ago is unattainable. But this holds true for any other figure of history, whether it be Julius Caesar, Cleopatra, the Buddha, Abraham Lincoln, or whoever.

What we *can* attain from the Gospels is some basic information about Jesus and his message. And there is more. What the Gospels, together with the rest of the Christian Testament, also offer us is an understanding of the meaning and significance of the historical Jesus for the people of his time. They tell us the story of the one whom Christians believe to be the Son of God—the one who fully reveals to humanity the very nature of God. Ultimately, is this not of much greater importance to us than mere historical facts? Hearing a person's

For Review

- Is the record of past events that we call "history" a totally accurate description of the events as they actually happened? Explain your response.
- What do the origins of the word *gospel* suggest about the purpose of the Gospels?
- Briefly explain what is meant by the term *religious truth* and discuss its relationship to the Scriptures.
- What can we gain from the Gospels besides some basic information about Jesus and his message?

The Gospels offer us an understanding of the meaning of the historical Jesus for the people and communities of his time.
Photo: An ancient village near the Dead Sea and Jericho

The Roman Catholic Church's Tradition and Jesus

The Roman Catholic church is often distinguished from other Christian churches by its commitment to both the Scriptures and Tradition as major sources for understanding Jesus and his message.

Most Protestant churches rely solely on the Christian Scriptures as the basis for their teachings and practices. The Catholic church, on the other hand, believes that as the church moves through history, the spirit of Jesus guides it to clarify, develop, and preserve particular teachings and practices. On that basis, Catholics accept as part of God's revelation some things other than those mentioned explicitly in the Scriptures. These official teachings and practices in the Catholic church are known as its Tradition, with a capital T, and Catholics view Tradition along with the Scriptures as companion, authoritative guides to truth.

For example, the commitment to Tradition has guided the Catholic church to have more sacraments than Protestant churches do. Protestant

churches generally accept only baptism and the Eucharist as sacraments because only these two can be found explicitly in the Christian Testament. In religious education, Protestants emphasize knowledge of the Christian Scriptures far more than Catholics do, which is one reason that some Protestants may be able to cite or quote scriptural passages with relative ease.

A summary of the development of the Roman Catholic teachings about Jesus will be offered in the last chapter of this textbook. The focus in this course, however, is primarily on a portrait of Jesus as seen in the Christian Testament. A thorough treatment of Jesus from the perspectives of both the Scriptures and Tradition is a task that goes beyond the scope of this course.

The Roman Catholic church believes that as the church moves through history, the spirit of Jesus guides it to develop particular teachings and practices.

Photo: **Today, Pope John Paul II represents the teaching voice of the Catholic church.**

The Development of the Gospels

Perhaps the most effective way to understand the nature and purpose of the Gospels is to look at how they came to be written. Scholars who have studied the Christian Testament have identified at least three major stages in the Gospels' development:

1. During the time that Jesus lived and worked, he had a profound effect on his disciples.
2. After the death and resurrection of Jesus, the disciples and the early church proclaimed the Good News throughout the Roman Empire.
3. Later, the Gospels were actually written by the Evangelists, who likely served as editors or collectors of material that had gradually developed through the years.

Stage 1: Jesus of Nazareth and His Disciples

It would seem to go without saying that the Gospels are based upon the words and works of Jesus of Nazareth, a historical figure from the land of Palestine who lived some two thousand years ago. However, the recognition and acceptance of this truth is central to our understanding and appreciation of the Gospels. For if the Gospels are not based on historical realities and events that truly happened, then all that they teach and call people to is little more than a flight of fancy or an idealistic vision that people have no reason to accept, much less live by.

It is essential to recognize that the foundation of the events and meaning recorded in the Gospels is Jesus of Nazareth, a man, a historical figure, one whose blood flowed through flesh as truly as does our own. Jesus' humanity is what is emphasized by the first phrase in the title of this textbook. When we talk about Jesus, we are definitely talking about the **Jesus of History.**

The Basic Facts

What can we say about the Jesus of History that can be accepted even by those who do *not* accept him as the Messiah, the Christ, the Son of God? From the Gospels and other sources, we are certain of the following points:

- Jesus was born a Jew sometime around the year 5 B.C.E. "in Bethlehem of Judea, in the days of King Herod" (Matthew 2:1). He was raised in the small village of Nazareth. As he grew, he learned and practiced the trade of carpentry.

We know that Jesus was born a Jew sometime around 5 B.C.E. in Bethlehem of Judaea.
Photo: **The town of Bethlehem at sunrise**

- At about age thirty, Jesus began a public career of preaching and teaching, proclaiming the beginning of a new era—the "Kingdom of God," as he called it. He apparently demonstrated some unusual powers and was referred to by historians of his day as a worker of wonderful deeds.
- Jesus' preaching and actions stirred great interest among the Jewish people, leading some to proclaim him as a great prophet and others to reject him as a sorcerer, a magician, someone who lacked reverence for God, and a threat to the Roman state. Those in power eventually brought him to trial, found him guilty of crimes under Roman law, and had him executed by crucifixion sometime around the year 30 C.E.

Virtually all people of any religious persuasion or belief could accept this much about Jesus simply by being open to historical records. However, the early Christians—both Jesus' immediate followers and those who had not known him while he walked the earth—clearly believed him to be much more than just a man, more than just Jesus of Nazareth, more than simply the Jesus of History.

The Resurrection: The Pivotal Event

What led the early Christians to believe that Jesus was more than just an extraordinary person was the event that his followers claim to have experienced *after* his death. This event completely and radically changed their understanding of everything Jesus had said and done while he walked the dusty roads of Palestine. What the followers of Jesus claimed was this: He did not remain dead. Approximately three days after he had been savagely executed on the cross, they experienced him alive again and present among them.

Belief in the resurrection of Jesus became the identifying mark of all those who claimed Jesus as

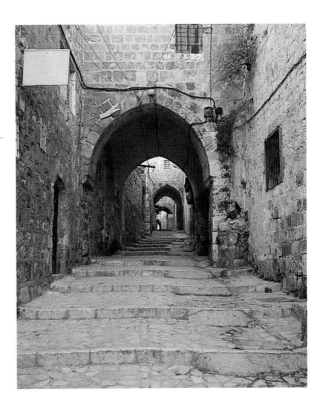

their Lord and Savior. Jesus' rising from the dead made his whole earthly existence—all that he had said and done prior to this event—believable and acceptable as truth. Without the Resurrection, the followers of Jesus would likely have run away in fear of their own execution. But with the experience of the Risen Jesus, they burst forth from their places of hiding and began proclaiming that "God has made him both Lord and Messiah, this Jesus whom you crucified," by raising him from the dead (Acts 2:36).

The Resurrection and its meaning will be discussed more fully in chapter 10 of this course, but this much can be said now: the conviction of Jesus' living presence after death is so central to the lives of Christians that Saint Paul, one of the most influential of all the early Christians, was led to say,

Photo: **A stepped street in Jerusalem leading off of the Via Dolorosa, the path believed to have been taken by Jesus on the way to the Crucifixion**

"If Christ has not been raised, then empty . . . is our preaching; empty, too, your faith" (1 Corinthians 15:14).

Christic: Not Jesus' Last Name

Some people in Jesus' time immediately rejected the proclamation of the Resurrection. They thought the news foolhardy, ridiculous, insane. For them, the Jesus of History would remain only the carpenter's son who preached a radical message and paid for it with his life. But others were nearly overwhelmed by the conviction that the proclamation of the Resurrection was true—that Jesus had in fact been raised by God from death itself and that he truly was, and would be forever, Lord and Savior. For these people, the Jesus of History was clearly much more than a carpenter's son. For the early Christians, the Jesus of History was also truly the **Christ of Faith**—an understanding of Jesus represented by the second phrase in the title of this textbook.

Unfortunately, over the years many people have come to think of the title *Christ* as simply a kind of last name or family name for Jesus. In fact, however, he was never known by that name during his earthly life. The name *Jesus* was a common one for Jewish boys. It is our translation of Jesus' Hebrew name, *Yeshua,* which he would have heard when called by his parents and others. The name *Yeshua* means literally "Yahweh (God) saves" or "Yahweh (God) is salvation." But the title *Christ* means literally "anointed one." It is based on the Greek word *Christos,* which is itself a translation of the Hebrew word *messiah.*

As will be discussed in more detail later, the Jewish people had long awaited the **Messiah,** "the One sent from God," the one who would save them from all oppression. To those Jews who accepted Jesus as the Messiah after his resurrection, he became known as "Jesus *the* Christ," which in turn became rather quickly shortened to what we now know as a single name: *Jesus Christ.* This development may have been an unfortunate one, for it clouds to some degree the recognition of a tremendous conviction held by Christians—that the Jesus of History is truly the Christ of Faith. This realization of Jesus as the Christ overwhelmed the disciples, and the whole of their experience of his life, death, and resurrection marks the first stage of the development of the Gospels.

Stage 2: The Disciples and the Early Community of Faith

What Would You Do?

Try to imagine yourself in the position of an early disciple of Jesus. You, along with the rest of the disciples, walk with Jesus; you hear his inspiring

Photo: Jesus' living presence in the world was obvious to those who believed in his resurrection.

message proclaimed from the synagogues and hill-sides; you touch him and are touched by him; and you witness the marvelous impact he makes on everyone he meets. Gradually you find yourself captivated by this man and his message. You find in him the answer to all your hopes and dreams, and you are certain that in this man from Nazareth you have discovered true freedom, joy, peace, love, and fullness of life.

But then you see the horror of Calvary: Jesus, whom you so deeply love, stretched out against the sky, nailed to a beam of wood, carrying all your dreams and hopes along with him to his death. You and so many who believed in him run away in fear—shattered, hopeless, convinced that all he promised was a sham, a lie, or at the very least a terrible mistake.

But then comes Easter. Suddenly you have the overwhelming experience of Jesus present again, alive and truly with you—in fact, even more truly with you than he was before. He is risen! Even death is conquered in this man! Incredible joy and peace surge into your heart, and you run from your place of hiding, shouting from the rooftops: "He's alive! Everything he told us is true!"

Now, what will you do next? It is doubtful that you will immediately sit down and begin to write an essay on what you have experienced. For one thing, you need some time just to sort out the significance of the incredible events that have taken place. Also, because of Jesus' promise at the time of his ascension into heaven—that he will come again to fully establish God's Kingdom—many of his followers are anticipating the almost certain end of the world as they know it. Perhaps based upon a misunderstanding of some of the things Jesus taught, they believe that he will come back soon—within their lifetime. These people believe

that they have little time to make up their mind about him. They suppose that either they will turn from their past ways, repent of their sins, and accept Jesus as Lord and Savior, or they will perish. Some Christians are even advising against marriage, and some are refusing to take jobs, feeling that these are silly considerations when the end of the world is right around the corner. With all of this commotion and speculation, writing about your experiences seems to be unnecessary. You have more important things to do.

Spreading the Word Near and Far

The situation just described is exactly the one the early Christians found themselves in after the Resurrection. Rather than write about their experiences with Jesus, they began an intense missionary campaign to proclaim his life, death, and resurrection to all people. In a matter of decades, the proclamation of the Good News of Jesus spread like wildfire throughout the Roman Empire—from Palestine, where it had begun, out to Egypt, Syria,

Photo: **A cross of victory leads the way during an Easter Week procession in Jerusalem.**

Greece, Asia Minor, and ultimately into the capital city of Rome itself (at that time, Rome was often referred to as "the ends of the earth").

Though it was clear to the early Christians that preserving their message for the future was not necessary—there was, after all, no "future" expected—they did not lose any of their love for the past. In fact, it was only in terms of history that Jesus' followers could understand him. They began to see how so much of what he had said and done took on meaning only in light of the ideas and past events recorded in the Hebrew Scriptures. As Saint Paul was to say to his fellow Jews, "'We ourselves are proclaiming this good news to you that what God promised our ancestors he has brought to fulfillment for us, their children, by raising up Jesus'" (Acts 13:32–33). This idea of the promises of God fulfilled in Jesus became a fundamental part of the preaching of the early Christians as they spread the word across the land.

Words and Deeds to Remember

It was within the context of preaching the Good News throughout the land that the process of picking and choosing what to remember about Jesus was begun. Incidents from his life and teaching were used to instruct people who were interested in joining the community of faith. Reflections on his life in terms of the prophecies in the Hebrew Scriptures became part of Christian worship services. And perhaps most importantly, Jesus' words were not only recalled but applied to the experiences of the early Christians as they began to share and celebrate and live out his message in their daily life.

In other words, Jesus' life and words and works were never recorded in a logical, day-by-day, biographical fashion. Not all of the available information about Jesus was preserved, but only those events and works and teachings that had a particularly profound impact on the early Christians. In many cases this meant eliminating descriptive details from the accounts. For example, if we look at the Gospel stories of Jesus' miracles, we find only the briefest descriptions, which often makes the stories seem stark and unreal. Or sometimes Jesus' words as recorded in the Gospels are so direct, so straight to the point, that they seem harsh.

For several decades this information about Jesus was shared primarily by word of mouth among the Christians, developing into what is called an **oral tradition.** On the basis of these carefully selected and highly polished recollections, and from their application to the early church's experience, the Gospels would eventually be written.

Many examples from the Gospels will be used throughout this course. In pursuing an understanding of Jesus and his message, it is important to not lose sight of this "oral tradition" stage in the development of the Gospels.

The Good News spread like wildfire through the Roman Empire.

Photo: **Caesarea, a Mediterranean port in Palestine named after the Roman emperor Augustus Caesar, was a stop in the travels of the church's early missionaries.**

Stage 3:
The Early Community of Faith and the Evangelists

Jesus died around the year 30 C.E., but it was approximately forty more years before the first Gospel was written. Only after proclaiming the Good News and developing an oral tradition did the early Christians decide that the free-floating stories and words and teachings of Jesus should be collected into permanent records by the editors we call the Evangelists.

It is generally held that the first Gospel written was Mark's, around the year 70 C.E. Luke's and Matthew's Gospels were perhaps written during the middle to late eighties; and John's Gospel, not until as late as 90 to 100. More will be said about the Evangelists and their unique Gospels in a moment, but first there is a more basic subject to address: What brought about this third stage in the Gospels' development, the actual writing of them? There seem to have been at least two major factors: the passage of time and the need for continued instruction.

The Passage of Time

By the latter half of the first century, the followers of Christ had begun to be recognized as the "church," that is, something more than just a radical Jewish fringe group. It was becoming clear that

Illustration: **While sharing meals, the early Christians passed on stories about Jesus and his teachings, and they reflected on the meaning of his message for their own daily life.**

the community of faith would probably be around for a long time. The first disciples' expectations of an immediate return by Jesus gradually faded with the passing years. Christians slowly realized that they had apparently misunderstood Jesus; they were forced to recognize that he was not going to return in glory as quickly as they had hoped.

With the realization that the church did indeed have a future, it became necessary to find a means for preserving its teachings and passing them on to future generations. This was certainly one of the motives for developing the Gospels as we now have them.

The Need for Continued Instruction

The preservation of Jesus' message for future generations was not the only reason for collecting the available material about Jesus into the Gospels. There was also a continuing need to instruct and inspire the already existing communities of faith that had been formed throughout the Roman Empire during the previous decades of missionary activity.

Each of the Gospel writers gathered pieces from among all the stories about Jesus that had emerged since his death and resurrection. Then the writer assembled these pieces into a coherent story that would respond to the needs of a particular audience in a particular location at a particular time. This accounts for the fact that each of the Gospels is unique and that certain activities and words of Jesus recorded in one of the Gospels appear to be described or expressed differently in another. **4**

Common Threads

No one Gospel provides a completely accurate understanding of Jesus. And, again, we cannot look at the Gospels as detailed biographies of Jesus. Rather, we must seek an understanding of the *common threads of meaning* that run through the Gospels and try to understand the Gospels' meaning and significance for today. We can do this in part by studying their roots and implications in the historical, religious, and cultural times in which they were written. (Chapters 3 and 4 of this course will contribute to this task.)

For Review

- Briefly describe the three major stages in the development of the Gospels.
- *Christ* is not Jesus' last name. Explain.
- What two major factors explain the transition from an initial oral telling of the Good News to the written form found in the Gospels?

Illustration: **Each Gospel writer gathered pieces from the stories told about Jesus and assembled them into a coherent story—a complete Gospel.**

4
Fold a piece of paper in half to create two vertical columns. Title the left column "Oral Storytelling" and the right column "Written Storytelling." List at least five benefits and five shortcomings of each type of storytelling. For example, what can be done with an oral story that cannot be done with a written one, and vice versa?

The Gospels:
Four Portraits of Jesus

The Gospels were not simply the result of four individuals named Matthew, Mark, Luke, and John sitting down independently and writing about Jesus based on their own personal recollections of him. Rather, each Evangelist had a wealth of material available to him:

- stories about Jesus that were told over and over again in community worship
- the words of Jesus, recalled day after day in prayer and then applied to life experiences
- insights that were drawn by preachers about the relationship between the life and message of

Jesus and the history of the Jewish people, and so on

Each Evangelist also had a particular audience in mind when he began to collect this material into a coherent and understandable whole.

It is doubtful that any *one* person was responsible for the total development of any of the Gospels. It seems instead that the work was done by at least several people, perhaps including friends or followers of the Evangelists who honored these men by attributing the work totally to them as individuals.

Even today, scholars are constantly studying and arriving at new speculations about the identities of the Gospel authors, their purposes in writing, and the dates when they wrote their accounts of the

The Development of the Gospels

Good News. When reading the following very brief summaries of the most commonly held judgments about these issues, recognize that for each point mentioned here, scholars could be found who disagree. This fact can make the study and discussion of the Gospels a bit confusing, perhaps, but also as fascinating and challenging as trying to grasp the plot of a well-written mystery story.

Also, note that while the following discussion identifies each Gospel as a separate and unique "portrait" of Jesus, no one Gospel tells us everything we need to know about Jesus. Rather, we need to view the Gospels as different portraits, each one offering different insights, each adding to

our understanding of the truth about Jesus and his message. **5**

Mark's Portrait: The Human Jesus

By Whom and When?

Mark was a common name during the time of Jesus, and the Mark credited with writing the first Gospel could have been almost anyone. None of the Gospels actually identify their author directly, and the name we attach to each one represents the early church's traditional opinion on who the author was. Some modern-day scholars believe the author of Mark's Gospel to have been a certain John Mark who lived in Jerusalem and who might have learned about Jesus from the Apostle Peter. In the Acts of the Apostles (12:25) and elsewhere, John Mark is mentioned as a companion of Saint Paul. In addition, a group of Christians regularly met at John Mark's mother's house for prayer (Acts 12:12).

Scholars generally agree that the Gospel of Mark was written sometime between 65 and 70 C.E., that is, thirty-five to forty years after the death of Jesus. For the purposes of this course, the year 70 will be used. Some suggest that an earlier version of the Gospel, one written before the year 65, was lost and that the one we now have is a revised version of the earlier one.

A heavy sense of suffering dominates the Gospel of Mark, with many references to trials and persecutions. This may reflect the persecution of the Christians by the Roman emperor Nero, who, some historians claim, blamed the Christians for the burning of Rome in the year 64 C.E. Also, we know that the Jews revolted against the Romans in a violent conflict between the years 66 and 70, and

---

Illustration: **The burning of Rome in 64 C.E. was blamed on the Christians, setting off a terrible persecution by the emperor Nero. Mark's Gospel was written against this backdrop of persecution.**

5
Write a short paragraph describing the differences between a *portrait* and a *picture* of someone. How do these differences relate to the notion of the Gospels as four "portraits" of Jesus?

many scholars feel that Mark's account reflects an awareness of the suffering of that period as well.

For Whom and Why?

Mark's Gospel seems to have been written in Rome for the church there and for **Gentile** (non-Jewish) readers. Jewish customs that would have been readily understood by Jews themselves, for instance, are explained in Mark's Gospel in a way that indicates the customs were not familiar to the intended readers.

The human suffering of Jesus in his passion and death is stressed in Mark's Gospel, perhaps as an encouragement to the Christians who were suffering terrible persecution at the time this Gospel was proclaimed. In fact, Jesus' death is such a central point of Mark's Gospel that everything else that precedes its description seems to be offered almost

solely by way of introduction. It seems certain, then, that one of Mark's intentions was to explain to the members of the early church how suffering is an essential part of Christian life and to give them the courage to endure it as Jesus had.

A heavy concentration on the humanity of Jesus comes through in Mark's Gospel. For example, it portrays Jesus as expressing strong emotions. Mark may have been trying to counter the claim of some Christians during his day that Jesus was not truly human but only divine and had simply pretended to be a man. Mark's account makes it very clear that Jesus was truly a human being, or as the Roman Catholic church would much later express this reality in its Tradition, that Jesus truly possessed both human and divine natures.

In summary, Mark's Gospel provides us with perhaps the most intimate portrait of Jesus. It is also the shortest of the four Gospels. For these and other reasons, many suggest that anyone just beginning their study of the Gospels will find it helpful to read Mark first, preferably in one sitting. In this way the reader can gain a basic sense of how a Gospel proclaims the Good News of Jesus.

Luke's Portrait:
Jesus as the Compassionate Savior

The Gospel of Luke is actually the first part of a two-volume history of early Christianity. The second part is another book of the Christian Testament—the Acts of the Apostles. The Gospel of Luke is often referred to as "the Gospel of Jesus," and the Acts of the Apostles as "the Gospel of the Holy Spirit." Acts recounts the workings of the Holy Spirit in the life of the early church. The two books are best read together.

Photo: **In 1989, a woman in a town in El Salvador flees with her baby, fearing aerial bombardment of her neighborhood by the Salvadoran military. As in Mark's time, many hearers of the Gospel today suffer from persecution.**

By Whom and When?

A notion has persisted that the author of the Gospel of Luke and the Acts of the Apostles was a physician, a well-educated Gentile who had converted to Christianity. In the Letter to the Colossians (4:14), a certain Luke is identified by Saint Paul as a doctor, and some scholars have pointed out parts of Luke's Gospel that seem to indicate medical knowledge. This point has probably been exaggerated, though, given the limited evidence.

Luke is mentioned three times in the Christian Testament, as a companion of Saint Paul. At one point Paul says that Luke is not a Jew. If what Paul says is true, then the author of Luke and Acts is probably the only non-Jewish writer of the Christian Testament. Luke did not know Jesus but had to rely upon information received from those who were eyewitnesses to Jesus' life and ministry. Luke probably wrote his Gospel in Antioch, Syria, which was one of the largest cities in the Roman Empire.

It is difficult to date the writing of Luke's Gospel. Much evidence suggests that Luke had Mark's Gospel available to him when he was writing—especially the fact that some of Luke's material comes *directly from* Mark's Gospel. Based on this, we know that Luke wrote after Mark's Gospel was in circulation, which means sometime after the year 70 C.E. Most scholars say that the Gospel of Luke was written sometime during the eighties. The rough date of 85 will be used in this course.

For Whom and Why?

In the opening lines of his Gospel, Luke mentions a certain Theophilus, to whom he is addressing his Gospel. Luke tells Theophilus that he is writing "so that you may realize the certainty of the teachings you have received" (1:4). Luke claims that he has studied all the available accounts of the life and ministry of Jesus and wants, "after investigating everything accurately anew, to write it down in an orderly sequence" (1:3). So it seems that Luke was writing to offer those who were already Christians help in better understanding their faith and its roots.

Evidence in this Gospel indicates that Luke himself was unfamiliar with the land of Palestine and was writing to an audience made up mostly of Gentiles and perhaps well-to-do Christians. He sets out early in his writing to demonstrate the continuity of Christianity with the Judaism of the Hebrew Scriptures. And throughout his Gospel, Luke emphasizes the central role of the Holy Spirit in Jesus' life. He even closes his Gospel by stressing the continuing presence of Jesus through the Spirit after Jesus' death and resurrection. Perhaps Luke was trying to support those readers who were discouraged that Jesus had not yet returned as they were expecting him to.

Photo: **Luke's Gospel illustrates that God accepts persons cast out by society—persons least expected to receive God's favor.**

Luke, more than any other Gospel writer, stresses the mercy and compassion of Jesus. Accompanying this emphasis is the idea that the Christian message is for everyone—Jews and Gentiles, men and women, rich and poor. Luke illustrates that God—through Jesus—accepts the persons who are least expected to receive God's favor. (Examples of such persons at the time of Luke were those with diseases and social outcasts of one kind or another—including women.) Also, Luke continually reminds the reader of the joy that is shared by those who experience God's forgiving love in Jesus. The Gospel of Luke, therefore, clearly depicts a Jesus who deeply loves all men and women. Because of this Gospel's beautiful writing and its portrait of the compassionate Jesus, many Christians consider it to be their favorite of the four Gospels.

Matthew's Portrait:
Jesus as the Messiah of the Jews

By Whom and When?

There is no clear agreement on either the author or the date for Matthew's Gospel. Early in the history of the church, tradition held that the author was Matthew, an Apostle and therefore an eyewitness to Jesus' life and work. However, the author seems to have used almost all of Mark's Gospel and relied on Luke's account as well. It would have been strange for an eyewitness of Jesus' life and work to rely so heavily upon other sources. Perhaps the final, unknown author relied heavily upon the stories used by the Apostle Matthew to teach about Jesus.

Regarding the date of Matthew's writing, the majority of scholars would opt for a date anywhere between 80 and 100 C.E. This course will settle on

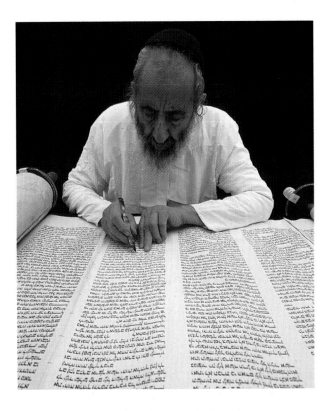

an approximate date of 90 because Matthew's insights into the meaning of Jesus seem more developed than those of Mark or Luke.

For Whom and Why?

The Gospel of Matthew is very different in structure from the Gospels of Mark and Luke. Some scholars suggest that its organizational pattern copies that of the first five books of the Hebrew Scriptures, indicating a particular desire by the author to show the Jews that Jesus was clearly the Messiah they had awaited.

The Gospel contains five great discourses, or speeches, by Jesus, demonstrating his role as a powerful teacher. The Gospel also emphasizes that all of Jesus' life was a fulfillment of the promises

Photo: **A Jewish scholar studies the Torah. The organization of Matthew's Gospel seems to follow the pattern of the Torah, which is the first five books of the Hebrew Scriptures.**

made by God to Israel. Jesus, for example, is presented as a true teacher of the Jewish Law, or as "the new Moses." More than 130 passages in the Gospel of Matthew refer either directly or indirectly to the Hebrew Scriptures.

The author shows interest in the church itself, which may provide a clue to his intent in writing. In fact, Matthew's Gospel is sometimes referred to as "the church's Gospel." It is the only Gospel to use the word *church* (see 16:18 and 18:17), and it

seems concerned with the church's organization and with the communal life and teaching among the believers.

Because the Gospel of Matthew contains Jesus' teaching in such a thorough, well-organized, and understandable manner, it quickly became the most popular and widely used of all the Gospels in the early church, especially when educating new Christians. Its sensitivity to the continuity between Christianity and Judaism also made the Gospel valuable for Jews who were inquiring about the faith. These qualities explain in part why the Gospel of Matthew appears first in the Christian Testament today.

John's Portrait: Jesus as the Divine Son of God

Different from the Synoptic Gospels

The Gospels of Matthew, Mark, and Luke are similar in so many respects that they are often referred to as the **synoptic Gospels.** (The word *synoptic* means "to see together.") It was noted earlier that the authors of the first three Gospels often seem to have used the same sources (stories told and insights drawn about Jesus) or one another's work in writing their accounts. Because of the similarities and overlapping, the synoptic Gospels can be fully understood only when seen or looked at side by side.

John's Gospel, on the other hand, is unique. Even just a quick reading of sections of it reveals this fact. Filled with symbolic language and images, this Gospel offers profound insights into the meaning of Jesus and his message. Some of its language is very beautiful, and it is often used as a basis for both communal and personal prayer.

Written for Jews, the Gospel of Matthew emphasizes that all of Jesus' life was a fulfillment of God's promises to Israel.

Photo: A Jewish man, wearing a prayer shawl, prays at the Wailing Wall, in Jerusalem.

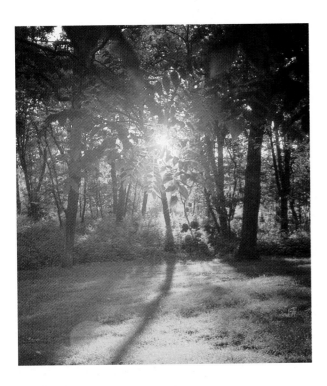

By Whom and When?

There is wide disagreement over who authored the fourth Gospel, and we may never resolve the issue. At least some of the confusion is based on the fact that the name *John* was quite common, and it can be difficult to distinguish one John from another in the Scriptures. For years the church suggested that the author was the Apostle John. It was believed that the Apostle John wrote the Gospel at the end of a very long life, after much prayer, reflection, and personal experience of actually living out his faith in Jesus. This would account for the reflective, prayerful, and thoughtful style of the Gospel. The church has traditionally also held that the same John wrote the Book of Revelation.

However, much current discussion regarding the authorship of the fourth Gospel centers on the rather mysterious person identified in several places in the Gospel as "the disciple whom Jesus loved" (see John 13:23, 19:26, 20:2, and 21:7). Most scholars now refer to this person as the *Beloved Disciple.* In the past, some thought that this person and John the Apostle were one and the same. Few now accept that thinking.

Currently, the most common position on the authorship of the fourth Gospel is that it was written by members of the community or "school" founded by the Beloved Disciple. These disciples or students meditated on their leader's understanding of Jesus and gained even more profound insights into the Risen Lord and his meaning. The three epistles of John, also in the Christian Testament, seem to have come out of the same group, but some scholars suggest that a Christian prophet, also named John but otherwise unknown, wrote the Book of Revelation.

Regarding when the Gospel of John was written, scholars suggest that the earliest possible date would be around 90 C.E. and that it could have been as late as 100. In this course a date of 95 will be used. This late date alone would make it highly unlikely, if not impossible, for a disciple of Jesus to have written the Gospel of John.

For Whom and Why?

The late date of the writing of the Gospel of John helps us gain an understanding of its unique style and the purposes for which it was written. Many years had passed since Jesus of Nazareth had walked among the people of Palestine, years during which the church continually deepened its understanding of his true identity. As noted earlier, it was only after the Resurrection that Jesus was fully recognized as the Christ, the Messiah, and the Son of God. The more time people had to reflect on

Photo: John's Gospel offers a profound, prayerful understanding of Jesus as the divine Son of God, "the light of the world."

these realities and their implications, the more central to their teaching and preaching did these realities become.

Therefore, in John's Gospel—more so than in the synoptic Gospels—we see a strong attempt to present a profound and prayerful understanding of Jesus as the divine Son of God. For this reason, many scholars feel that if we are to attempt an accurate historical portrait of Jesus as he lived and taught in Palestine, we should rely more heavily on the synoptics than on John. This does not mean that John's Gospel is not truthful, but rather that the truths it attempts to share are more deeply theological and reflective than the truths in the other Gospels.

On the other hand, the almost poetically prayerful nature of John's Gospel and its familiar and treasured imagery of Jesus as "the bread of life," "the light of the world," and "the good shepherd" have made this Gospel a favorite source for meditation on the divine significance of Jesus' life.

The synoptic Gospels are the primary sources for the information in chapters 5 through 10 of this course. However, brief excerpts from or comments on John's Gospel will be included. These will often be presented as short commentaries set off from the rest of the text and identified with the title "Focus on John."

For Review

- For each of the four Gospels, summarize the following information: *author, approximate date when written, primary audience, central themes.*

Like a Many-Layered Drawing

One scholar describes the Gospels' development in this way:

> When we have a complicated diagram to reproduce (an industrial design, for example, or the anatomy of the human body), we may sometimes build up a series of sheets of tracing paper. The first will contain a basic framework (perhaps the human skeleton), and on top of that we may put other drawings made to the same scale on tracing paper, representing the muscles, the various organs, and so on. In this way we can look at each drawing separately or, if we wish, we can put them together and see one superimposed on top of another.

> We can understand the Gospels in the same way. On top of the portrait of Jesus of Nazareth that they had kept in their memories, the Evangelists superimposed their understanding of the Risen Jesus as they had only begun to understand him after Easter. When we read the Gospels in a rather naive if not incorrect way, everything about Jesus as the Christ of Faith proclaimed by believers might seem very clear. It seems in reading the Gospels, for example, that Jesus often directly presents himself as the Son of God, and that many people immediately recognize him as such. In fact, the modern reader might be amazed that anyone could have failed to recognize the Jesus

of History as the Christ of Faith or as the Son of God.

Everything seems so clear to us, however, because we are looking at all the "drawings" together. This was not the case of the people of Jesus' time, those who witnessed his life and ministry. The Gospels, therefore, can only be fully understood in light of faith in Jesus of Nazareth as the Risen One, the Messiah, the Christ, the Son of God. (Based on Charpentier, *How to Read the New Testament,* page 19)

Continuing the Search

Many people today live with the illusion that it would be much easier to believe in Jesus if only they could see him, touch him, hear his voice, walk with him. They seem to think that the people who actually experienced Jesus during his earthly life in Palestine had a much easier time understanding and accepting him than people do today. The facts, however, do not support this notion.

If it was, in fact, so easy to recognize and accept Jesus in his own day, why did so many people have such a hard time doing this? If the message of Jesus was so understandable for those who heard it firsthand, why did so many of them reject it? In some ways, it is probably easier for people to accept Jesus today than it was when he lived. We today have the benefit of nearly two thousand years of historical experience with the person and message of Jesus. So much is known today that was not known in his day. History has recorded the profound impact of his vision on the world. Despite the shortcomings of Christian people throughout the years who have failed to live Jesus' message fully, it is still considered one of the most powerful and life-changing visions ever offered to humanity.

The next two chapters discuss several dimensions of Jesus' life and times. This can help us a great deal in understanding the meaning, impact, and significance of the message he proclaimed. Specifically, exploring his social, cultural, and religious background as a Jew and laying out some of the historical setting in which he presented his vision are key requirements in a search for a full understanding of the one called Jesus the Christ.

Each Gospel offers its own portrait of Jesus, emphasizing different aspects or dimensions of him. Together, the Gospels form a more complete portrait of who Jesus was and is.

Photo: **A modern African wood sculpture, "Christ with the Crown of Thorns," offers a distinctive outlook on Jesus.**

3

The World of Jesus:
History and Politics

HE came to Nazareth, where he had grown up, and went according to his custom into the synagogue on the sabbath day. He stood up to read and was handed a scroll of the prophet Isaiah. He unrolled the scroll and found the passage where it was written:

"The Spirit of the Lord is upon me,
  because he has anointed me
    to bring glad tidings to the poor.
He has sent me to proclaim liberty to captives
  and recovery of sight to the blind,
    to let the oppressed go free,
  and to proclaim a year acceptable to the Lord."

Rolling up the scroll, he handed it back to the attendant and sat down, and the eyes of all in the synagogue looked intently at him. He said to them, "Today this scripture passage is fulfilled in your hearing." And all spoke highly of him and were amazed at the gracious words that came from his mouth. (Luke 4:16–22)

Jesus the Jew

Understanding the Life and Times of Jesus

An essential piece of information we need to know about Jesus in order to understand him and the message he proclaimed is this: he was a deeply faith-filled and profoundly committed Jew of his day. In a startling and highly disturbing interview, the television host Phil Donahue one day confronted a major leader of the Ku Klux Klan with this fact. With an icy stare and hate-filled conviction, the man strongly denied that Jesus could have ever been a Jew, claiming with an almost incredible lack of understanding that Jesus was instead "the first Christian."

For most people, of course, a lack of sensitivity to the Jewish roots and religious experience of Jesus is not motivated by such bigotry. But the fact is, unfortunately, that many Christians over the centuries have not clearly grasped the tremendous importance of having a solid background in Jewish religious, social, and political history in order to truly understand Jesus Christ.

Jesus in the Synagogue

Take another look at the scriptural passage that introduces this chapter. It is perhaps one of the most popular and frequently quoted of all passages from the Christian Testament, one often used in prayer services because of its dramatic presentation of the mission of Jesus. But note the number of details in it that can be recognized and comprehended only within the context of the history of Israel:

1. Jesus went into the synagogue (what is a synagogue?)
2. on the sabbath day (what is so special about that day?)
3. according to his custom (why was it his custom?)
4. he stood up to read (what gave him the right to do that?)
5. from a scroll of the prophet Isaiah (who was Isaiah, and what is a scroll?) 1

What Jesus read was a very old and sacred passage from the Hebrew Scriptures. It was one that Jesus felt identified both who he was and what he was all about, because, as he said, it was being fulfilled that very day in him.

History, Politics, and Religion

The point of the above questions is this: we simply cannot understand Jesus and his message outside the context of his Jewish heritage. This chapter

---

To understand Jesus, we must understand his Jewish roots. Central to the history of the Jews was the covenant that God made with the Israelites through Moses on Mount Sinai.

Photo, facing page: The Sinai Range, shortly after sunrise, as viewed from what is believed to be Mount Sinai

1
In writing, answer the questions in parentheses concerning the story of Jesus in the synagogue. Do the best you can without using a source other than the story itself.

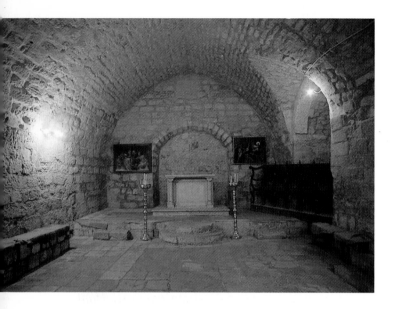

will offer some insights into the basic history of the Jews and then briefly discuss the political situation in which the Jewish people found themselves at the time of Jesus. This discussion will help provide a context for understanding many of the stories of Jesus that are presented in the Gospels.

Chapter 4 will then look at the land, daily life, and religious practices of the Jewish people of Jesus' time. Along with the religious history of the Jews, this information about the basic lifestyle of the people—the homes they lived in, the food they ate, the nature of their family life, their key religious feasts, and so on—can make the Jesus of History much more real and personal to us. Background of this kind can make the Gospels not only more understandable but more enjoyable and personally enriching to read.

With an Open Mind

Without question, the rough sketch of Jewish history that follows will greatly oversimplify the pro-

found and incredibly moving history of the people of faith we now call the Jews. Nevertheless, it can at least serve as a starting point for understanding Jesus' heritage as a Jew. The many names, events, and religious places and celebrations surveyed in this chapter and the next were realities that touched Jesus deeply. Every moment of Jesus' earthly life grew out of, was touched by, and spoke directly to the Jewish community of his day. Without understanding that, we cannot truly understand Jesus.

And just as when listening to a new friend tell us the story of his or her life and where he or she came from—his or her "history"—we need to keep our sometimes less-than-enthusiastic feelings about studying history from getting in the way of our learning more about Jesus. Exploring Jesus' roots can help us understand, for example, why Jesus would weep over Jerusalem, or why his cleansing of the Temple was such a striking event both for those who witnessed his powerful religious convictions and for himself as well. This is the only way we can hope to comprehend the drama of a scene like the one that introduces this chapter, where Jesus stands up before a hushed crowd, his heart pounding as he unrolls that very sacred scroll and proclaims for himself a role that will eventually lead him to the cross. Getting in touch with Jesus' roots is a way of getting in touch with him.

So with an attitude of openness to the many lessons of history and with a desire to truly comprehend the meaning and message of Jesus, let's review Jesus' roots as a Jew.

For Review

- Explain why studying Jewish history is important to understanding Jesus and his message.

Jesus a faith filled, profoundly committed Jew of his day → can't understand him outside context of his heritage

Photo: **An old synagogue in Nazareth. In a setting perhaps like this one, Jesus read from the prophet Isaiah and proclaimed, "Today this scripture passage is fulfilled in your hearing."**

A Brief History of the Jewish People

By this time in your religious education, you may already have acquired a sense of the basic history of the Jewish people. What follows, therefore, are only the most central highlights of that history, as a kind of quick review. Your teacher will be able to explain particular events in greater detail if necessary. 2

The Story Begins: 1900 B.C.E.

Abraham

Sometime between 1900 and 1750 B.C.E.—nearly two thousand years before the time of Jesus—Jewish history began. At that time, the Jews were simply part of a number of tribes collectively known as **Hebrews.** Only later would they take on the name

Jews. Their history as a special people started with the profound religious experience of a man named Abram. Abram followed a single loving God in an age when people believed in countless gods, few of whom entered into any kind of friendly relationship with people. The God of Abram called him into a very special kind of personal relationship. As one sign of their unique relationship, God gave Abram a new name: *Abraham.*

This type of special relationship between God and people—either as individuals or as communities—is a **covenant**. The covenant with Abraham was just the first in a series that God would establish with the Hebrew people. In the covenant, God promised to take care of Abraham's people. Abraham and his people, in turn, were called to follow God loyally and lovingly.

Isaac and Jacob

Though Abraham and his wife Sarah were very old, Sarah gave birth to a son named Isaac. Some years later it was revealed to Abraham that he had to sacrifice Isaac as a sign of his loyalty to God. But God then withdrew that command at the last minute, recognizing that Abraham's willingness to sacrifice his son was testimony enough to the strength of the covenant.

Later, Isaac and his wife Rebekah gave birth to a son named Jacob. The covenant was renewed with Jacob when, in a dream, God told him, "'Know that I am with you; I will protect you wherever you go, and bring you back to this land. I will never leave you until I have done what I promised you'" (Genesis 28:15).

Jacob eventually fathered twelve sons and later, like Abraham before him, was given a new name—*Israel*—as a sign of his special relationship with God.

2
As you read this history of the Jewish people, record and briefly identify the major characters, in the order in which they appear. Use the information as a study guide.

■
Abraham probably belonged to a tribe of nomads—people who wandered from place to place, supporting themselves chiefly by raising herds of sheep and goats.

Photo: **The nomadic lifestyle of the Bedouin tribes in the Middle East today resembles that of Abraham and his family.**

Settlement in Egypt

One of Jacob's twelve sons was named Joseph, and because he was Jacob's favorite, all of Jacob's other sons were jealous of him. The depth of their jealousy became apparent when they sold Joseph as a slave to some merchants who were on their way to Egypt. But Joseph ended up serving as a steward in a rich Egyptian's house and eventually worked his way up to the position of prime minister of the country. From that position of authority he invited his father, Jacob, and all his brothers, whom he had long since forgiven, to join him and live in Egypt. After Jacob died—in about 1650 B.C.E.—the Hebrews became prosperous in Egypt.

The End of the Patriarchal Period

The settlement in Egypt ended the *patriarchal period* of Jewish history. That period was dominated by Abraham, Isaac, and Jacob—the three **patriarchs.** (The word *patriarch* means "father and leader of a family or a people.") References to "the God of Abraham, Isaac, and Jacob" and "the God of our fathers," which appear throughout the Christian Scriptures, point to the patriarchal period.

Unfortunately, the recorders of Jewish history—like those who have recorded much of the world's history—often ignored or minimized the important role of women. Certainly women—some of them mothers, or **matriarchs**—played key roles throughout Jewish history. As will be seen later, in his time Jesus uniquely recognized and affirmed the dignity of women.

Because Jacob had been given the name *Israel* by God, his people became known as the **Israelites** during the period of history that centered around him and his sons. The prosperity of the Israelites in Egypt did not last. After about 150 years of living under kind pharaohs who came from a people related to their own, the Israelites came to be dominated by Egyptian pharaohs who enslaved them. The Israelites were given the backbreaking jobs of brick making and constructing public buildings. For a people who had always been free, this enslavement was miserable, and the Israelites dreamed of being liberated. The one who would lead them to freedom would be born several generations later.

The Story of Moses: 1250 B.C.E.

The man called to free the Israelites from slavery in Egypt was the powerful figure Moses. Moses sensed God's call to this mission during a profound religious experience. In the biblical account of this experience, God tells Moses, "'The cry of the Israelites has reached me, and I have truly noted that the Egyptians are oppressing them. Come, now! I will send you to Pharaoh to lead my people, the Israelites, out of Egypt'" (Exodus 3:9–10). It is at this point that God does something truly startling, something that we can understand only if we have a firm sense of the Israelite mentality: God reveals the name of God to Moses.

A Special Revelation

God's revelation to Moses on Mount Sinai (also known as Mount Horeb) is expressed through the biblical imagery of the Book of Exodus:

"But," said Moses to God, "when I go to the Israelites and say to them, 'The God of your fathers has sent me to you,' if they ask me, 'What is his name?' what am I to tell them?" God replied, "I am who am." Then he added, "This is what you shall tell the Israelites: I AM sent me to you."

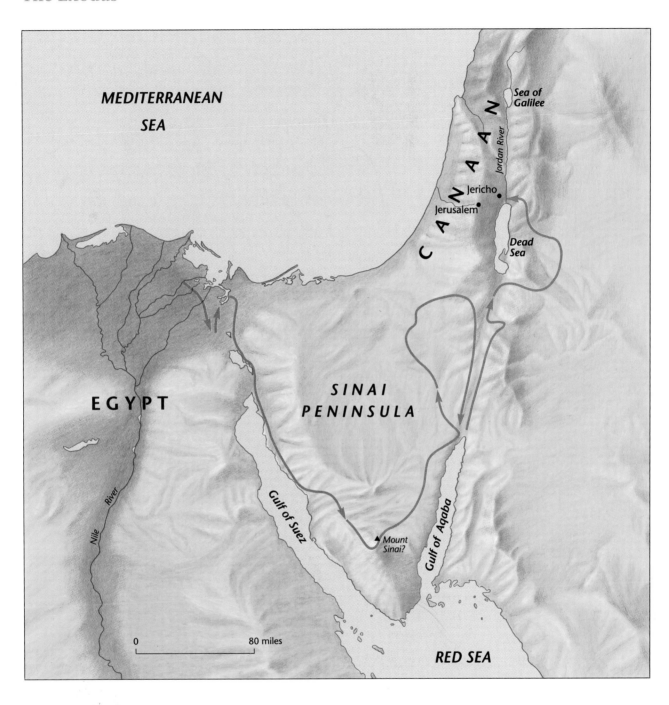

MEDITERRANEAN
SEA

EGYPT

CANAAN

Sea of Galilee

Jordan River

Jericho

Jerusalem

Dead Sea

SINAI
PENINSULA

Nile River

Gulf of Suez

Gulf of Aqaba

▲ Mount Sinai?

0   80 miles

RED SEA

Map: **The red line indicates the traditional but much-debated route of the Israelites as Moses led them out of Egypt to the Promised Land of Canaan. Later, the Greeks would rename the** Promised Land *Palestine,* **which is what it was called in Jesus' time. The "sea of reeds," believed to have been crossed by Moses and the Israelites, was most likely one of the lakes to the north of** what is now known as the Gulf of Suez.

49

A Clarifying Word About God's Name

The name *Yahweh* continues to be treated with great reverence by Jews today. In an effort to demonstrate sensitivity to Jewish religious beliefs, some writers and Bible translations today use the word *Lord* rather than *Yahweh* when referring to the Hebrew name for God. (The all-capital letters in *Lord* are meant to reflect the Hebrew symbol YHWH.) This is the case with the two main translations of the Bible quoted in this course.

Further confusing this treatment of the name for God, however, is the fact that Jesus is often referred to as "Lord" in the Christian Testament. In some cases the title is intended to show Jesus' total unity with God (a concept that will be discussed later in this course). The point is, if we use the same title both for Yahweh, the God of the Jews, and for Jesus himself, we can become quite confused. Therefore, in order to avoid such confusion, this course will continue to use *Yahweh* as the Hebrew name for God.

God spoke further to Moses, "Thus shall you say to the Israelites: The Lord, the God of your fathers, the God of Abraham, the God of Isaac, the God of Jacob, has sent me to you.

"This is my name forever;
   this is my title for all generations."

(Exodus 3:13–15)

Many versions of the Hebrew Scriptures translate the word **Lord** (see the word in the biblical passage above) as **Yahweh,** the most important name for God in the Hebrew Scriptures. The name *Yahweh* is thought to come from the Hebrew word for the verb "to be," and it signifies that God is the Creator, the Ruler of nature and history, and the One who is always present.

The significance of God's name being revealed to the Israelite people (rather than the people coming up with their own name for God) lies in the fact that for the Israelites, the act of naming anything indicated the power of the namer over the named. By revealing God's name first, God claimed sovereignty over the people. Also of significance is the fact that at a time when many gods were believed in, the Israelite people were told who the one true God was.

Over the years, the Israelite people would come to regard as very sacred the name that God had revealed to them, and they would not even pronounce this name for fear of misusing it. In their Scriptures, the Israelites actually used only the symbol YHWH and accompanied it with the word *Adonai* (meaning "my great Lord") to remind the reader to say "Lord" rather than "Yahweh." To call God by name would have been the greatest sacrilege, implying that people had control over God.

As will be seen later, Jesus himself would grapple with this understanding of his God—the God of

אֶהְיֶה אֲשֶׁר אֶהְיֶה

Abraham, Isaac, and Jacob—and he would offer his own startling and profound insights into God's very nature. Jesus would even offer a new name for God, which would not only astound but deeply anger the faithful Jews who heard him speak.

The First Passover

Moses was sent by God to convince Pharaoh to free the Israelite people from bondage. But Pharaoh was not easily persuaded, and God had to provide a great deal of help so that Moses could accomplish the mission. Pharaoh's hand was forced when a series of ten plagues revealed God's power over the lives of people. The tenth plague—the one that ultimately freed the Israelites from Pharaoh's grip—also resulted in key religious rituals that to this very day highlight the spiritual life of the Jewish people.

The tenth plague was to involve the death of all the firstborn children in Egypt. But God gave the Israelites a sign that would protect them—and them alone—from this disaster. They were to slaughter either sheep or goats from their flocks and then take some of the blood from the slaughter and put it on the doorposts and above the doors of their homes. The flesh of the slaughtered

Illustration: **At the time of Jesus, as today, the annual feast of Passover helped the Jews celebrate God's freeing their people from slavery in Egypt. They recalled that God had brought the Israelites unharmed through the "sea of reeds."**

animals was to be eaten along with unleavened bread and bitter herbs. Later, as the firstborn children in all of Egypt were killed, God *passed over* the homes on which the blood had been poured, saving the Israelites and convincing the Egyptians to let them go. And God said to the Israelites, "'This day [Passover] shall be a memorial feast for you, which all your generations shall celebrate with pilgrimage to the LORD, as a perpetual institution'" (Exodus 12:14). A discussion of key Jewish feasts, including Passover, will come later.

The Covenant of Sinai

Following their exodus from Egypt, the Israelites wandered in the desert. After fifty days, God ratified the covenant with them in one of the most important events recorded in all of the Scriptures. In a dramatic encounter (see Exodus, chapters 19 and 20), Yahweh called Moses to the top of Mount Sinai and there said to him:

"Thus shall you say to the house of Jacob; tell the Israelites: You have seen for yourselves how I treated the Egyptians and how I bore you up on eagle wings and brought you here to myself. Therefore, if you hearken to my voice and keep my covenant, you shall be my special possession, dearer to me than all other people, though all the earth is mine. You shall be to me a kingdom of priests, a holy nation. That is what you must tell the Israelites." (Exodus 19:3–6)

So God had now extended the offer of the covenant to an entire people—the implications of which will become clear in a moment.

A covenant is a two-way relationship, and because God chose the Israelites as God's people, something was expected of them by God. Their end of the bargain was to follow the elab-orate system of the Jewish Law, of which the cornerstone was the **Ten Commandments.** The Law would one day be misused and would be a stumbling block between Jesus and his own people. But at this point in Jewish history, it was recognized for what it truly was—a wonderful gift that uniquely established a relationship of love between Yahweh and Yahweh's people.

As was said earlier, the covenant of Sinai is one of the central events in all of the Scriptures and in the history of the Jews. Yahweh transformed a crowd of poor slaves into a nation—God's own special people. Until this point Yahweh had spoken only to individuals (Abraham and Jacob, for example), and these individuals were, at most, only leaders of small clans of people. At Sinai the *People of God* were born, with the special name *Israel*. So the people became a covenant community, and it is only in terms of that community that we can come to understand the Jews and, for that matter, the real meaning of today's church.

Following the marvelous events at Sinai, the Israelites roamed the desert for forty difficult years. Even though the faith of the Israelites wavered at times, Yahweh remained firm in commitment to this covenant community. Yahweh was indeed their God, and they were God's people—though, as will be seen later, they were not always a faithful people.

Life in the Promised Land

Following the death of Moses, the Israelites crossed the Jordan River into the land that had been promised to them by Yahweh: the Promised Land of Canaan. The next few hundred years, however, were brutal ones, with many wars and seemingly endless turmoil for Israel as it sought to settle in a land already occupied by other peoples. During

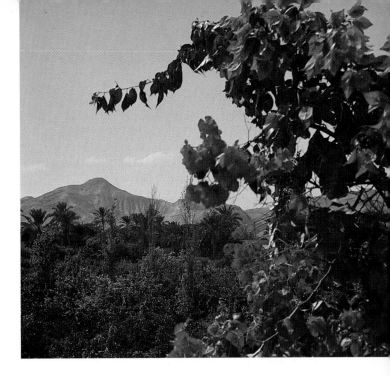

this time, *judges*—great warriors rather than judges in our usual sense of the term—were periodically appointed to fight and defeat Israel's enemies. As land was gradually conquered, it was divided among the *twelve tribes of Israel,* one tribe descending from each of the twelve sons of Jacob.

In about 1050 B.C.E., nearly 150 years after beginning the conquest of the land of Canaan, Israel confronted a new enemy: the Philistines. With new weapons, and fighting a now-divided Israel, the Philistines proved to be way too strong for the Israelites. The Philistines captured the treasured ark of the covenant, in which Moses' written version of the Ten Commandments was stored and honored. If the Israelites were to defeat their enemies and survive as a people, they needed a strong leader. In desperation they appointed their first king, a man named Saul.

The Kingdom of Israel: 1000 B.C.E.

Saul: A Warrior-King

Saul, the first king of Israel, was actually more of a warrior than a king in today's sense, and though he was a brave man in battle, he was a weak man personally. He was very jealous of a young man named David, one of the leaders in his army, who had gained public acclaim for leading the people in some of their victories over the Philistines.

By the time Saul became king, the twelve tribes of Israel were divided into two main groups. The ten tribes who lived mostly north of Jerusalem retained the name *Israel,* and the two tribes living to the south of Jerusalem went by the collective name *Judah.* Although all twelve tribes recognized Saul as their first king, the two groups disagreed about who should be Saul's successor. While the ten northern tribes recognized one of Saul's sons as their new king, the two southern tribes recognized David. Saul's son was a weak leader and was murdered after just a short time on the throne.

David: Uniting the People of Israel

Upon the death of Saul's son, the people turned to David as their only king. He was thirty-seven years old when he united all twelve tribes of Israel into one nation, around the year 1000 B.C.E., and he led Israel in defeating the Philistines and conquering much of the surrounding territory. Jerusalem became known as "the city of David," where he built a palace and desired to build a great temple in which the reclaimed ark of the covenant could be kept and honored. Jerusalem therefore became the center of not only the political life of the people of Israel but also their religious life. David is still recognized as the greatest of all the kings of Israel.

Solomon: Son of David

Before David died, he made sure his son Solomon was publicly crowned successor to the throne.

The Israelites crossed the Jordan River to enter the Promised Land. The first Canaanite town they conquered was Jericho.
Photo: The oasis of Jericho

Solomon served as king for some forty years. It was a period of great building, increased trade, and prosperity, during which Solomon built the magnificent Temple that David had dreamed of. But to build the Temple, Solomon had to resort to heavily taxing the people and drafting thousands of workers a month. Though the Temple was beautiful and attracted the people to worship Yahweh, Solomon himself turned to idolatry, building pagan shrines and worshiping pagan idols. **3**

The Kingdom Divided: Israel and Judah

After Solomon died, one of his sons was immediately proclaimed king of the two tribes of Judah, in the south. Solomon's son could have been accepted as king of all the northern tribes as well, if he had been willing to listen to the demands of the people there. The people of the north wanted relief from their taxes and the labor draft. Solomon's son refused to grant them their wishes, however, and alienated them. The ten tribes in the north refused to accept him as their king and instead formed themselves into a new kingdom of Israel, thereby destroying the unified kingdom of David.

The Time of the Prophets

What followed for both Israel and Judah was a history of weak kings and religious disgrace. Great **prophets** arose, trying to call the people back to the covenant, but the people continued to weaken. Eventually, in 721 B.C.E., the northern kingdom of Israel was destroyed by the Assyrians.

The southern kingdom of Judah was able to last about a century longer than the northern kingdom because Judah's leaders, successors of David, were somewhat more loyal to the covenant with Yahweh than were the kings of the north. The great prophet Isaiah, however, recognized that one day the southern kingdom also would be destroyed. He made a prediction: Comparing the royal family of David to a tree that had been cut down, Isaiah said that only a stump would be left to represent the family that had started with David's father, Jesse (this family tree is the origin of the religious symbol of the Jesse tree, which is often referred to at Christmastime). However, said Isaiah, from this stump would come a shoot, a new branch—and this future king of David's line would be someone powerful and good, someone who would bring peace. (See Isaiah 11:1–9.) Christians, of course, would much later recognize that someone in the person of Jesus, one born from the line of David.

The Babylonian Exile: 598 B.C.E.

In 598 B.C.E. Jerusalem was overrun by the Babylonians, and the leading citizens of the kingdom of Judah were carried off as captives into Babylon— the southern kingdom had been destroyed just as Isaiah had predicted. Another prophet, by the name of Jeremiah, wrote to the captives in Babylon and urged them to settle as residents there, promising that someday Yahweh would return them to their home.

Back in Jerusalem everything worsened, and in 587 B.C.E. the city itself was destroyed and thousands more captives were led off into exile in Babylon. Many of the people who were not captured left the country for places along the Mediterranean Sea, where small colonies of the faithful began to grow. These people made up a settlement called the **Diaspora**, from a word meaning "dispersion" or "those who have been dispersed." (The people

---

3
Choosing from among all the characters of Jewish history identified up to and including Solomon, write a brief paragraph on the one you would most like to meet and talk with.

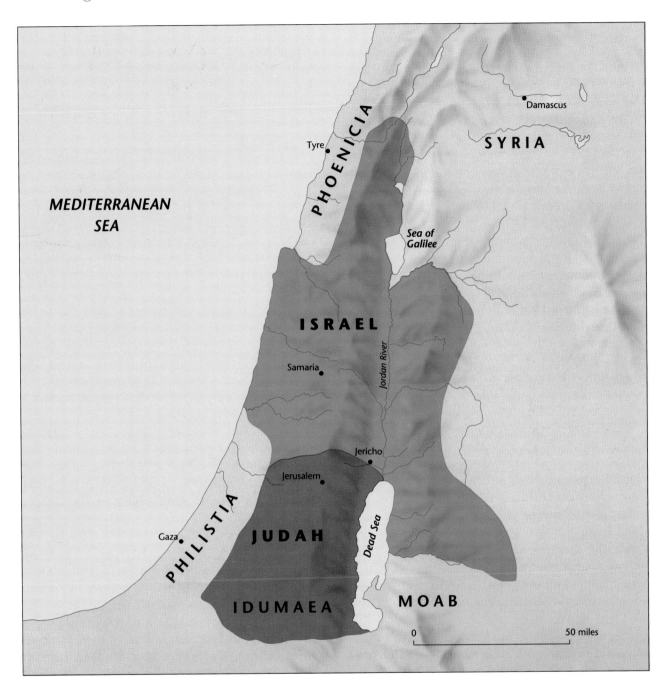

Map: After Solomon died, the kingdom of the Israelites split into the northern kingdom of Israel and the southern kingdom of Judah. By 721 B.C.E., the northern kingdom had fallen to the Assyrians. The kingdom of Judah was conquered by the Babylonians in 587 B.C.E., and many of its citizens were exiled.

Summary of Jewish History: 1900 to 515 B.C.E.

Key persons and events are indicated by **bold** type.

1900 B.C.E.
Jewish history began about 1900 B.C.E. with **Abraham** in the land of Canaan. Abraham's wife Sarah gave birth to **Isaac.** Isaac and his wife Rebekah had two sons, one of whom was **Jacob.** Jacob had twelve sons, from whom the twelve tribes of Israel were derived. One of the twelve sons was **Joseph,** who settled in Egypt, where he was later joined by his father and brothers. One hundred fifty years of prosperity followed for the people of Israel.

1500–1250 B.C.E.
From about 1500 to 1250 B.C.E. the Israelites suffered **slavery in Egypt.**

1250–1000 B.C.E.
Around 1250 B.C.E. **Moses** led the Israelites out of Egypt (the **Exodus**), and Yahweh formed the **covenant of Sinai** with the people. The Israelites then settled in the Promised Land, Canaan. From 1200 to 1000 B.C.E. the **judges** led the Israelites against their enemies.

1000 B.C.E.
The kingdom of Israel was formed. **Saul** was the first king, followed by **David** (1000 B.C.E.), who would be the greatest of all the kings. David established Jerusalem as the central city of his people. He was succeeded by **Solomon,** who built the **Temple.** After the death of Solomon, the kingdom split apart into the **northern kingdom of Israel** and the **southern kingdom of Judah.**

721–587 B.C.E.
The northern kingdom was destroyed by the **Assyrians** in 721 B.C.E. The southern kingdom survived until 598 B.C.E., when its leading citizens were taken into captivity by the **Babylonians.** In 587 B.C.E., Jerusalem was destroyed and thousands more were led into captivity (the **Exile**).

539–515 B.C.E.
In 539 B.C.E. the **Persians** defeated the Babylonians, and the exiles were allowed to return to Jerusalem. From this point on they were known as **Jews** (from the word *Judah*). The **rebuilding of the Temple** was completed by 515 B.C.E.

---

of the Diaspora would later become important in the ministry of Saint Paul, who would travel to the widespread communities to share the message about Jesus.)

Through the voice of the prophet Jeremiah, Yahweh assured the people of everlasting love and a new covenant. It was clear that Yahweh would never abandon them: "The days are coming, says the LORD, when I will make a new covenant with the house of Israel and the house of Judah. . . . I will place my law within them, and write it upon their hearts; I will be their God, and they shall be my people" (Jeremiah 31:31–33).

Renewal of the Covenant Community

A Faithful Remnant
Somehow the experience of being in exile, with Jerusalem destroyed, led many of the exiled people to a renewed appreciation of their faith in Yahweh. Certainly many of those held in Babylon gave up

in hopelessness, and the time of the captivity was perhaps the saddest in all of Jewish biblical history. But a certain number of these people—called the **remnant**—began to live much more closely to Yahweh than ever before. The **Exile** was seen not so much as punishment by God, but rather as God's way of bringing the people back to recognition of Yahweh.

A Prophet's Promise

In 539 B.C.E. the Persians overcame the Babylonians, and the Persian leader allowed all the exiles in the new empire to return to their native lands with freedom of worship. This had been predicted by perhaps the greatest of all the prophets, one whose name we have never even known. His writings were added to those of the prophet Isaiah, so we have come to call this prophet Second Isaiah. He wrote some of the most beautiful passages in all of the Scriptures, including the famous "suffering servant" passages, which speak of a great servant of God who will one day save his people through his own suffering and death rather than through military conquest. (See especially Isaiah 53:1–12.) To Christians of the twentieth century, those fully aware of the life and death of Jesus, such a prophecy makes sense. However, to the exiles, who first heard it in the middle of the sixth century before Christ, it was a bewildering kind of talk. They were a people who expected victory by *fighting* for it. The thought of gaining victory by suffering willingly must have seemed like utter nonsense.

The Return to Judah

By 537 B.C.E. the faithful remnant began returning to their homeland in caravans. They worked on rebuilding the Temple, a project completed in 515 B.C.E. They were no longer a political nation united under a king, but rather a religious community under a new form of leader: the *high priest.* Because these people were a remnant from the southern kingdom of Judah, it is at this point in their history that we begin to speak of **Judaism** as we know it today. And it is also from this term, *Judaism,* that we have derived the word *Jew* for those who follow that faith.

Gradually, two main classes of leaders developed among the Jews: the **priests**, who were responsible for offering sacrifices in the Temple, and those called **scribes**, who were responsible for teaching the Law of Moses. 4

Before continuing with this look at Jewish history, you may wish to pause and review the summary chart of this material on page 56. When you feel that you adequately understand the information summarized there, you can with confidence move on to the rest of the history.

For Review

- List two major characters in ancient Jewish history that received new names. Give both their original and their new names. Briefly explain the significance of their receiving a new name from God.
- What name did God reveal to Moses, and what does the name mean? Why was God's giving of that name so significant?
- Briefly explain the origin and meaning of the term *Passover*.
- Identify *Saul, David,* and *Solomon* and briefly explain the relationships among the three.
- Define the term *Diaspora*.

4
Consult a dictionary and write down the definitions of these words: *prophet, priest, scribe.*

The Political World of Jesus

The first part of this chapter reviewed Jewish history from 1900 to 515 B.C.E., the year the Jewish remnant returned from the Exile, the Temple was rebuilt, and the religion of Judaism formally began. The second part of this chapter will cover the developments in Jewish history from roughly three hundred years before Jesus' birth until about forty years after his death. What is offered is a broad overview of that history, keying in on only those persons, groups, or events that played a direct role in the Gospel story.

Greek Domination of Palestine

One man seemed to dominate the world about three hundred years before the time of Jesus. He was *Alexander the Great,* and he was unquestionably one of the most remarkable figures in all of history. He lived only thirty-three years, but in that time he towered over his world. Though born in a country north of Greece, he was a Greek in spirit, educated by the great philosopher Aristotle and convinced that the Greek vision of life offered civilization its greatest hope of fulfillment and excellence. He was just twenty when he became king of his own country, but he quickly won the hearts and minds of the Greeks as he led his armies in victories over all the enemies of Greece. By the time he died, in 323 B.C.E., he had conquered much of the Mediterranean world and lands as far east as India.

Alexander's Empire Divided

After Alexander's death, the land that he had conquered was divided among the leading generals of his army. The concern in this course is what happened to one part of the empire, namely the Middle East, which included Palestine, the land in which Jesus would be born some three hundred years later.

Palestine was divided between two of Alexander's generals. Though the generals were both Greek, they did not see eye to eye. These two men and their successors dominated Palestine for 150 years. One of these lines of generals was centered in Syria, to the north of Palestine; the other, in Egypt, to the southwest. Palestine was located directly between the two centers of power, and it was inevitably caught in the struggle for control between them, a struggle that lasted for many years. Many of the factions and groups we find in the Gospels developed out of that conflict.

Greek influence: For about the first one hundred years after Alexander's death, most of the people of Israel were ruled by the power located in Egypt. Because of the distance that separated Egypt from Palestine, that Greek power seldom interfered in the internal affairs of the Jews. Nevertheless,

Alexander the Great, a Greek ruler, conquered much of the Mediterranean world, including Palestine, three hundred years before the time of Jesus.

Photo: **A bronze statue of Alexander the Great**

A Land, a People

The names used for the region in which the Gospel story takes place can vary and, therefore, cause confusion. For example, it is common today for people to variously refer to the area as Palestine, Israel, or the Holy Land. The issue is complicated even more by the fact that the country we now know as Israel involves a smaller area of land than the region in which the Gospel story took place. Below is an explanation of how the place names are used in this course. Not only is the following the most accurate usage, but it also reflects the way in which these terms are used in the Scriptures themselves.

- *Palestine* is the name used for the *geographic setting* in which the Gospel story takes place. Whenever we are talking about Palestine, therefore, we are discussing the land itself. The name *Palestine* was given to the region by the Greeks and derives from the Greek word for "Philistines," the ancient rivals of Israel who at one time dominated the region and whom king David defeated.
- Throughout the Scriptures, *Israel* is the name given to the *People of God* themselves, that is, the political and religious group. Therefore, Israel as a people might exist regardless of what land they occupy and, in fact, even if they have no home at all, as when they roamed the desert after the exodus out of Egypt.

Greek culture in some way had an impact on all the people who inhabited Palestine. For example, the Greek language was increasingly used throughout the land.

In Galilee (the northern region of Palestine), which the Syrian Greeks controlled, the influence of Greek culture on all levels of Jewish life was profound—so much so that the region is often referred to as "Galilee of the Gentiles" in the Bible. (Gentiles are non-Jews, and by Jesus' time, a Jew born in Galilee—like Jesus himself—was seen in Jewish eyes as someone "born on the wrong side of the tracks.")

The end of tolerance: The tolerant kind of Greek occupation practiced by the power in Egypt ended in the year 198 B.C.E., when all of Palestine came under control of the power to the north, in Syria. At first the people of Israel were allowed to maintain local control of their affairs, but that situation changed gradually as the rulers developed a need for increased finances. The Romans, from the west, had defeated the Syrian Greeks in a naval battle and then demanded an enormous amount of money as a price of defeat. To pay off Rome—as well as to support other Greek war efforts—the rulers in Syria began a heavy taxation of the Jews. Any peace and goodwill that had existed between the Greeks and the Jews was shattered by this.

Reactions to Greek Rule

All of this historical development is important in a study of Jesus because of the Jews' reactions to it and the emergence of groups that became identified with those reactions.

There were two basic reactions to the Greek influences on the people of Israel, particularly by those living in the region of Palestine called Judaea, where the city of Jerusalem was located:

1. The Jewish leaders, the wealthy landowners, and the priestly class tried to get along with the Greeks, simply because they had the most to lose in any conflicts with them.

2. Another group, called the *Hasidim,* meaning "the pious ones," resented the Greek rulers and felt that any compromise with them amounted to a rejection of the Jewish faith.

Out of these basic philosophical and religious differences developed many of the factions that appear in the Gospels—particularly the Sadducees and the Pharisees. These groups will be defined more clearly later.

An incredible victory: The Greek domination of Israel led to one of the greatest events in the entire history of the Jews, one that eventually resulted in a religious festival that is celebrated by the Jews even today. At one point, rebels within the Jewish community tried to overthrow their Greek overlords and regain their freedom. However, the Greek leaders in Syria, already angry about their defeat by the Romans, took out their rage on the rebelling Jews. They not only crushed the Jewish rebellion but sacked Jerusalem and desecrated the beloved Temple. They even went so far as to build an altar to the Greek god Zeus in the Holy of Holies, the most sacred part of the Temple.

The Greeks had clearly gone too far and had underestimated the power of a people whose religious convictions ran as deeply as those of the Jews. All of Judaea erupted in outrage at what the Syrian Greeks had done. Though the odds were strongly stacked against them, the rebelling Jews won a decisive victory over their oppressors! (One of the Jewish leaders was nicknamed Maccabeus, meaning "the hammer," because of his ferocious fighting. The revolt itself came to be known as the

Maccabean War, or the Maccabean Revolt, and its story is told in two books of the Hebrew Scriptures—1 and 2 Maccabees.) In 164 B.C.E. the hated altar of Zeus was removed and the sacred Temple was rededicated, an event still remembered and celebrated by Jews today, with the Feast of Dedication, or *Hanukkah.* By 142 B.C.E. the Greeks had granted complete freedom to Israel, and about a century of national freedom followed. A period of independence for the Jews would not be experienced again until, incredibly, the founding of the modern state of Israel in our own era.

Jewish Independence

Unfortunately for the Jews, strong leaders did not emerge to guide them during the period of independence. In fact, Jewish independence was undermined even before it was fully gained. Before

Greek culture and rule had a profound impact on all who inhabited Palestine.
Photo: **The temple of a Greek god, Hephaestus, in Athens, Greece**

Hasmonean

complete independence was granted by the Greeks, the Jewish family that eventually assumed leadership of the Jewish state acted improperly. One member of this ruling family accepted the "gift" of the high priesthood from the Greek leaders. The leadership position of high priest was important among the Jews during the time of foreign domination, and it had traditionally been restricted to only certain families from one of the original twelve tribes of Israel. Not only did the Greeks have no authority to choose whomever they wanted for the position of high priest, but the family member who accepted the gift had no right to accept it. Thus the family was seen as publicly violating the traditions of their own people. The act also greatly lessened the prestige and respect accorded to the priesthood—a fact represented by the tensions in the Gospel stories—and it planted a seed that would soon give rise to factions among the Jews.

Political Factions Within Judaism

The violation of the priesthood and the role of high priest by the ruling family evoked a number of different responses, and different political factions began to take shape:

The Sadducees: The priestly class worked out accommodations with the new Jewish political leaders, just as they had earlier with their Greek overlords. The members of this priestly class became known as the Sadducees.

The Essenes: Some people reacted so strongly to the weaknesses of the Jewish political leaders that they withdrew from Jewish society altogether in order to observe strict religious traditions. These people were called the Essenes. Though they are never mentioned in the Bible, it is likely that Jesus knew

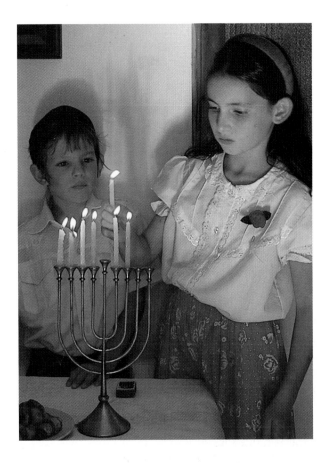

of the Essenes and may even have been influenced by their deep religious convictions and practices.

The Pharisees: Another group, the Pharisees, tried at first to find some kind of middle ground between the political accommodation of the Sadducees and the withdrawal of the Essenes. In the end, however, they refused to compromise their religious beliefs and therefore lost some influence in the higher levels of religious and political power. But among the common people they gained a strong reputation for strict faithfulness to the covenant, and they were very much respected and

Photo: **Jewish children light the menorah, a candelabrum used to celebrate the Feast of Dedication, or Hanukkah. This "Feast of Lights" recalls the rededication of the sacred Temple after the Jews'** **decisive victory over their Greek oppressors in the Maccabean Revolt.**

therefore influential among those people. The Pharisees were an extremely important Jewish group and are mentioned often in the Christian Testament. **5**

Geographical Factions in Palestine

Much of the prejudice and bitterness between various sections of the country in Jesus' time originated during the period of Jewish independence.

The region of Judaea: Judaea was the region of central Palestine that had been settled by the faithful remnant, who had returned from the Exile in the year 537 B.C.E. Because Jerusalem was located there, Judaea had become the religious as well as the geographic center of Judaism. During Jewish independence, groups holding political power further abused their position of authority by trying to expand from their central power base in Judaea out to the other regions of Palestine.

The region of Idumaea: On the map on page 63 you will see that just south of Judaea was the territory of Idumaea. Under the leadership of the Jews holding political power, this region was quickly absorbed by Israel and *forced* to accept Judaism. The fact that the Idumaeans' "acceptance" of the Jewish faith was brought about by force would always make the Idumaean Jews suspect to the mainline Jews of Judaea.

The region of Samaria: The people of Samaria, the territory just north of Judaea, were also suspect. The Samaritans were among the descendants of the old northern tribes of the kingdom of Israel (conquered by the Assyrians in 721 B.C.E.), who had stayed in the north and lost touch with their

5
Imagine yourself as a young Jewish person living during the time of Jewish independence and facing the problem of weak and untrustworthy leaders. Which political faction would you most agree with—the Sadducees, the Essenes, the Pharisees, or none of these? Explain your response in a paragraph.

■
People in Samaria were considered suspect by their Jewish "cousins" to the south in Judaea. *Photo:* The modern city of Sebastiyeh is located on the site of the ancient city of Samaria.

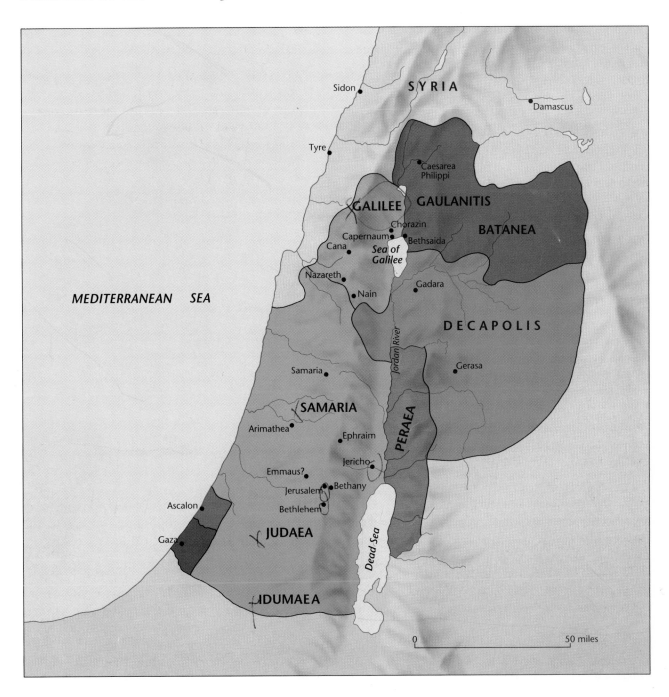

Map showing: SYRIA, Sidon, Damascus, Tyre, Caesarea Philippi, GALILEE, GAULANITIS, BATANEA, Chorazin, Capernaum, Bethsaida, Cana, Sea of Galilee, Nazareth, Nain, Gadara, DECAPOLIS, Jordan River, Samaria, Gerasa, SAMARIA, PERAEA, Arimathea, Ephraim, Jericho, Emmaus?, Jerusalem, Bethany, Bethlehem, Ascalon, Gaza, Dead Sea, JUDAEA, IDUMAEA, MEDITERRANEAN SEA, 0 — 50 miles

Map: **The Gospels mention many towns and geographical regions of Palestine. The area around Capernaum is sometimes referred to as Gennesaret. Peraea is also called Transjordan, or "across the Jordan," in the Gospels. Decapolis was a loose federation of ten cities and their surrounding territory.**

Jewish "cousins" in the southern kingdom of Judah. They had *not* been sent into Babylon during the Exile. Many of their religious practices and traditions—including their scriptures—were different from those of the mainline Jews in the south. When the remnant returned from the Exile, they completely rejected the Samaritans and would not allow them any participation in Jewish religious or national life.

During the period of independence, the leaders of the Jews, in their effort to expand their power, went so far as to destroy the temple that the Samaritans had built in their own territory. The Jewish leaders tried to force the Samaritans to accept orthodox Judaism. The intense bitterness between the two peoples deepened, and by the time of Jesus great hatred existed between them.

Imagine now the impact of the story Jesus would one day tell about the good Samaritan, who comes off as a hero when compared with the Jewish priest in the story (Luke 10:29–37), or Jesus' public conversation with not just a woman—which would have been scandalous enough—but a *Samaritan* woman, no less (John 4:1–30). No wonder Jesus seemed to cause problems and controversy wherever he went!

The region of Galilee: Galilee, too, was annexed by the Jewish leaders, and the non-Jews there were forced to either accept Judaism or leave the region. Many accepted, and by Jesus' time most of Galilee was Jewish. Nevertheless, the mainline Jews held a negative, haughty attitude about Galileans. The Galileans' late acceptance of the Jewish faith added to their reputation as second-class citizens.

As mentioned earlier, and as you can see from the map on page 63, Nazareth—where Jesus was raised—was located in Galilee. This explains a

comment that the mainline Jews make about him in the Gospels: "'Can anything good come from Nazareth?'" (John 1:46).

An Appeal to Rome

The century of independence under inept Jewish leaders thus quickly deteriorated—nearly to the point of civil war—because of bitter factions. Finally, both the Pharisees and the Sadducees appealed to Rome for help in settling their conflicts. The Romans had just been waiting for such an invitation, and when it came they were ready to offer more "help" than the people had bargained for. In 63 B.C.E., some sixty years before the birth of Jesus, the Romans occupied Palestine and took complete control.

The Romans occupied Palestine and took complete control in 63 B.C.E. Roman domination marked the Jewish world of Jesus' day.

Illustration: A Roman soldier's uniform and gear

The Roman World in the Time of Jesus

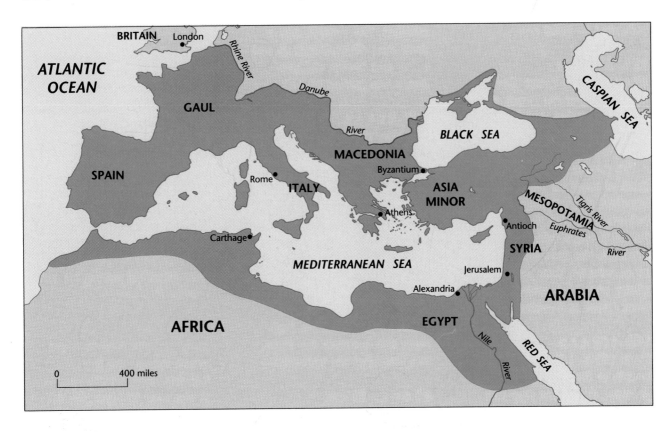

Israel Under Roman Domination

One of the reasons the Romans were able to build such a powerful empire in their day was the wise way in which they governed the people they conquered. For example, when they defeated a country and took control of it, the Romans would carefully select leaders from among the conquered people themselves. This practice gave stability to the entire empire. By 37 B.C.E. the Romans had selected a shrewd Idumaean Jew named Herod to rule Israel. (Remember, Idumaean Jews were not respected by mainline Jews because the faith had been forced upon the Idumaeans.) Herod would rule until his death in 4 B.C.E., and toward the end of his reign, Jesus would be born. The sons of Herod would continue his dynasty until almost the end of the first century after Jesus.

Herod "the Great"

If one were to judge Herod on purely political grounds, with no regard to his morality, he would have to be judged a success as a ruler. He combined the qualities of political cunning and absolute terror. He was a master builder, and he began restoring the Temple to its original splendor during Jesus' time. But he was also an incredibly cruel man. For example, in Matthew 2:13–18, we find

Map: **The green area represents the extent of Roman political domination in the time of Jesus.**

Key persons and events are indicated by **bold** type.

323–200 B.C.E.

Alexander the Great died in 323 B.C.E., and the Greek empire was divided. Greek leaders located in both Syria and Egypt were given control of Palestine.

The Greeks in **Egypt** ruled most of Israel for about one hundred years. Though Greek influence was felt throughout Palestine (especially in Galilee), generally the Jews were allowed to conduct their internal affairs without interference from Greek authorities.

198–142 B.C.E.

From 198 to 142 B.C.E. the Greeks in **Syria** controlled all of Israel. The rulers imposed heavy taxation, and political and religious factions began to develop among the Jews. After the **desecration of the Temple** by the Greeks, the outraged Jews successfully rebelled. The Temple was re-dedicated (**Hanukkah**) in 164 B.C.E., and Jewish independence was gained by 142 B.C.E.

142–63 B.C.E.

The Jews were independent from 142 to 63 B.C.E. Unfortunately, they had poor leaders. Factions within Judaism became defined: **Sadducees** (more concerned about politics than religion), **Essenes** (religiously strict and withdrawn), **Pharisees** (more concerned about religion than politics). Tension grew between the mainline Jews and the Galileans and between the mainline Jews and the Samaritans.

63 B.C.E.–36 C.E.

From 63 B.C.E. until well after the time of Jesus, the **Romans** ruled Palestine. In 37 B.C.E. **Herod the Great** was appointed its ruler. He was a political "success" but extremely cruel. He ruled until 4 B.C.E., and the **birth of Jesus** was very near the end of his reign (6 or 5 B.C.E.). After Herod's death came the **division of Palestine** among his three sons. One of them, **Herod Antipas**, was ruler of Galilee. Another son was put in charge of Judaea, but he was such a poor leader that he was replaced with a Roman procurator. From 26 to 36 C.E. the procurator of Judaea was **Pontius Pilate**, and **Jesus was crucified** during his term (about 30 C.E.).

66–70 C.E.

In 66 C.E. the **Zealots** began a revolt against the Romans, but they were totally crushed. In the year 70 came the **destruction of Jerusalem and the Temple**, and it was only on the strength of the Pharisees that Judaism was able to survive.

the story of Herod's execution of all male children age two and under, in the hope of destroying the Messiah, who might assume the role of "king of the Jews." This event, called the Slaughter of the Innocents, has not been historically verified, but Herod's reputation for brutality certainly makes it seem possible. (Also, the story is told that when Herod lay dying, he ordered that all prominent men in the town be executed right at the moment of his own death, so that the grief of the townspeople would be real!)

It was Herod's political ability that managed to hold the country together during his reign. But when he died, the Romans allowed his power to be passed on to his sons, most of whom seemed to have all of his cruelty but none of his political intelligence. This political situation in Palestine be-came the backdrop for the Gospel story.

Herod Antipas

One of Herod's three sons was given control of the northeast region of Palestine. A second son, *Herod Antipas* (sometimes called simply Antipas to avoid confusion with his father) was given control of Galilee and Peraea, a region just east of the Jordan River. Antipas's marriage to the wife of his half brother brought about the rage of John the Baptist, which in turn led Antipas to have John beheaded (Matthew 14:3–12). Jesus referred to Antipas as "that fox" in a discussion with the Pharisees (Luke 13:31–33). The Gospels refer to him simply as Herod or occasionally as "Herod the tetrarch," a title based on the Greek word for "four" and referring to a person who governs one-fourth of a province.

A Procurator: Replacement for a Son of Herod the Great

The third son of Herod the Great was by far the worst leader of the three, but he was given the most important area to rule: Judaea, Samaria, and Idumaea. He was so inept as a ruler that he was eventually removed and sent into exile by the Romans, who replaced him with a Roman official variously called a "procurator," a "prefect," or less often, a "governor." The first procurator was installed by the Romans in 6 C.E., and by the time of Jesus' public ministry, five different men had held the position. The fifth procurator began his rule in the year 26, just a year or so before Jesus began his public life. The man was *Pontius Pilate,* and he would play a key role in the trial and execution of Jesus.

The Destruction of Jerusalem

The political confusion and division within Palestine lasted throughout Jesus' lifetime and beyond. Eventually the strong anti-Roman feelings among the Jews built to the point of exploding, fueled by the memory of the Jews' successful rebellion against their Greek overlords years earlier. Under the leadership of a revolutionary group known as the *Zealots,* an open rebellion against the Romans began in 66 C.E. But this time the Jews took on a power far too great in strength. The Romans totally crushed the rebels and destroyed Jerusalem and its Temple by the year 70. The Jewish hopes for freedom were destroyed, and only because of the strength of the Pharisees was Judaism able to survive and become the major world religion it is today.

This survey of the religious and political history of the Jewish people has been brief but certainly not simple. As the discussion of Jesus in the Gospels unfolds in the next several chapters, you may occasionally wish to refer to the brief summaries of this material offered on pages 56 and 66.

For Review

- Briefly explain how the Greeks—in particular the Syrian Greeks—came to dominate the people of Israel.
- Identify two major Jewish reactions to Greek rule.
- Identify and define three major political factions within Judaism that developed during the period of Jewish independence.
- Explain the origins of the Jewish hatred for the Samaritans.

An Oppressed People Dream of a Liberator

Out of this complex history there emerged within the minds and hearts of the Jewish people the dream that someday God would send them a great leader—the Messiah, the anointed One, the person whose title from the Greek language is "the Christ." The Jewish people dreamed of one who would overthrow their oppressors and restore them to the glory they had known in the days of David and Solomon. By the time of Jesus, the yearning among the Jews for the one who was to set them free had grown to great intensity.

From David's Line

The hope and expectation of God's promised deliverer was strongly associated with the kingship of David, the greatest of the Israelite kings. As discussed earlier in this chapter, the Israelites had turned to a king to unify them and lead them at a time when they were in chaos as a people and their very existence was threatened by their enemies. It was under David's kingship that all the tribes of Israel were finally united, and it was David who led the armies of Israel in defeating the nation's enemies.

For generations the Jews had yearned for a "son of David," one from the line of that beloved king who would restore them to their place of prominence in the world, who would lead them to victory over new enemies, who would bring them into an age of peace and prosperity.

Great Expectations

From the time of King David—about one thousand years before Jesus—"the One who is to come" was spoken of and described in different ways by different people. Over the many years of waiting, the son of David that the people yearned for took on mythic qualities.

Jews of Jesus' day remembered how, centuries before, Moses had led the Israelites out of slavery in Egypt.

Photo: The Desert of Midian, where the Israelites wandered after leaving Egypt; the site thought to be Mount Sinai is in the background.

By the time the Jews were living under the complete domination of the Romans, the Messiah had taken on the image of a mighty warrior-king, a great military leader, one who would overthrow the Romans and make the Jews a mighty and free nation once again. This militaristic image of the Messiah would clash dramatically with the life and message of Jesus and have major implications in the Gospel story. **6**

Behind the Jewish "No" to Jesus

A detailed development of the Jewish understanding of the Messiah, his nature, and his characteristics is too complex to be treated in this course. However, though the Jewish people undoubtedly had various understandings about the nature and role of the Messiah, it is certain that the Jews would *never* have considered the Messiah to be the "divine son of God," as Christians understand him to be.

Remember that the Jewish understanding of God was such that the Jews could not even bring themselves to utter God's holy name. The idea of a human in some way "being God" would have been nothing short of unthinkable for the devout Jew. (The Jewish understanding of God would also have great implications for the Jewish response to Jesus' message in the future.)

Christians, in light of the Gospel story, profess that the One eventually sent by God was unlike any human expectation. Jesus of Nazareth was and is the One True Liberator. **7**

One More Stop Before Jesus

Before moving directly into the story of Jesus, one final dimension of the world he entered and to which he proclaimed his marvelous message will be explored in chapter 4. The Gospel portraits of Jesus are filled with stories and images drawn from the daily life and religion of the Jewish people—their homes, occupations, meals, customs, and more. A general understanding of this information can provide a rich texture to the Gospel story and make the message of Jesus come alive for us.

For Review

- Briefly explain the origins of the ancient Jews' expectations of the Messiah.

6
List groups of people besides the Jews, either past or present, who have experienced long-term domination and control by another group. Write about what their life might be like.

7
Imagine what it would be like to yearn for a messiah in today's world. List five or more qualities that such a person would have to possess in order to be recognized as a great leader by people today.

◼
Photo: **The typical Jew of ancient Palestine dreamed of a great leader, the Messiah, who would overthrow the Roman oppressors and liberate the Jewish people.**

4

Daily Life in Jesus' Time:
Culture and Religion

THEN the disciples of John [the Baptist] approached [Jesus] and said, "Why do we and the Pharisees fast much, but your disciples do not fast?" Jesus answered them, "Can the wedding guests mourn as long as the bridegroom is with them? The days will come when the bridegroom is taken away from them, and then they will fast. No one patches an old cloak with a piece of unshrunken cloth, for its fullness pulls away from the cloak and the tear gets worse. People do not put new wine into old wineskins. Otherwise the skins burst, the wine spills out, and the skins are ruined. Rather, they pour new wine into fresh wineskins, and both are preserved." (Matthew 9:14–17)

Jesus: Born in a Particular Time and Place

The Gospels are filled with passages like the one quoted above, expressing images and experiences from the day-to-day lives of first-century Jewish people. Along with reading about wineskins and old cloaks, we read about festivals and parties, the lilies of the field and the birds of the air, storms at sea, planting and harvesting, bread baking, young children playing, old people dying, and more.

One message of the Gospels, then, is this: Jesus was a Jew, born in a particular place within a particular culture at a particular time in history. A true understanding of Jesus must include a basic sense of his daily world. We need an appreciation for the subtle influences of his culture that were so much a part of who he was and the message he shared.

Jesus Spoke the Language of His People

Jesus' immersion in the world of first-century Palestine enabled him to speak to his fellow Jews using images they understood and situations they could identify with. He, like them, was steeped in all the religious and social traditions of the day. He was nourished with the food and drink of his homeland and brought to laughter by the parties and weddings of his people. Even the sickness, disease, and death that haunted daily life touched Jesus' life and often moved him to tears. Here are just a few examples of how Jesus' life experiences were woven into his teachings:

- The Pharisees and the Sadducees asked Jesus to show them a sign from heaven to prove he was the Messiah. Jesus' response: "'In the evening you say, "Tomorrow will be fair, for the sky is red"; and then, in the morning, "Today will be stormy, for the sky is red and threatening." You know how to judge the appearance of the sky, but you cannot judge the signs of the times'" (Matthew 16:2–3). Jesus' reference to forecasting the weather came out of his culture, and the message he conveyed with that reference was of great significance to his listeners.

Photo, facing page: **Many Gospel passages express everyday images and experiences of first-century Jews, such as planting and harvesting.**

Photo, above: **The sun sets on the Sea of Galilee. Jesus' contemporaries forecast the weather by looking at the sky. A red sky at sunset meant that the weather would be fair the next day.**

- The scribes challenged Jesus because of his dinner companions "'Why does he eat with tax collectors and sinners?'" (Mark 2:16). Jesus said to them, "'Those who are well do not need a physician, but the sick do. I did not come to call the righteous but sinners'" (Mark 2:17). Discerning the meaning of this scene requires an understanding of the tremendous importance of meals in the life of the Jewish people.
- Jesus' first disciples heard his call to follow him while they were working as fishermen by the Lake of Gennesaret. Under Jesus' direction they netted such a huge number of fish that their nets began to tear. They caught so many fish, in fact, that two boats almost sank under the weight. From this experience of an almost too successful fishing trip, Jesus drew the point he wanted to make: "'Do not be afraid; from now on you will be catching men'" (Luke 5:10).
- Jesus was a carpenter, and the vocabulary of his trade found its way into his teaching: "'Why do you notice the splinter in your brother's eye, but do not perceive the wooden beam in your own eye? . . . You hypocrite, remove the wooden beam from your eye first; then you will see clearly to remove the splinter from your brother's eye'" (Matthew 7:3–5). The image of a beam sticking out of one's eye may illustrate Jesus' occasional use of exaggeration to make a point, but without doubt his point is clearly made. **1**

This chapter will provide some general background on the geography and daily life of Jesus' time. It will also highlight key features of Judaism as it was practiced in Jesus' day. As was true in the discussion of Jewish history in chapter 3 of this text, only short glimpses into the past will be provided here. This information should, however, help to illuminate the rich human texture of the Gospels. It is hoped that this information will enable you to read between the lines of the Christian Testament, and thereby gain a deeper appreciation for the profound message that is so often contained in and expressed through common life experiences.

For Review

- Why is a basic sense of Jesus' daily world important to understanding Jesus and his message? Illustrate your response with an example.

■
***Illustration:* When making points, Jesus drew on common images of his day, such as the occupation of fishing.**

1
Select one of the four examples of Jesus' teachings given above. Keeping in mind the point Jesus was trying to make, rewrite the scene as you imagine it might occur today. For example, what words would Jesus use? Where would the scene take place?

Palestine:
Great Variety in a Small Land

Today, the homeland of Jesus is commonly known as the Holy Land. In Jesus' time it was called the land of Canaan, the Promised Land, the land of Israel, or the land of Judah. As mentioned earlier, it was called Palestine by the Greeks.

A Land the People Knew Intimately

The Palestine that Jesus knew was roughly the size of Massachusetts, stretching just 145 miles from north to south and anywhere from 25 to 87 miles from its western coast at the Mediterranean Sea to its eastern border. Yet this small area was the only world that Jesus ever knew. This may be astonishing, given the fact that today Jesus' home country can be traveled from one corner to another by car in a matter of just a few hours.

Even though the people of Jesus' time most often had to walk from town to town, it was still relatively easy for them to get around. The Jews were great walkers, thinking nothing of walking distances we might hesitate to drive. An average walker could go from Nazareth to Jerusalem (approximately ninety miles) in about two days, for example. This accounts in part for why Jesus and his disciples seem to move continually from one place to another in the Gospels. The small geographic size of Palestine explains in part the profound love the people had for their land—they simply knew it very well, just as a farmer knows every acre of her or his land "by heart." **2**

A Land of Beauty and Diversity

Geographical Diversity

Though Palestine was a rather restricted area in terms of size, it held tremendous geographical diversity. The Gospels speak of lakeshores and hillsides, of deserts and forests. The area surrounding the Dead Sea was desolate and forbidding, and the area surrounding the Sea of Galilee (also known as the Lake of Gennesaret or the Sea of Tiberias) was lush and inviting. As one author puts it, "A walk of

---

Palestine, in Jesus' time and now, displays tremendous geographical diversity.

Photo: **The barren Desert of Judah, near the Dead Sea**
Photo, inset: **The lush western shore of the Sea of Galilee**

2
Write a paragraph comparing what it means to know a *thing* (such as the land on which you live) by heart with what it means to know a *person* by heart.

a single hour [took] one from the richest of plains to the bare hills where the sheep [grazed]; and the caravans, toiling under the hot wind of the desert, took hope again from the sight of the snow shining on [the mountain]" (Daniel-Rops, *Daily Life in the Time of Jesus,* page 15). The "mountains" of Palestine were really only large hills, but they gave a texture and a majesty to the land that would impress even the traveler of today.

Varied Climate

In modern-day Palestine, the average temperature for the year is 72 degrees Fahrenheit, with an average monthly high of 77 degrees and an average monthly low of 59 degrees. But the variations can be quite extreme, with frigid nights and hot days. Though rare, snow does fall in the region, yet the temperature around the barren Dead Sea can reach 122 degrees. Rainfall is a problem, with most of it falling in October and March. Often the rain takes the form of violent storms, like the one mentioned in Matthew 7:24–27, where Jesus reminds his listeners of a time when "'the rain fell, the floods came, and the winds blew.'"

Gifts of Life from the Land

Water: A Precious Resource

The question of having enough water was a serious one in Jesus' time, and it is often referred to in the Gospels. The people had to dig many wells, and strict rules governed the use of water. The scarcity of water enhanced the people's deep love for those bodies of water that *were* available to them. They particularly treasured the Jordan River (which the Hebrew people crossed to enter the Promised Land and in whose waters Jesus himself was baptized) and the gorgeous Sea of Galilee.

In this context of scarce water, think of the imagery used by Jesus when, in talking to a Samaritan woman by a well, he referred to himself as "living water":

"Everyone who drinks this water [from the well] will be thirsty again; but whoever drinks the water I shall give will never thirst; the water I shall give will become in him a spring of water welling up to eternal life." (John 4:13–14) **3**

Bread and Wine

With a great variation in climate and rainfall, it is not surprising that a wide variety of vegetation and foliage grew in the Palestine that Jesus knew. Trees and fruits were abundant, with juniper and oak the most common trees, and olive and fig trees the most valuable because of the fruit and oil they

---

Illustration: **In the desert region of Palestine, water was an especially precious resource.**

3
List at least ten characteristics of water that make it a symbol or image rich with meaning.

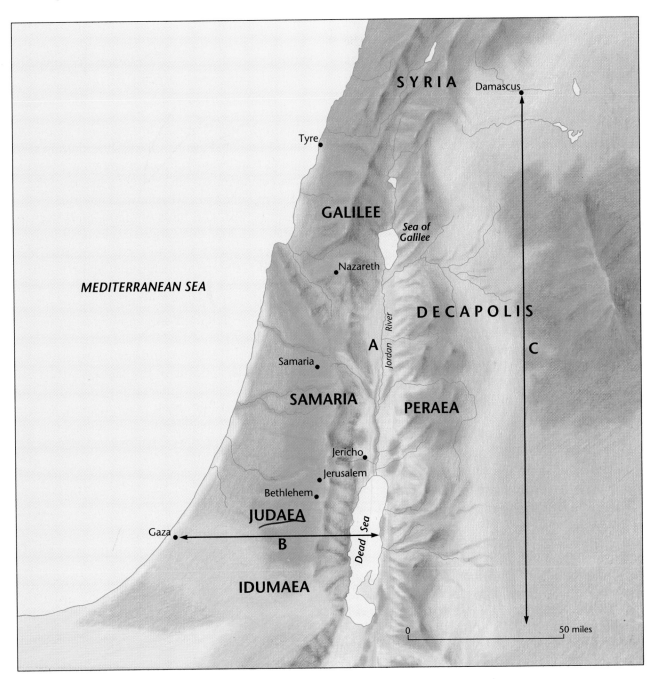

A: The Sea of Galilee and the Dead Sea are about sixty-five miles apart, but the meandering Jordan River, which connects these two bodies of water, is nearly three times that long.

B: A journey from Gaza to the eastern shore of the Dead Sea would cover about seventy miles–about the distance from San Francisco to Sacramento, or Chicago to Milwaukee.

C: A straight path from Damascus in Syria to the southern tip of the Dead Sea covers about two hundred miles, roughly the same distance as from Boston to New York City, or Dallas to Austin.

The Christian celebration of the Eucharist, of "breaking bread together," has its origins in the central place that bread—and wine—occupied in the lives of the people of Jesus' day.

Animals

Both wild and domestic animals were abundant and varied in Palestine. Among the common wild animals that Jesus would have known were boars, foxes, porcupines, hyenas, wolves, leopards, bears, and lions—many of which are mentioned in the Scriptures. Fish and birds of many kinds were also plentiful. The domesticated animals included sheep, oxen, donkeys, and cows. There were also pigs, which the Jews considered unclean animals, not to be eaten. Roosters, hens, and geese were common. The donkey was the most useful animal because of its strength and endurance; in fact, it was so highly valued that it could never be offered as a sacrifice. Perhaps surprising to us, given our modern understanding of the Middle East, is the fact that camels were quite rare in Jesus' day. The only people on horseback were probably Roman soldiers. There were no family cats in Jesus' culture, and most of the dogs were half-wild relatives of the wolves.

provided. And of course the people had the wonderful "fruit of the vine," the grapes from which the people made their deep, full-bodied red wines, so rich and thick that they had to be mingled with water before being served. Jesus referred to himself as "the true vine" (see John 15:1–17), and the Gospels refer many times to the vineyards and those who tended them.

The common cereals of Jesus' time included wheat—the most precious—along with oats and barley. Bread was the essential food of Jesus' day, so much so that bread alone could sometimes be a full meal. Bread was treated with great respect, and many Jewish laws governed its preparation and use. So when Jesus identified himself with the bread and wine at the Last Supper, it was clear to those gathered with him that he was revealing himself as one who could give them complete sustenance and fulfillment. He was in fact "the bread of life," who could totally satisfy the deepest hungers of people (see John 6:22–59).

For Review

- What is one explanation for the sense that Jesus and his disciples continually move from place to place in the Gospels?
- Explain why the people of Jesus' day had a great concern for water.
- What was Jesus telling the people when he described himself as "the bread of life"?

Photo: Olive trees were highly valued because of the fruit and oil they provided.

"Give Us This Day . . ."

Some of the richest imagery used in the Gospels is that of bread and all the tasks that surrounded the planting and harvesting of the grain from which bread was made. Some insight into these tasks is good to have when we come across such imagery in the Gospels.

The farmer of Jesus' day sowed the seed for cereal crops during November or December. By this time the autumn rains had softened the ground. Using plows pulled by oxen, some farmers plowed up the soil before sowing, while others sowed the seed first and then plowed the seed into the ground. Rainfall during the winter and spring helped the crops grow, and the harvest took place between March and May.

The farmer reaped the crop with a sickle. The crop was then carried to a hard, flat piece of the ground used as a *threshing* floor. There the grain was separated from the straw by oxen either treading

on it or pulling a wooden device, similar to a sled, over it.

The next task was *winnowing*. The farmer threw the threshed crop into the air with a pitchfork, and the breeze (either natural or created by a winnowing fan) carried away the light husks, or *chaff,* and the heavier grain fell back on the floor. The chaff was collected and burned, and the grain was sifted and bagged, ready to be

ground into flour for bread making.

All of these steps in the harvesting process, as well as the later process of bread making, were well known by people of Jesus' day. In light of this brief description, consider the following passage from Matthew's Gospel, a passage that might normally mean little or nothing to the contemporary reader. In this passage, John the Baptist is telling his listeners about Jesus, whom he will shortly be baptizing in the Jordan River:

> "I am not worthy to carry his sandals. He will baptize you with the holy Spirit and fire. His winnowing fan is in his hand. He will clear his threshing floor and gather his wheat into his barn, but the chaff he will burn with unquenchable fire."
> (Matthew 3:11–12)

(Adapted from Hughes and Travis, *Harper's Introduction to the Bible,* page 104)

Illustration: **Harvesters used a sickle to reap grain.**

The People and Their Daily Life

Nearly every lesson Jesus teaches in the Gospels is expressed through the common experiences of his people and their daily life—their food and meals, their housing and occupations. Here are some glimpses into these aspects of daily life in Jesus' time.

The Food and Meals of the Jews

Sharing a Meal: A Sacred Act

To the ancient Jewish people, the sharing of a meal was a sacred act. To "break bread" (bread was never cut but always broken) was an outward sign of unity and friendship. Whenever a meal is shared in the Gospels, you can be sure that something very significant is happening. No wonder people of the time reacted so strongly when Jesus ate with obvious sinners. The people were shocked by what they considered a demonstration of Jesus' outright approval of both the sinners and their sins. What Jesus was trying to demonstrate by his actions, however, was that he was offering a continually forgiving love to sinners, despite his disapproval of the sins they committed. "'I did not come to call the righteous but sinners'" (Matthew 9:13). 4

Meat: On Special Occasions Only

Most people in Jesus' day ate very little meat. This food was considered a luxury and was available on a regular basis only to the wealthy. When Jesus told the parable of the prodigal son, he used this fact to effectively express the profound joy that the father felt when his son returned home:

"'Take the fattened calf and slaughter it. Then let us celebrate with a feast, because this son of mine was dead, and has come to life again; he was lost, and has been found.'" (Luke 15:23–24)

The people listening to Jesus knew that one only ate meat on very special occasions or during major celebrations, such as the Passover feast, when lambs were prepared and eaten.

Common Fare

The most common food other than bread was fish, and together bread and fish formed the most typical meal of Jesus' day. The people often dried and salted fish to preserve it, and they cooked fresh fish over a charcoal fire, as we see Jesus doing during an appearance to his disciples after his resurrection (John 21:9–10).

The most common food was bread.
Photo: **A Jewish woman, *right*, and her Arab neighbor prepare bread in Israel.**

4

According to many religious leaders, several of the problems of modern families can be explained by the fact that family members rarely eat meals together. Explain in writing why you agree or disagree with that claim.

Fruit was also an abundant food, as were nuts like walnuts, almonds, and pistachios. The only drink more common than wine was water. The wine was stored either in large jars or in containers made of goatskin. Jesus refers to these wineskins when teaching a lesson (as in Matthew 9:17).

The Dinner Table

Meals were often eaten in the open air and at flexible times of the day, for the people of Palestine had few of the concerns about precise times and schedules that often frustrate us today. At formal meals the people ate in a reclining position rather than a sitting position. They generally ate with their hands from a flattened metal cup rather than using forks, spoons, and plates. Though most of their meals were simple, the Jews loved their occasional feasts and parties, because of the sense of family togetherness and community these gatherings provided. Many times in the Gospels, a feast or another celebration forms a backdrop for the message of Jesus. **5**

Illustration: **For most people of Palestine in Jesus' time, daily life revolved around the activities of the village.**

5
Choose any one of the four Gospels and page through it. Jot down the chapter and verse numbers for every instance in which eating a meal is mentioned.

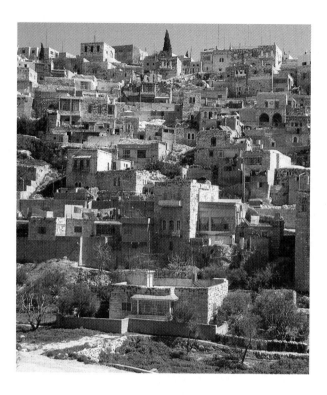

the rich were made of stone. In the same way, most house floors were simply hard-packed earth, but the floors of the wealthy were covered with baked clay tiles.

The roof of the common house was made of *wattling*, which consisted of poles bound together by reeds and grass and then covered with earth. The wattling could be lifted off easily, as can be seen in the story of the cure of the paralyzed man:

- Jesus was at home. In order to get a paralyzed man to Jesus, the people who were carrying the man "opened up the roof above [Jesus]. After they had broken through, they let down the mat on which the paralytic was lying" (Mark 2:4).

The roof usually had just enough slope to carry off rainwater. The people often kept tools on the roof, spread linen there to dry after washing, and even slept there on cool evenings. It was also quite common to sit on the roof during times of prayer and meditation.

The Typical House: Simple but Adequate

Design and Construction

For the most part, the houses of Jesus' time were neither large nor impressive. The majority of people were part of what we today would call the lower class, and their houses were usually one-room, whitewashed cubes. The houses normally had only one door, and the one room was often divided in half, with the people living on one side of the room and their animals living on the other. Some houses were built into the side of a hill, so that part of them was actually a cave.

Most houses were made of clay, which was sometimes baked into bricks. Only the homes of

Furnishings

Only the houses of the rich contained wood-burning stoves, but every village had at least one communal oven that all could use for baking bread and cooking food. The people's furniture was simple, consisting perhaps of just a chest for storage and a bushel basket or wood container used for measuring grain at the market and then turned over for use as a table in the home. Small lamps were used for light. These were placed on lampstands and fueled by rancid olive oil, giving a familiar but not very pleasant odor to all the houses. Jesus referred to these items when he said that people would not put a lamp under a bushel basket to be hidden, but rather would place it on a lampstand, where it could give light. "'Just so, your light must shine before others, that they may see your

Photo: **The village of Silwân (formerly Siloam), just outside Jerusalem, contains residential architecture reminiscent of ancient Jerusalem.**

Focus on John: Images from Daily Life

A quick scan of John's Gospel reveals frequent references to the daily life of the people of Jesus' time. John always tapped into apparently simple, commonplace realities to express profound insights into the meaning of Jesus and the God whom Jesus revealed. You may want to read one or more of the following passages from John, reflecting on them in light of the content of this chapter.

- The wedding at Cana (2:1–11)
- The multiplication of the loaves (6:1–15)
- Jesus as the bread of life (6:22–59)
- Jesus as the source of "living water" (7:37–39)
- Jesus as the good shepherd (10:1–21)
- "Unless a grain of wheat dies . . ." (12:20–26)
- The vine and the branches (15:1–17)

good deeds and glorify your heavenly Father'" (Matthew 5:15–16; see also Mark 4:21–23; Luke 8:16–18).

The people slept on mats, which they rolled out in the evening, and they used pieces of wood or even stones as pillows. For warmth at night they wrapped themselves in their cloaks. These cloaks were made of camel or goat hair and were very thick, heavy, and waterproof. They were so sturdy, in fact, that they could stand up on their own! During the daytime these cloaks could be worn over lighter woolen tunics or coats. When Jesus told his followers, "'If anyone wants to go to law with you over your tunic, hand him your cloak as well,'" he was telling them to turn over a very valuable possession—literally the shirt off their back (Matthew 5:40).

Although the average person's home was simple by our standards, it did provide adequate shelter.

Above all, a person's home was the center around which his or her entire life revolved, primarily because Jewish family life was considered sacred—as will be seen later in this chapter.

Common Occupations

Agriculture

The Jewish people of Jesus' day had a particular love for work related to the earth.

Farmers: Many people were farmers and shepherds, and images from these occupations fill the Gospels: the sower and the seed, the fields of wheat, the picking of corn (a grain unlike the corn we raise today), the people tending their sheep or cattle, and the laborers in the vineyard. Plowing, sowing, and harvesting all enter into the teachings of Jesus.

Photo: **Jesus used the familiar image of a shepherd to describe himself and his relationship to his disciples.**

Fishers: Given the nature of the land and the diet of the people, it should not be surprising that fishing was another common and respected occupation. Jesus called his first disciples from this work (see Matthew 4:18–22; Luke 5:1–11), and he used imagery from fishing in many of his teachings. The basic qualities that made one a successful fisher may have attracted Jesus to those whom he chose as his first disciples. They were men of courage and patience, and they had hearty spirits. (In the Gospel of Mark, Jesus calls two of them, James and John, "sons of thunder.") Perhaps most importantly, they had a basic reliance upon and trust in the goodness of God, who, after all, supplied the fish they needed for their livelihood.

Trades

Many different trades were practiced in Jesus' day, and the Christian Testament mentions no fewer than twenty-five of them. These range from carpentry, which was the trade of Jesus and Joseph, to tent making, which was the trade of Saint Paul. Though many necessary items were made in the home, skilled workers provided for the other needs of the people.

The trade of carpentry was well-respected. As a carpenter, Jesus may have built cabinets, made tools and other equipment for farmers, constructed small bridges, and so on. We can imagine that his years in that work gave him a sensitivity to the needs of the people he lived and worked with. His trade would have also put him in touch with the glories of God's creation as he roamed the forests in search of good wood and then struggled to create something useful out of the varied woods he found there.

Jewish society provided the earliest social legislation governing trade masters and their apprentices,

and trade unions were even beginning among the Jewish laborers.

For Review

- What status did meals have among the Jews of Jesus' day?
- What qualities of fishers might have attracted Jesus to them when he was seeking disciples?
- What might Jesus have learned about life from his years as a carpenter?

Illustration: **A carpenter's saw, typical of the kind Jesus would have used**

The Jewish Family: A Community of Faith

Not surprisingly, much of Jewish family life revolved around religion, including many family traditions and customs, the education of children at the synagogues, and so on. (More on Jewish religious practices will be offered later in this chapter.) The family was clearly recognized as the essential basis of Jewish society, and the Law upheld the permanence and authority of the family. In fact, for the Jews, the family unit was a true religious community in and of itself, with the father being the chief leader, or celebrant, of many family religious feasts.

Betrothal and Marriage

People in Jesus' day married early in life. The men usually married at no later than age twenty. The women normally married as soon as they were physically able to bear children, which the Law defined as twelve and a half years of age. Mary, the mother of Jesus, was probably no older than fourteen when she bore him.

A Period of Engagement

Marriages were most commonly arranged by the parents, chiefly the father of the prospective husband. The actual marriage was preceded by a period of betrothal, or engagement, which lasted for about a year. This period gave the couple time to get to know each other. The Law, however, already recognized many of the rights and obligations of marriage during the time of betrothal. For example, a betrothed woman found guilty of adultery was stoned to death, just as she would have been if she were married; she was already considered the property of her future husband. Generally such punishment applied only to the woman. Adultery by a man was a crime only if it involved a married or betrothed woman other than his own, because in that case the act injured the stability of a family. This helps explain why Joseph wanted to quietly divorce Mary, rather than publicly accuse her of adultery, when he found out she was pregnant. If he had accused her, the Law would have demanded that she be killed. (See Matthew 1:18–19.)

The Wedding Feast

The actual wedding was a great event, sometimes lasting for more than a week. There was much eating and drinking, as illustrated by the wedding at Cana. At that wedding Jesus' mother recognized that the lack of wine might ruin the party, and Jesus responded with his first **sign**, or miracle (John 2:1–11).

The Husband's Role

After the marriage, the husband was recognized as truly the head of the family. His wife even called him "lord" or "master." Sons and daughters were recognized as his property, and the Law even allowed the father to sell them into slavery if they committed a crime. The commandment to "love thy father and mother" was so strong that historically the father had the right to put to death a child who disobeyed! This severe tradition was virtually gone by the time of Jesus, however.

Monogamy: The Ideal

Polygamy, or having more than one spouse at the same time, had been allowed for men early in the history of the Jews. By the time of Jesus, however, *monogamy,* the commitment to one spouse, was recognized as the ideal. Jesus himself, though never directly condemning polygamy, elevated the role of women in his day dramatically and spoke out strongly on the sanctity of the marriage commitment.

Men and Women in Ancient Jewish Society

A Patriarchal Society

As the ancient laws governing adultery suggest, women were considered the property of men. In fact, in just about every way imaginable, women were considered inferior to men. For example, the women did not eat with the men but instead ate while standing and serving them. Women kept a distance from men on the streets and were restricted to certain areas of the Temple.

Only after learning of this male domination can one appreciate the tremendous impact of many of Jesus' words and actions with women in the Gospels. Take, for example, the apparently simple yet remarkable scene in which Jesus carries on a

discussion with a woman at a public well. His disciples "were amazed that he was talking with a woman" (John 4:27), because the practice was not tolerated. Consider also that in the Gospels, some of the first followers to learn of Jesus' resurrection and proclaim it are women. What is so astonishing about this is that at the time, the testimony of women was not even recognized or accepted in a court of law.

A Just Society in Other Ways

Despite the inequalities just mentioned, Jewish women and children actually had a better life and were more respected and loved than those of many other cultures of the time. Women did have some recognized rights in Jewish society—for example, the right to be housed, clothed, and fed—and Jewish men took this responsibility seriously. Children were always recognized as a great blessing to Jewish families. Girls, however, were less desired than boys because girls married at such a young age and then became the property of someone else. Even so, the ancient Jews, to their credit, never resorted to the horrible pagan custom of the day in which unwanted children were simply and cruelly destroyed. In Jewish society, in fact, children were recognized as adults, with adult responsibilities and rights, at age thirteen. **6**

For Review

- Why did Joseph want to quietly divorce Mary when he discovered she was pregnant?
- What was unusual about Jesus' actions and attitudes regarding women?
- Why were female children in Jesus' day regarded as less desirable than male children?

■

Photo: **Muslim women of the Druze sect living in Israel today take a break from daily activities.**

6

Fold a piece of paper in half to create two vertical columns. In the left column, list the major characteristics of Jewish family life in Jesus' day. In the right column, note how modern family

life compares on each point listed in the left column.

Social Classes in the World of Jesus

Every society, it seems, gradually develops a series of social classes or groups: the "haves" and the "have-nots," the prestigious and the scorned, the politically powerful and the oppressed. Jesus' world was no different, except that the level of inequality between the various classes was perhaps far greater than what most of us experience in today's world.

Predictably enough, in the Jewish society, part of what determined social position was religious tradition. The priestly class, for example, could claim some degree of social importance or nobility on religious grounds, though they had lost some of their historical power and influence to the scribes by the time of Jesus.

A Few Rich, Many Poor

No Middle Class

As in most cultures, social standing in Jewish society had a lot to do with money. Jesus talked often about the rich and the poor, primarily because the gap between the two was so great. A middle class in today's sense of the term simply did not exist. There were very few rich people, only those who had somehow acquired land and the power that went with it or who had accumulated wealth through trade or political influence. The vast majority of the people were part of the working class, who did not have much by our standards. Jewish society also had its very poor, who were comparable with today's homeless people.

Slavery in Jesus' Time

Slavery existed at the time of Jesus, and it enters into several of his parables (though in the Christian Testament, the term often used for slaves is *servants*). But slavery among the Jews was not nearly as common as it was among the Romans and the Greeks, where as much as one quarter of the entire population may have been slaves. Historical records show that in the Greek city of Delos, ten thousand slaves might be traded in one day. And a wealthy Roman of the first century C.E. might have owned as many as two thousand slaves. Most Jews could not afford slaves.

The Law of Moses called for much better treatment of slaves than what was required in Roman culture, though no doubt Jewish legal principle

Photo: **Jesus' respectful attitude toward women in the Gospels is particularly noteworthy because at that time women were considered inferior to and the property of men.**

was not always followed. The Jewish Law did demand, however, that all slaves be freed after seven years of service, and this fact made a Jewish slave worth much less money than a pagan slave. Therefore, Jewish slaves were less popular and fewer in number than pagan slaves, and this may partly account for the fact that Jesus did not seem greatly concerned about the slavery issue directly. Certainly, however, Jesus' entire message of love and human freedom contradicted every argument people could develop to try to justify slavery.

In-groups and Outcasts

As noted earlier, the ancient Jewish society included many occupations and trades. People who worked hard were greatly respected. Some workers, however, were held in higher esteem than others. Sandal makers and woodworkers were thought to be better, for example, than tanners (who smelled bad) and perfume salesmen (who were in continual contact with prostitutes).

As discussed in chapter 3, mainline Jews felt great contempt for groups such as the Samaritans. (The Gospels make clear how deeply despised the Samaritans were.) Other social outcasts included those who were labeled "unclean" (lepers, for example), the extremely poor, the sick, and of course, women. Judaism excluded all of these people from the center of religious life, thus cutting them off from most everything of value in Jewish society. **7**

The Social Classes and Jesus' Ministry

Imagine the incredible impact of Jesus' ministry and message in the ancient Jewish social setting.

Jesus challenged and even condemned his own society on virtually every level.

- The society rejected the poor and the weak, yet Jesus made these people the very center of his message and those to be most honored.
- The Jewish people deeply hated the Samaritans, yet in Jesus' preaching the Samaritan is seen as good, while the selfishness of the Jewish priest is condemned (Luke 10:29–37).
- The society, at best, tolerated women, but Jesus freely associated with them and accepted them as central participants in his ministry.
- Jesus embraced with love and compassion the sick and the "unclean," who were rejected by his people. He attacked those with wealth and power who refused to share with those in need.

Jesus was more than a social revolutionary, more than someone committed to changing the social conditions of the people. He proclaimed a freedom deeper than freedom from social, economic, or political oppression. But it can never be ignored or minimized that his message included the condemnation of all social oppression—hunger, racial and sexual discrimination, political domination, and all the things that kept people from experiencing the fullness of life that was due them as sons and daughters of a loving God.

For Review

- Why did Jesus often speak about the rich and the poor?
- Give two reasons that slavery was not practiced as much among the Jews as among the Greeks and the Romans.
- Give three examples of how Jesus challenged his society's social structure.

7
List the groups considered outsiders in the religion or the culture you are most familiar with. For each group, provide at least one example of how the members are discriminated against.

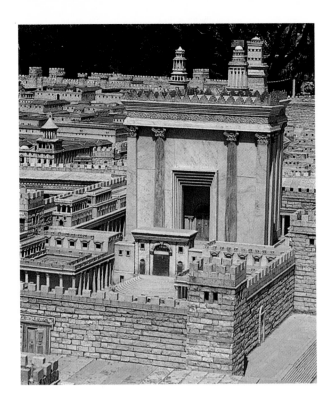

Major Features of Judaism

For the Jewish people, political history and religious history were heavily intertwined. Political events were understood as religious events, and political and religious leaders were often the same. Although much of the material in chapter 3 and thus far in chapter 4 has touched on aspects of Jewish faith, the following section will highlight some of the significant places, practices, and people of Judaism in Jesus' day. It will especially focus on those features that play a part in the Gospel stories. **8**

Special Places

Jerusalem: The Holy City

Jerusalem was clearly a unique and central city for the Jews of Jesus' time. Its geographical position, in central Palestine, made it ideal as a capital, a fortress, and a center of marketing. But more importantly, it was recognized as a holy city, and had been so for ten centuries before Jesus. The Jews of the Diaspora, who lived outside Palestine, dreamed of one day seeing Jerusalem's beautiful gates, walking its bustling streets, and setting their eyes on the **Temple**, the wondrous building that symbolized and celebrated the Jews' entire history as a people of faith. At the time of Jesus, Jerusalem was a major city of some 150,000 people, but that number could swell almost incredibly to 500,000 during the great religious feasts. For the Jew, to take steps on the soil of the city of Jerusalem was to walk on holy ground.

To this central and holy Jewish city, Jesus would cry out,

"Jerusalem, Jerusalem, you who kill the prophets and stone those sent to you, how many times I yearned to gather your children together, as a hen gathers her young under her wings." (Matthew 23:37)

The Temple

Rebuilt by Herod: Just before Jesus' time, Herod the Great began adding the last beautiful touches to Jerusalem, which the remnant had begun to rebuild five hundred years earlier. The crowning achievement of his building efforts would be to rebuild the Temple as it was in Solomon's time. Herod's work on the Temple began about fifteen years before Jesus' birth. It was not completed until nearly thirty-five years after Jesus' death, only to be totally destroyed by the Romans a short time after its completion. The present Wailing Wall, in Jerusalem, is all that remains of Herod's efforts.

It is hard for us to gain a sense of the Temple's splendor. Thirteen gates opened into the Temple proper, and one of them—the Nicanor Gate—was

---

The Temple in Jerusalem was the center of Jewish life.
Photo: A model of Herod's Temple, part of the scale model of ancient Jerusalem displayed at the Holyland Hotel, Jerusalem

8
As you read the following section on the major features of Judaism in Jesus' day, make a list of those features. For each one, try to identify a parallel feature in modern Roman Catholicism.

The Hebrew Scriptures

The Hebrew Scriptures were originally sacred stories and teachings that the people of Israel passed on by word of mouth from generation to generation. Some of these stories and teachings—the Psalms, for example—were actually songs or chants before they were committed to writing.

The Jews became known as "the People of the Book" because of their total commitment to their Scriptures. So thoroughly did these writings dominate their lives that not a single written work from ancient Israel has been found that is not directly related to their Bible.

The works of the prophets held particular importance for the Jews. Two of these prophets—Isaiah and Jeremiah— were referred to in chapter 3's brief overview of the history of the Jews. Other prophets, like Elijah, Amos, Hosea, and Ezekiel, were also cherished by the Jews. This accounts for the recurring phrase, in the Gospels and elsewhere, about the Jewish commitment to "the Law and the prophets."

The Hebrew Bible developed over a very long period. Even the individual books of the Hebrew Bible took a long time to develop, with the Book of Psalms, for example, taking as long as eight hundred years to be compiled. The Hebrew Bible eventually consisted of forty-six different books. About two hundred years before Jesus' time, a Greek edition of the Bible developed within the Jewish community. This was the Bible that the Apostles and the early church used.

Jesus was deeply and prayerfully aware of the Hebrew Scriptures, and many of his sayings and teachings reflect this fact. Anytime we hear Jesus say, "You have heard it said . . ." or "It is written that . . .," he is referring to the Bible of the Jews or, less often, to the teachings of the rabbis regarding those sacred Scriptures.

made entirely of bronze and was so large that it took twenty men just to open it! The sound of this gate opening signaled the beginning of the day for the people of Jerusalem.

A place of offerings, prayer, and governing: The Temple was at the center of the lives of the People of God. Sacrifices were offered there. Particularly important sacrifices accompanied all major feasts, and lesser sacrifices were offered as signs of thanksgiving or by those seeking forgiveness for their sins. Such rituals were officially recognized by the Jews as outward signs of an honest and interior personal religious attitude. Still, many of the people actually viewed these sacrifices as having almost magical power.

The Temple was for prayer as well as sacrifice. (The story of the Pharisee and the tax collector, in Luke 18:9–14, illustrates this fact.) It was also the seat of the religious, political, and judicial body of the Jews, which was called the *Great Sanhedrin.* The Temple was so large that it could hold literally thousands of priests and tens of thousands of believers at once.

A den of thieves? By recognizing the centrality of the Temple to the religious life of the Jews, we can begin to appreciate why at one point Jesus offered in the synagogues, but precious scrolls containing the Hebrew Scriptures were kept there.

A synagogue was open three times a day for prayer and occasionally for other gatherings, but weekly Sabbath worship was the chief gathering held there. It is hard to overestimate the importance of the synagogue in the lives of the believers of Israel. In John's Gospel, for example, it is mentioned that those Jews who followed Jesus were threatened with the denial of their synagogue privileges as a severe threat and punishment.

The synagogue remains to this day the center of Jewish communal life. It assured the Jews' survival as a people over the last two thousand years, as Judaism became strictly a "religion of the word," based on the sacred Hebrew Scriptures.

Central Religious Practices

Daily Life:
Consecrated to God in Prayer

The faithful Jew was expected to live a life of personal prayer in the home. At dawn and at nightfall the Jew recited the famous Shema prayer:

"Hear, O Israel! The Lord is our God, the Lord alone! Therefore, you shall love the Lord, your God, with all your heart, and with all your soul, and with all your strength." (Deuteronomy 6:4–5)

This was the absolute minimum of religious observance.

The truly faithful Jew also set aside three other times for prayer each day: morning, afternoon, and evening. These were primarily times for prayers of praise and prayers asking for God's blessing. Thus Jesus grew up in a religious tradition based heavily on personal and communal prayer as well as on the sacred Scriptures.

stormed into the Temple. He was enraged by the way the money changers had been desecrating it and cheating the people. Turning over tables and scattering chairs and pigeons alike, he shouted words of the Hebrew Scriptures: """My house shall be a house of prayer, but you have made it a den of thieves""" (Luke 19:46).

Synagogues

After the Temple's destruction by the Romans in 70 C.E., the synagogues became the central places of worship. Some traditions say that these houses of prayer originated during the Babylonian Exile as a substitute for the Temple.

Each village had at least one synagogue, and any adult male Jew had the right to erect one or even turn his house into one. Sacrifices were never

After the Romans destroyed the Temple in 70 C.E., the synagogues became the places of worship. *Photo:* The local synagogue is still at the core of Jewish communal life today.

The Impact of Religion: Greater than We Think

Jesus was a devout Jew, immersed in the history, religious traditions, and rich prayer life of the Jewish people. In order to gain a sense of the importance of Jesus' religion to him, consider for a moment the ways in which religious heritage touches all dimensions of the lives of Roman Catholics. Try to imagine, for example, how Catholics would be affected by the following:

- if all Catholic churches in every part of the world locked their doors for one year so that Catholics and their families could not celebrate communal worship
- if Christmas and everything surrounding it—the worship, the carols, the gift giving, the manger scenes, the family traditions—were dropped for one year
- if Easter and all the joyous events that surround it were not allowed for one year
- if every religious symbol and expression in a Catholic's home—from a religious picture on the wall to family prayer before meals—were taken away for a year
- if a practicing Catholic could be controlled in such a way that she or he were unable to pray even privately for one year, never able to turn to God in moments of need
- if every Bible in every home, church, and school were confiscated and locked away for a year

Granted, this is hard to imagine, but that is precisely the point. The purpose of this exercise is to illustrate that religious traditions are part of a person's identity, not simply realities that are artificially attached and therefore easily discarded. Many religious impulses arise from within— as in the need to reach out to God in prayer at certain moments in life, or in yearning to celebrate great and joyous events with other people. As individuals become more deeply involved in communal religious experiences, these communal experiences become a deeper part of life— personally valuable and life-giving.

The Week:
Consecrated to God on the Sabbath

A sign of the covenant: The **Sabbath** is a weekly day of rest and prayer for the Jews. It is such a significant religious observance that it is mentioned nearly seventy times in the Gospels alone. The Sabbath day is based on the Creation story from the Book of Genesis, in which God rests after creating the world. The day is also linked historically to the Exodus experience. In the early history of the Jews, people who violated the Sabbath laws were put to death, but this severe practice was no longer the case in Jesus' time. Nevertheless, the Sabbath was recognized as a central and sacred sign of Yahweh's presence with the people and of their covenant relationship with God.

Unlike our days, which begin at midnight, a day for the Jew begins at sunset. Therefore, the Jewish Sabbath actually lasts from what we know as Friday evening through the daylight hours of Saturday. In ancient times, the Sabbath was the only day of the week that had a name of its own. All other days were either numbered or identified in relation to it. For example, a Jew might have referred to "the day before Sabbath."

Prohibitions and regulations: Strict prohibitions and regulations governed the Sabbath observance: No housework or cooking could be done by the women; no labor of any kind could be performed. It was unlawful to light a fire, so the people had "Sabbath lamps," which were fueled and tended by the woman of the house during the Sabbath observance. It was even against the law to walk using a wooden leg on this day! After the Friday evening meal, the people could not eat again until after the Saturday morning synagogue service, and special prayers then accompanied each meal during the remainder of the Sabbath.

The rabbis constantly argued with others and among themselves about how closely the Sabbath laws were to be followed. Jesus spoke for many of the rabbis when he proclaimed, "'The sabbath was made for man, not man for the sabbath.'" But he added, "'The Son of Man is lord even of the sabbath,'" a claim that could not help but offend and greatly anger many of the people (Mark 2:27–28).

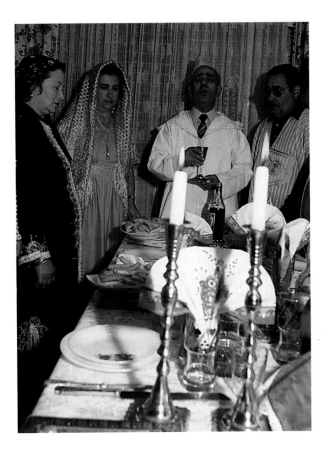

The Jewish Year: Consecrated to God Through Religious Feasts

The Gospels indicate the central role of several key religious festivals and feasts in Jewish religious life. These were occasions to glorify, thank, and petition Yahweh. Some of the feasts were celebrated in the people's homes or in small groups with a master and his disciples. But even these feasts had a strong communal character, with the individual Jews sensing their unity as one nation turned to its God. Each feast had public ceremonies as well, and for the Jews of the Diaspora, many feasts were occasions for pilgrimages to Jerusalem.

Initially some of the Jewish feasts were probably nature feasts borrowed from other people—for example, feasts of spring and the harvest—which gradually took on religious dimensions through the Jews' long history. Many of the feasts were serious and penitential in nature, reminding the Jews of their failures to follow the will of Yahweh. Other feasts were highly festive and had a cheerful, carnival atmosphere.

We must be conscious of three major Jewish feasts if we are to fully understand the Gospel accounts of Jesus' life. These religious feasts are still celebrated by Jews around the world.

Pentecost: Also called the Feast of Weeks, Pentecost is a celebration of Yahweh's giving the Law to Moses. The word *Pentecost* itself is based on the

Photo: **A Jewish family gathers for Friday evening Sabbath prayer.**

Greek word for "fiftieth" and reflects the fact that it was fifty days after leaving Egypt before Moses received the Law on Mount Sinai. Historically, this feast also celebrated the Jews' harvesttime, a time for experiencing and expressing deep gratitude for the wonderful gifts of Yahweh. (The Christian feast of Pentecost celebrates the coming of the Holy Spirit to the Apostles, which occurred during the Jewish feast of Pentecost.)

The Day of Atonement: In autumn, a series of three feasts follow in quick succession—all within twenty-two days of each other: the Feast of the Jewish New Year, the Day of Atonement (Yom Kippur), and the Feast of Tabernacles. The **Day of Atonement** is of such central importance to the Jews that if a person simply mentions "the Day," everyone knows that he or she is referring to this special feast. It is a time for the Jews to solemnly repent of all their sins.

In Jesus' time—as today—the Day of Atonement involved moving ceremonies, fasting, prayer, and ritual bathings. Also on this day, the high priest would enter the sacred Holy of Holies in the Temple to purify it with the mingled blood of a goat and a bull.

Passover: Of all the feasts of the year, the holiest and most celebrated is **Passover,** celebrating the miraculous liberation of the Israelites from Egypt. Lasting a week, this marks the beginning of the Jewish religious year. It traditionally included the Temple sacrifice of lambs (known as the **paschal lambs,** from the word *pasch,* meaning "to pass over") and the ritual of a special meal recalling the one eaten by Moses and the Israelites before the Exodus. Obviously, Passover is a very cheerful feast for the Jews. It played a central role in the Gospel events surrounding the final days of Jesus' life.

Key Religious-Political Groups and Persons

The Gospels repeatedly refer to various factions within Judaism. The following groups or classes of people are particularly significant. (The Sadducees and the Pharisees were discussed briefly in chapter 3; see pages 61–62.)

The Priestly Caste

Priests were known in Jewish history as far back as the time of Moses, but they took on special importance during the time of the kings, when the Temple became a national institution. The priests served as go-betweens, or intermediaries, between God and the people, offering sacrifices in the Temple. They were considered the guardians of worship.

Originally a man could be recognized as a priest simply because he was a member of a certain tribe. By the time of Jesus, however, the powerful officials of the Temple—the Great Sanhedrin (see the description below)—chose priests from among the many members of that particular tribe. The priests were supposedly selected on the basis of "respectability," but that often meant wealth or social prestige. The priesthood, therefore, became a very exclusive class and was often hated by the common people.

The high priest: The **high priest** was the head of the priestly caste. He held a special kind of authority that went beyond his role as a spiritual leader. He was anointed in much the same way that the kings of his day were anointed, he lived in a lavish palace, and he dressed in very colorful and highly recognizable clothing. The appointment of the high priest was made by political masters of the country, and a lot of intrigue—and sometimes

Sadducee

Zealot

Tax Collector

money—entered into the selection. As the spiritual leader of his people, the high priest had so much influence that politicians always wanted to stay on his good side.

All of this helps explain the role of the high priest in the Gospels, particularly in the trial of Jesus. During the trial, the high priest is a man named Caiaphas. Pontius Pilate treats Caiaphas with real caution and consideration because of his position of importance and influence among the Jewish people.

Sadducees

The **Sadducees** were mainly the aristocracy of the priestly caste. Though not all Sadducees were priests, all were part of the Jewish upper class—meaning that they had a lot of political power. The power base of the Sadducees was Jerusalem because of their great commitment to the Temple and its sacrificial worship. They were liberal in politics (in that they were willing to compromise with the people in power), but they were very conservative in religion. For example, they accepted only the first five books of the Hebrew Scriptures (called "the Pentateuch," "the Torah," or simply "the Law"), and they rejected all attempts to add to or interpret the basic Law contained there. They also rejected any belief in a resurrection after death, which at Jesus' time was a rather recent religious belief among some Jews. An example of the Sadducees' conflicts with Jesus on this point can be found in Mark 12:18–27, in which they pose a problem for him. With the destruction of the Temple by the Romans in 70 C.E., this group eventually lost power and died out.

Pharisees

The **Pharisees** were the chief political and religious rivals of the Sadducees, so there was often great tension between the two groups. The Pharisees originated from the Hasidim, the group known as "the pious ones" because of their strict adherence to the Law. By the time of Jesus, however, the Pharisees were far more liberal in religious matters than were the Sadducees. For example, the Pharisees were open to new developments in Jewish thought, such as accepting other books of the Hebrew Scriptures besides the first five when judging matters of the Law. This openness led them to create an extensive oral commentary on the Law to help people live it more fully. Their commitment to the Law rather than the Temple, as in the case of the Sadducees, enabled the Pharisees to survive beyond the destruction of the Temple in 70 C.E. The Judaism of today is derived from Pharisaism.

Unlike the Sadducees, the Pharisees were conservative politically; that is, they rejected any attempts to compromise with their political rulers. Because of this attitude they were greatly respected by the common people.

A caution on stereotyping: Perhaps no single group receives a more negative treatment in the Gospels than the Pharisees. Jesus' comments about this group (and about the scribes) in Matthew 23:13–36 can make the reader wince, nearly embarrassed by the rage of Jesus against these people. The strongly negative image of the Pharisees presented in the Gospels may well reflect some of the early church's conflicts with this group; this is particularly the case in John's Gospel. We should be careful, however, about stereotyping the Pharisees according to this limited impression of them.

No doubt, Jesus did have serious conflicts with the Pharisees over their interpretation of the Law and their tendency to be overly legalistic. But certainly Jesus must have greatly admired some of the Pharisees for their religious fervor. Note, too, that the Pharisees had no official part in the trial and execution of Jesus.

An exaggerated negative understanding of the Pharisees, especially when used as a description of the Jewish people in general, has led in part to bitter *anti-Semitism,* or social rejection of the Jews, throughout the Jews' long history. Christians have an obligation to help change this false perception of the Jews, and nothing will accomplish that more than a clear presentation of the facts.

The Great Sanhedrin

The word *sanhedrin* literally means "assembly" or "senate." The **Great Sanhedrin** was the official governing body of the Jews, and it was recognized as such by the Romans. It consisted of seventy members plus a president. The position of president was often filled by the high priest, and the members of the Great Sanhedrin were representatives of the priestly families, the scribes and doctors of the Law, and the elders (*elders* was the name given to outstanding Jewish laymen). Both the Pharisees and the Sadducees were represented, but the Sadducees had much greater influence because of their strong relationship with the political powers. The Great Sanhedrin voted on the laws, had its own police force, and controlled everything to do with religion—which, as has been noted, meant virtually all of Jewish life. In the trial of Jesus, the Great Sanhedrin acted like a kind of supreme court.

Zealots

The beginnings of the **Zealots**—at least the beginnings of the attitudes they represented—may have gone back to the time of the Jewish revolt against the Greek overlords from Syria, almost two hundred years before Jesus' time. The Zealots maintained that Jewish independence could be attained only through a military overthrow of the Romans. It is possible that some of them may have been attracted to Jesus at first because of his strong leadership, but his obvious commitment to nonviolence likely led them to reject him eventually.

Tax Collectors

As mentioned in chapter 3, the Syrian Greeks began taxing the Jews to help pay off debts to the Romans. The Jews were also expected to pay a Temple tax to their own leaders, and this double taxation became nearly unbearable, amounting to some 40 percent of a family's total income. In order to collect the taxes from the Jews, the Romans hired Jewish agents who were expected to attain a certain quota of taxes, after which they could keep whatever "extra" money they managed to collect. These agents were the notorious **tax collectors** we read about in the Gospels, and they were clearly a despised group of men. (The tax collectors were also called *publicans*.)

Scribes

The scribes had their origins during the exile in Babylon. They were both writers (as the term *scribe* indicates) and jurists, or interpreters of the Law. They had the task of carefully studying the Law and passing judgment on those who broke it. This group organized the Hebrew Scriptures much as we know them today. The most respected of the scribes were given the title *doctor of the Law,* and when scribes were in a position of teaching, they were given the title **rabbi,** meaning "master" or "teacher." They taught in the synagogues. The scribes, as previously noted, are often mentioned in the Gospels along with the Pharisees, but the two groups were not identical. Though many of the scribes no doubt belonged to the Pharisaic party, not all of them did. **9**

For Review

- Why did the synagogues become more important for the Jews after the time of Jesus?
- What was the origin of the Sabbath day, and what was it a sign of?
- Identify and briefly describe the three major religious feasts of the Jews.
- Identify the major characteristics of both the Sadducees and the Pharisees. Why did the Sadducees have greater political power than the Pharisees?

On to the Story of Jesus

Chapters 3 and 4 have sketched out the social, political, and religious world that Jesus entered, preached to, and was largely rejected by. As you have learned, it was a complex setting of deep religious convictions and great political tensions. The oppression and near despair of the People of God was profoundly real, and their hunger for salvation and a savior was intense. Chapter 5 will turn to the story of Jesus and the message he proclaimed to that desperate world.

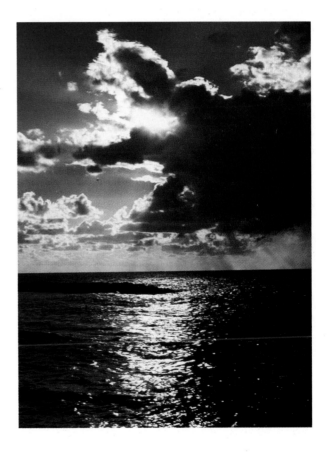

9
Using an encyclopedia or other sources, write a one-page essay that expands upon any feature of ancient Judaism discussed in this chapter.

■
Jesus entered a world where Jewish people suffered oppression and despair.
Photo: An approaching storm on the Sea of Galilee

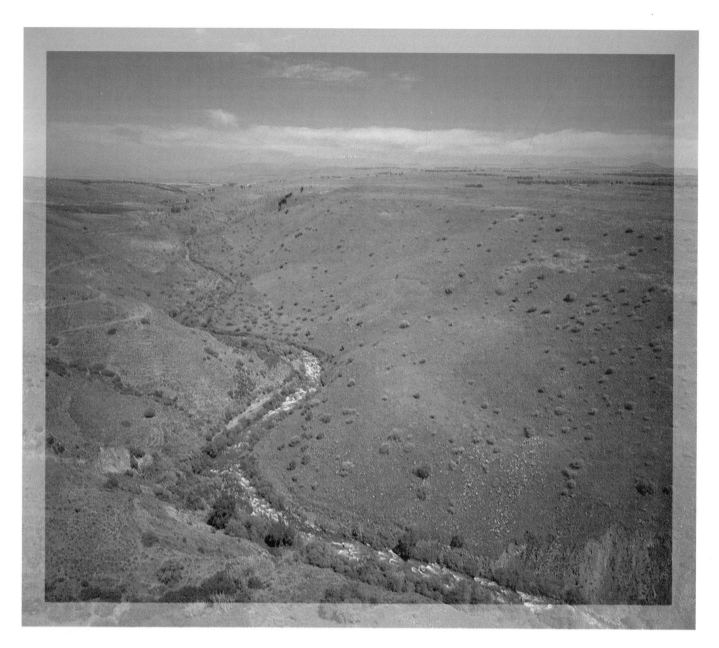

5

The Mission Begins:
Preparing the Way of the Lord

THE beginning of the gospel of Jesus Christ [the Son of God].

As it is written in Isaiah the prophet:
"Behold, I am sending my messenger ahead of you; he will prepare your way."

. . . .

John [the] Baptist appeared in the desert proclaiming a baptism of repentance for the forgiveness of sins. People of the whole Judean countryside and all the inhabitants of Jerusalem were going out to him and were being baptized by him in the Jordan River as they acknowledged their sins. . . . And this is what [John] proclaimed: "One mightier than I is coming after me. I am not worthy to stoop and loosen the thongs of his sandals. I have baptized you with water; he will baptize you with the holy Spirit."

It happened in those days that Jesus came from Nazareth of Galilee and was baptized in the Jordan by John. On coming up out of the water he saw the heavens being torn open and the Spirit, like a dove, descending upon him. And a voice came from the heavens, "You are my beloved Son; with you I am well pleased."

At once the Spirit drove him out into the desert, and he remained in the desert for forty days, tempted by Satan. (Mark 1:1–13)

And so the mission of Jesus began—at least as it is described by the Evangelist Mark. After this brief introduction to his Gospel, Mark begins a discussion of the public ministry of Jesus.

But pause for a moment and ask yourself, Isn't there something missing here? Is this where the story of Jesus begins—with John the Baptist and the baptism of Jesus? What about the birth of Jesus, the event that Christians throughout the world celebrate to this day with elaborate and joyous traditions? What about his childhood?

These questions surrounding Jesus' birth and early years were precisely the ones raised by the early Christians as the Gospels began to develop. Many people could recall from personal experience the early days of Jesus' public ministry. Many had heard his words and seen his works. But where did he come from, what was his childhood like, and what did he do *before* he came among them as a thirty-year-old man?

The Infancy Narratives

Familiar Scenes and Stories

In an effort to provide a faith-filled response to the natural questions of the early faith community, Matthew and Luke began their Gospels with writings that have come to be known as the *infancy narratives*—stories about the birth of Jesus and his early life. The Gospel of John, like that of Mark, does not describe the birth or childhood of Jesus. Instead, John's Gospel begins with a profound and poetic statement of what it meant for the "Word of God" to become human in the person of Jesus. (See "Focus on John: 'In the Beginning . . .'" on page 98.) 1

In the Gospel of Matthew

In the Gospel of Matthew we do not read about the public preaching of John the Baptist or the baptism of Jesus until the third chapter. That material is preceded by an introduction.

- The introduction begins with the genealogy, or family tree, of Jesus, tracing his roots back to Abraham (1:1–17).
- The genealogy is followed by the story of Mary and Joseph (including the statement that she

---

■
John the Baptist baptized Jesus in the Jordan River.
Photo, facing page: **The upper end of the Jordan River**

1
Make a list of words, phrases, objects, places, and names associated with Christmas—as many as you can think of. While reading about the infancy narratives, put a check mark by the items on

your list that seem to have a basis in the Gospels.

"And the Word Became Flesh"

While Matthew and Luke describe the origins of Jesus through their infancy stories, John speaks of the origins of Jesus and the profound nature of his ministry in a complex, poetic, highly philosophical prelude to his Gospel, called the *prologue* (John 1:1–18). As is true of the prologues in most works, this one was likely written after the rest of the book had been completed. Here is just a part of what John has to say about Jesus' origins and his ministry:

> In the beginning was the Word,
>   and the Word was with God,
>   and the Word was God.
>
> . . . .
>
> He was in the world,
>   and the world came to be through him,
>   but the world did not know him.
> He came to what was his own,
>   but his own people did not accept him.
>
> . . . .
>
> And the Word became flesh
>   and made his dwelling among us,
>   and we saw his glory,
>   the glory as of the Father's only Son,
>   full of grace and truth.
>
> (1:1,10–11,14)

Revealing the Very Essence of God

The Gospel of John was the last Gospel to be written, and it reflects many years of prayerful reflection about the nature of Jesus and his message. To decipher the full meaning of Jesus, John goes back in time further than Jesus' human birth in Bethlehem. John explores the origins of Jesus in the heart of God before the beginning of time. To do this, John speaks of Jesus as "the Word" of God. As is true of all words, Jesus as the Word is an expression or revealer of another reality, namely Yahweh. John tells us that in Jesus we encounter the fullest expression, the very essence, of God.

The other Gospels, for the most part, slowly and gradually reveal Jesus' true identity as the Son of God; that is, they tend to move from the Jesus of History to the Christ of Faith. John's Gospel proclaims Jesus as the Son of God at its starting point.

"And the Word became flesh and made his dwelling among us."
Photo: A view of earth from the *Apollo II* spacecraft; most of Africa and portions of Europe and Asia can be seen.

becomes pregnant with Jesus "through the holy Spirit") and then a simple description of Jesus' birth and the giving of his name (1:18–25).

- We then learn of the visit of the Magi, or Wise Men, who follow a star to the place of Jesus' birth and present gifts of gold, frankincense, and myrrh (2:1–12).
- The story of the Magi is followed by that of the flight of Joseph, Mary, and Jesus into Egypt as Herod begins to slaughter innocent children, in the hope of eliminating a possible rival to his throne (2:13–18).
- Last, we read of the return of Jesus' family to Palestine and the town of Nazareth in Galilee, where Jesus is to be raised (2:19–23).

These are very familiar scenes to most Christians. The touching images are recalled by families and parish communities each Christmas season.

In the Gospel of Luke

If we look at Luke's treatment of the early life of Jesus, we discover information not contained in Matthew's account.

Luke's preface to the stories about Jesus' birth: Luke begins his infancy narrative with events that happened before Jesus was born, mainly dealing with Jesus' announcer, John the Baptist.

- In Luke's preface we find a rather detailed description of how John the Baptist came to be born to a priest named Zechariah and his elderly wife, Elizabeth (1:5–25).
- The preface is followed by the angel Gabriel's announcement to Mary that she is to bear a son named Jesus, who will be called the "'Son of the Most High'" (1:26–38). (Catholics celebrate this event even today with the Feast of the Annunciation, on March 25.)

- We then learn of Mary's visit to Elizabeth, who is her relative (1:39–45). Upon discovering that Mary is pregnant, Elizabeth exclaims, "'Blessed is the fruit of your womb.'" So in chapter 1 of Luke's Gospel, we find the origin of part of the prayer we now know as the Hail Mary.
- In a prayer now called the *Magnificat,* we read Mary's beautiful response to the realization that she is to bear a special son (1:46–55). Mary's prayer is actually a collection of many verses from the Hebrew Scriptures.
- Last, we find several scenes centering on John the Baptist: his birth, his circumcision and naming, and a prophetic prayer by his father, Zechariah (1:57–80).

Luke's stories about Jesus' birth and early life: It is only after all of the above information has been shared that Luke begins to describe the birth of Jesus and the events that follow it. Much in

---

■

Matthew's Gospel includes the story of the Magi, or Wise Men, who follow a star to the place of Jesus' birth.

Photo: A depiction of the adoration of Jesus by the Magi, a fifteenth-century painting by Fra Angelico and Fra Filippo Lippi

Luke's version of these events has found its way into Christmas traditions and therefore into the minds and hearts of most Christians. Some of these ideas are found only in Luke's Gospel.

- Luke offers this familiar description of the birth of Jesus: "[Mary] wrapped him in swaddling clothes and laid him in a manger, because there was no room for them in the inn" (2:7).

- As noted earlier, in Matthew's Gospel the Magi are led by a star to the place where they find Jesus. But in Luke's Gospel, poor shepherds hear of the marvelous birth from an angel who announces, "'For today in the city of David a savior has been born for you who is Messiah and Lord'" (2:11). Luke does not mention the Wise Men, nor does Matthew mention the shepherds.

- After telling us of the poor shepherds, Luke describes the circumcision of Jesus, his presentation in the Temple in accordance with the Law, and prophecies about Jesus by a man named Simeon and a woman named Anna (2:21–38).

- Finally, Luke is the only Evangelist to offer the familiar story of Jesus at age twelve when his parents lose track of him during a trip to Jerusalem (2:41–50). They eventually find him in the Temple, "sitting in the midst of the teachers, listening to them and asking them questions, and all who heard him were astounded at his understanding and his answers."

Luke's closing statement: Luke closes his discussion of the early life of Jesus with this important statement: "[Jesus] went down with [his parents] and came to Nazareth, and was obedient to them; and his mother kept all these things in her heart. And Jesus advanced in wisdom and age and favor before God and man" (2:51–52).

The Infancy Narratives in Light of the Gospels

Most Christians learn about the birth of Jesus through a lifetime of experiences with Christmas traditions. Manger scenes, Christmas carols, and other religious customs retelling the story have developed throughout the history of the church. Sorting out all of these traditions in terms of the Gospels can be difficult at times. Yet we must do this because the Gospels are the documents that ultimately serve as the foundation and source of the Christian understanding of Jesus. And, as was said early in this book, the intention of this course is not to provide simple answers but sound ones, answers that will help you move toward a more

Illustration: **Luke's Gospel emphasizes the humble, poor circumstances of Jesus' birth.**

mature, adult, and therefore more fulfilling and meaningful understanding of Christianity, particularly Catholic Christianity. **2**

The differing stories of Jesus' birth and early years as they are presented in the Gospels of Matthew and Luke can be explained when seen in light of the nature, purpose, and development of the Gospels. A brief refresher on the major points raised in chapter 2 will provide the framework needed for understanding the stories of Jesus' early life. Recall these important points made about the Gospels:

1. The Gospels are testimonies of faith. The Gospels are not biographies of Jesus. Rather, they are testimonies of faith, proclamations of the Good News written by people after they had experienced Jesus as the Risen Lord.

2. The Gospels present different portraits of Jesus. Each Gospel was written by a different person, at a different time, to a different group of people, and for a different purpose.

- Mark's was the first Gospel to be written. It was directed to non-Jewish Christians, and it stressed the humanity and suffering of Jesus.
- Luke's Gospel was written approximately fifteen years after Mark's. It was directed to Gentiles, and it emphasized the fact that the Good News of Jesus is offered to all people—rich and poor, men and women, Jews and Gentiles.
- Matthew's Gospel was written not long after Luke's, and it was directed to devout Jews. It stressed the conviction that Jesus fulfilled the Law of Moses and was the Messiah the Jews had been awaiting.
- John's Gospel is very different from the other three. It offers a profound portrait of Jesus as the Messiah and divine Son of God, often expressing

that conviction through poetic and symbolic language and stories.

As noted earlier, this course's portrait of Jesus will rely primarily on the three synoptic Gospels, because of the unique nature and purposes of John's Gospel.

3. The Gospels are stories about meaning. The intention of the Gospel writers as believing Christians was not merely to provide historical facts about Jesus. Their chief aim was to describe the *meaning, significance, and impact of Jesus' life and teaching* upon the people and events of his time.

The Infancy Narratives and the Christ of Faith

Biblical scholars agree that a great deal of symbolism is involved in the Gospel stories of Jesus' birth and early life. After all, very few people besides Jesus' parents were there to witness the events themselves. In other words, Matthew's and Luke's

---

2
Write a brief essay describing the Christmas when you felt most in touch with the true meaning of the season. Explain what made that celebration of Christmas so special.

Every age and culture imagines the birth of Jesus in its own way. *Photo:* **The Nativity, as seen through the eyes of a modern-day peasant artist in Nicaragua**

The Visit of the Magi

Adding to the Story

Matthew's Gospel includes the familiar story of the Magi, a story frequently recalled at Christmas (though not always with biblical accuracy) in manger scenes and Christmas carols. A careful reading of the original Bible story will reveal that some of the details often associated with the story have been added over time. Popular belief during medieval times, for example, added the notion that there were three men (probably based on the three gifts of gold, frankincense, and myrrh); that the men were kings; and that their names were *Gaspar, Melchior,* and *Balthasar.* None of this information can be found in the Gospel account.

Looking for Historical Accuracy

Over the years people have tried to demonstrate the historical accuracy of the story of the Magi. Some, for example, have tried to explain through astronomy the presence of the star that guided the Magi. (The Magi are commonly understood to have been astrologers who observed and tried to

interpret the movement of the stars.) Some suggest that the "star" they saw may have been the planets Jupiter and Saturn coming close together. In ancient thought, Jupiter was a star associated with royalty and Saturn was the star of Israel. Modern-day astronomers tell us that Jupiter and Saturn come together this way only every 794 years; they calculate that this would have occurred in 7 B.C.E., roughly around the time of Jesus' birth.

Others offer another suggestion: Chinese records state that a *nova,* a brilliant fire caused by the explosion of a star, appeared in the eastern sky in 5 B.C.E. Perhaps this was the star that the Magi witnessed.

Making the Point in a Memorable Way

All attempts to explain the historical accuracy of the story of the Magi seem to miss the larger and more central question that is constantly being asked in this course: What does this story mean? The story of the Magi illustrates a major point that Matthew wished to make: Jesus as the Messiah was accepted by many Gentiles and rejected by many Jews. One must admit that the story of the Magi makes that point in a memorable way.

Photo: **A bright star over Bethlehem**

infancy narratives tell us as much, if not more, about Jesus as the Christ of Faith as they do about the historical Jesus. The following are the main points Matthew and Luke wanted to teach about Jesus as the Christ of Faith through their infancy narratives.

Matthew's Intentions: Three Themes

Jesus is the Messiah. Matthew wanted to show his Jewish readers as clearly as possible that Jesus was the Messiah they had been waiting for. In the genealogy of Jesus at the beginning of his Gospel, for example, Matthew refers to Jesus as "the son of David, the son of Abraham" (1:1). Then he starts with Abraham and works his way up to Jesus. He carefully notes that Joseph was born in the town of Bethlehem from the line of David. Throughout Jewish history, the people had expected the Messiah to descend from David, and David's hometown was Bethlehem.

Jesus was accepted by Gentiles, rejected by Jews. Matthew included the story of the *Magi*, non-Jewish men who were members of the priestly caste of the Persians and who served as chaplains to and representatives of the Persian royalty. The Magi were known for their understanding of astrology and the occult, the mysterious dimension of life. (Our words *magic* and *magician* come from the same root word.) By way of the story of the Magi, Matthew was showing his Jewish readers that Gentiles often accepted Jesus as the Messiah even though many Jews rejected him. This theme is repeated throughout Matthew's Gospel.

Jesus is "the new Moses." Matthew filled his entire infancy account with quotes and images from the Hebrew Scriptures, all of which would have had a profound impact on his Jewish readers. For example, in Matthew's Gospel, the Holy Family flees to Egypt, and then an angel calls them out of Egypt to Israel after the death of Herod. Who else was called out of Egypt by God? The Israelites, of course, who were led out of their bondage in Egypt by Moses. So Matthew recognized Jesus as "the new Moses," one who totally fulfilled the Law, the Messiah, who would lead the people to salvation.

Luke's Intentions: The Good News Is for Everyone

Luke had a different audience and a different message in mind as he wrote his story of the birth and early years of Jesus. Though Luke made it clear that Jesus was the Messiah, who fulfilled Jewish hopes and expectations, he did not use a lot of quotes from the Hebrew Scriptures. Luke's readers, who were Gentiles, would not have been as concerned about this as Matthew's Jewish readers. As mentioned before, Luke's Gospel stresses that the Good News is for everyone, especially those who are poor and downtrodden. That was Luke's reason for including the shepherds in his story, indicating that the poor would be the first to recognize and respond to Jesus.

Luke's emphasis on the fact that Jesus offers the Good News to everyone is also illustrated later in a genealogy he offers for Jesus (3:23–38). Luke's version of Jesus' genealogy differs dramatically from Matthew's. Matthew, as noted, starts with Abraham and works his way up to Jesus. Luke, on the other hand, begins with Jesus and works all the way back to *Adam*. As the "first man," Adam is the father of *all* people, not just the Jews, and with this clever point Luke again affirms the universality of the message of Jesus.

Focusing on the Meaning

When we look at the meaning the Gospel writers were trying to convey, the reasons for the differences in the infancy narratives become clearer. The writers were trying not so much to provide historical facts but to explain the *meaning and significance* of historical events. In fact, in their infancy narratives, Matthew and Luke may have moved beyond historical concerns altogether, focusing instead on insights into the origins of Jesus that only people of faith would be concerned about.

This course does not seek to explain the meaning of every line of the Gospels. But certainly we cannot understand any of the events described in the Gospels without asking questions about the meaning of Jesus and his message as understood by the Gospel writers. From this point on—whether in discussing specific events in the life of Jesus, his miracles, or the parables he shared—the constant emphasis will be on the following questions:

- What do these things mean?
- What point were the Gospel writers trying to make?
- What can *we* understand about Jesus from this?

These questions are at the core of trying to understand the Jesus of History as the Christ of Faith.

For Review

- Define *infancy narrative* and name the Gospels that contain an infancy narrative.
- List the major intentions of each writer of the infancy narratives. Give an example of how each intention is reflected in the writer's narrative.

Luke included the shepherds in his story of the Nativity, indicating that the poor and downtrodden would be the first to recognize and respond to Jesus.

Photo: A shepherd and his flock, near Bethlehem

The Hidden Years of Jesus' Life

Beyond what Matthew and Luke tell us about Jesus' birth and early years, much of his life prior to his public ministry is unknown to us. The entire period before the start of Jesus' public life is often referred to as Jesus' "hidden years." In addition to the infancy narratives, information about the history of the Jewish people, their beliefs, their religious practices, their family and social life, and so on, can help answer the question, What were the hidden years of Jesus' life like?

With some reservation it can be said that the historical Jesus experienced life as a typical Jew of his day. Note that this claim is made "with some reservation." Jesus was a special person even as a young boy. He must have been particularly gifted, intelligent, and sensitive. This much can be surmised just by studying him as an adult. **3**

Jesus: One with Us in All Things but Sin

Jesus was obviously special, but we must be careful not to think of him as strange, weird, or so different from us as to seem almost inhuman.

In the early church, there were writings and stories about Jesus that did not find their way into our Gospels. One of the stories described Jesus as a young boy who, in order to entertain and impress his friends, would take clay models of birds and magically make them come alive and fly away! Many of us have impressions of Jesus that are not far from this kind of fanciful image. For instance, we might think of the baby Jesus lying in the manger with the power to know all things, to read

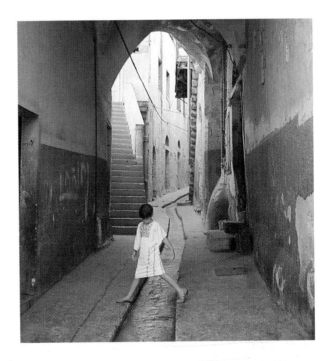

people's minds, or to go without food and drink. Such images can make Jesus seem like a freak of sorts, rather than what the church has continually claimed him to be—the Son of God, certainly, but also a person who was one with us in all things but sin.

In one of his epistles, Saint Paul says this about Jesus:

Who, though he was in the form of God,
    did not regard equality with God something to be
      grasped.
Rather, he emptied himself,
taking the form of a slave,
coming in human likeness;
and found human in appearance,
he humbled himself,
becoming obedient to death, even death on a
    cross.

                (Philippians 2:6–8)

3
Based on what you know of the adult Jesus, write a description of what Jesus might have been like when he was fifteen years old. For example, how would he have related to his parents? Would he have been popular among his peers or a "loner"?

Jesus experienced his childhood in Nazareth as a typical Jewish boy of his day.
Photo: **An old street in Nazareth today**

Saint Paul is saying that Jesus became as human beings are, with all the physical, emotional, intellectual, and spiritual needs each of us experiences.

Jesus' Birthday

Based on our understanding of the Jewish people and their history, we can say a number of things about Jesus' early life, beginning with his birthday.

Born During Herod's Reign

This course has stated that Jesus was born in or around 6 or 5 B.C.E. If, as traditionally held, our calendar begins with the year 0, marking the birth of Jesus, the above proposed date for his birth can be a bit confusing! The reasons for this discrepancy are too complex to discuss in full here. Basically what happened is this: When our modern calendar was first developed during the sixth century C.E., a miscalculation was made in determining the year in which Jesus was born, and that mistake was never corrected.

We know from the Gospels, however, that Jesus was born during the reign of Herod the Great, and we know with certainty from other sources that Herod died in the year 4 B.C.E. So Jesus was certainly born before that year. Scholars differ on the precise year of his birth, claiming anywhere from 8 to 5 B.C.E. It is obvious that the people of Jesus' day, and the Evangelists, did not share our concern for precise information about such an event. In a typical biography today, one of the first bits of information we would gain about the subject would be his or her date of birth. That detail did not concern the authors of the Gospels at all! So we need not expect to find such information there.

Circumcised According to the Law of Moses

Eight days after his birth in Bethlehem, Jesus was circumcised according to the Law of Moses. Circumcision was a religious practice that involved removing the foreskin of the male child's penis as a permanent sign of the child's membership in the covenant community of the Jews. This practice can be traced back to Yahweh's first covenant with Abraham (see Genesis 17:9–14), in which God said, "'Circumcise the flesh of your foreskin, and that shall be the mark of the covenant between you and me. Throughout the ages, every male among you, when he is eight days old, shall be circumcised.'"

At the time of his circumcision, Jesus was given his name. (As mentioned earlier, *Jesus* was a popular Jewish name of the day, and it meant "Yahweh saves" or "Yahweh is salvation.") Then Jesus' parents took him to the Temple in Jerusalem, where they consecrated him to Yahweh with the offering of a pair of turtledoves, or pigeons, the common sacrifice of the poor.

Photo: **Goods are sold on the street at a bazaar in Nazareth, Jesus' boyhood home.**

Jesus' Childhood in Nazareth

A Carpenter for a Father

Jesus' hometown of Nazareth was a community of just a few thousand people. He probably lived in the kind of one-room house described earlier. His father, Joseph, was a carpenter by trade, and as was the common practice of the day, Jesus worked along with his father and eventually became a carpenter himself. The carpenter of Jesus' day was a relatively skilled craftsman, and the occupation was a respected one.

A Good Education

Jesus seems to have had a good education. He knew Hebrew, which was fairly rare among the lower-class of people of his day. Because of the historical setting in which he was raised, and also due to the location of Nazareth geographically, Jesus probably spoke three languages: Hebrew, Greek, and Aramaic, the common language of Palestine. From age eight to age thirteen he likely attended school in a room attached to the synagogue, where his study revolved around the Hebrew Scriptures and the faith and history of his people, the Jews.

Photo: **Children play in the hills near contemporary Nazareth.**

Jesus' education was also enhanced by life in Nazareth itself. Though Galilee was held in low esteem by many Jews, it was an area in which the growing and maturing Jesus would have encountered many of the new ideas of the Greeks and the Romans.

A Faith-Filled Family Life

Ultimately, Jesus' strong Jewish faith had its source and solid foundation in the faith of his parents. Both Joseph and Mary were devout Jews, and as we know, the Jewish family was recognized as a religious community in itself. Most likely the family of Jesus was deeply prayerful and committed to faithfully following not only the Law but the spirit of the Jewish religion.

From that early foundation of a strong, loving, and truly religious family, Jesus grew. He developed a profound love and understanding of the Hebrew Scriptures and became fully committed to the personal and communal worship of his people. For some thirty years he "advanced [in] wisdom and age and favor before God and man" (Luke 2:52).

Jesus was unquestionably a man of deep prayer, as is constantly reflected in the Gospels. He had an intense religious awareness, an understanding of Yahweh and Yahweh's relationship with people that would one day put him in direct conflict with his people, his friends, and perhaps even his family (see Matthew 12:46–50). His vision would eventually lead him to death on the cross, which would offer all people the possibility of fullness of life. 4

For Review

- Why must we be careful about the images we have of Jesus during his early life and hidden years?
- Identify at least four factors that influenced Jesus while he was growing up.

4
Of all the things that influenced Jesus while he was growing up, which do you think had the greatest impact on him? Explain your opinion in a paragraph.

Photo, left: The Gezer calendar, a simple aid for remembering the agricultural seasons, etched in stone in Hebrew, was probably used by schoolchildren in Jesus' culture.

Photo, right: Jewish boys in Israel read from the Scriptures to prepare for their bar mitzvah, a ceremony that indicates they have reached the age of religious duty and responsibility.

The Beginnings of Jesus' Public Life

John the Baptist was one of the many wandering prophets at the time of Jesus. He was different, however, in that he did not proclaim himself as the Messiah, Savior, or Liberator yearned for by the Jewish people. Rather, he pointed to "'one mightier than I'" (Luke 3:16). John's task was to prepare the way for Jesus' ministry by calling people to an awareness of their sin and to repentance. He announced that a whole new "kingdom," a new society, was about to begin and that the people were to get ready for it by having a change of heart.

The sign John used to express this change of heart, this openness of mind and spirit, was a ritual bathing called *baptism*. The act of bathing in water as a sign of spiritual purification was a common practice for many religions of the time, including Judaism. By accepting baptism from John in the Jordan River, people acknowledged both their own sinfulness and their desire to join the new kingdom by changing the way they were living. Later Jesus would praise John, saying that "'among those born of women, no one is greater than John'" (Luke 7:28).

Jesus' Baptism

Differences Between the Gospel Accounts

All of the synoptic Gospels record the baptism of Jesus, and John's Gospel alludes to it, but there are some significant differences between the accounts.

Mark's account: In Mark's account (1:9–11) Jesus is baptized, and then he sees "the heavens being torn open and the Spirit, like a dove, descending upon him." A voice comes from the heavens, saying, "'You are my beloved Son; with you I am well pleased.'"

Matthew's account: In the account of Matthew (3:13–17) Jesus is baptized only after some disagreement with John about whether John should baptize him. After the baptism, Jesus sees "the Spirit of God descending like a dove," and a voice from the heavens proclaims, "'This is my beloved Son, with whom I am well pleased.'"

Luke's account: In Luke's account (3:21–22) Jesus is seen at prayer *after* the baptism has taken place, and it is then that the Spirit descends upon him "in bodily form like a dove." A voice from heaven proclaims, "'You are my beloved Son; with you I am well pleased.'"

John's Gospel: Unlike the synoptic Gospels, John's Gospel does not describe the baptism of Jesus. However, it does include a passage of testimony by John the Baptist that seems to echo the baptism scenes of the synoptics (see John 1:29–34). This passage also includes some language that is familiar to contemporary Catholics in their experience of the Mass: it is here that Jesus is referred to as "'the Lamb of God, who takes away the sin of the world.'"

Symbolism in the Baptism Accounts

Certainly some symbolism appears in all of the accounts of Jesus' baptism:

- *The dove:* In ancient times, the dove was often a symbol for Israel as a whole and, less often, a symbol for the Spirit of God.
- *The voice from the heavens:* At times in the Hebrew Scriptures, Yahweh is depicted as speaking to the people in a voice from the heavens. Often Yahweh is concealed by a cloud.

The Evangelists likely used these images to express Jesus' interior experience of God during his baptism. That is, the dove and the voice from the heavens may not have been seen and heard by those gathered about Jesus. Note, for instance, that it is Jesus who sees the Spirit of God descending and that, in two of the accounts, the voice speaks directly to Jesus: "'*You* are my beloved Son . . .'" rather than "'*This* is my beloved Son . . .'"

The Development of the Baptism Accounts

It is interesting to note the development of the accounts of Jesus' baptism from the earliest version (Mark's) to the later versions (Matthew's and Luke's). Mark is straightforward and direct in describing the scene, while Matthew introduces the disagreement with John the Baptist over whether Jesus should be baptized at all. Luke almost skips

Illustration: **Jesus' baptism in the Jordan was apparently a pivotal time of self-discovery for him, a time when he began to recognize what Yahweh was calling him to do.**

over the actual baptism and shows Jesus in prayer after the event, and John virtually ignores Jesus' baptism. Scholars claim that this reflects the Evangelists'—and the early church's—increasing discomfort with the whole notion of Jesus' accepting baptism.

Why Jesus Accepted Baptism— According to Matthew

As the early church reflected on the identity of Jesus and grew more and more to recognize him as the divine Son of God, it was faced with this question: Why would Jesus, as Messiah and sinless Son of God, accept a baptism that John the Baptist himself proclaimed was one of "repentance for the forgiveness of sins" (Mark 1:4; Luke 3:3)? Matthew's statement about John's reluctance to baptize Jesus (3:14) was an attempt by the Evangelist to offer an explanation. According to Matthew, Jesus accepted baptism because "'it is fitting for us to fulfill all righteousness'" (3:15). That is, Jesus saw the act as part of God's design or plan, and he accepted it on that basis. Matthew wanted to show that Jesus' acceptance was not an admission of sin. Rather, it indicated his willingness to completely immerse himself in the life and concerns of his people, to live as they had to live. For Matthew, Jesus' water baptism was the first step on the road to the cross. (Jesus would later refer to the cross as a baptism he could not avoid [see Mark 10:38; Luke 12:50].)

Jesus' Baptism: A Moment of Self-discovery

The accounts of Jesus' baptism reflect some interesting concerns of the early community of faith, but they also reveal Jesus' growing understanding of himself and his mission. Jesus, like each of us, struggled to find his place in the world. His baptism was apparently a pivotal time of self-discovery, a kind of "aha! moment" in which he came to some recognition of what he was being called to by Yahweh.

Jesus learned two chief lessons from his baptism, both symbolized by the writers of the Gospels with vivid, biblical imagery:

1. Jesus recognized that he was chosen in a special way to proclaim and begin a new kingdom. The words spoken from the heavens echoed those of Isaiah 42:1, which told of the "suffering servant of Yahweh," who would one day save Yahweh's people.
2. Jesus learned that he would be given the power to fulfill his role through the Spirit of God, represented by the descending dove. (That same Spirit of God drove Jesus into the desert immediately following his baptism, and would continue to lead him throughout his ministry.) **5**

Temptation in the Desert

In the scriptural quotation at the beginning of this chapter, Mark simply states that immediately after Jesus' baptism, "the Spirit drove him out into the desert, and he remained in the desert for forty days, tempted by Satan." The Gospels of Matthew and Luke expand this scene and describe a threefold temptation that Jesus experiences while in the desert (see Matthew 4:1–11; Luke 4:1–13).

In Matthew's Gospel, the tempter, or "devil," asks Jesus first to turn stones into bread, then to throw himself down from a high point of the Temple and have God catch him (in order to prove his special relationship with God), and finally to fall at the feet of the devil and worship him, for which Jesus would then receive "all the kingdoms of the

5
Based on recollections by your parents and others, write a short description of your own baptism.

world." In Luke's Gospel, the order of the second and third temptations is reversed, but the content is essentially the same.

According to what we find in Matthew's account, Jesus responds to all three temptations by giving direct quotes from the Book of Deuteronomy, which is part of the Hebrew Scriptures. In response to the three temptations, Jesus says, in turn:

1. "'"Not by bread alone does [one] live, but by every word that comes forth from the mouth of the Lord"'" (Deuteronomy 8:3).
2. "'"You shall not put the Lord, your God, to the test"'" (Deuteronomy 6:16).
3. "'"The Lord, your God, shall you fear; him shall you serve"'" (Deuteronomy 6:13).

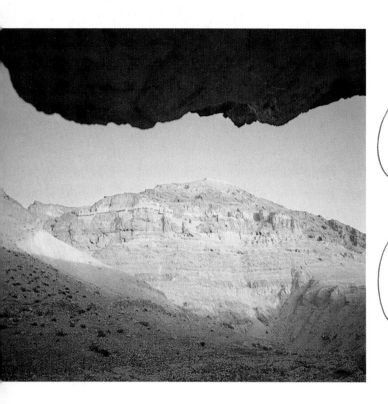

Jesus' Priorities in the Desert Experience

Again we must ask, What does this story mean? What were the Gospel writers trying to say about Jesus and his mission?

"The new Israel" did not fail. Each of the synoptic Gospels refers to the forty days that Jesus spent in the desert, and every Jew of Jesus' time would immediately have been reminded of the forty years that the people of Israel spent wandering in the desert in search of the Promised Land. The Israelites were severely tempted in the desert, and they ultimately failed to stay true to Yahweh. Jesus, as "the new Israel," was tempted as well, but he did not fail.

Jesus refused the messiahship expected by his people. A major lesson from the Gospels is that Jesus flatly rejected the political and militaristic messiahship that the Jewish people had come to expect and hope for. The story of the three temptations illustrates this point quite well, for it deals with the kinds of power that Jesus *refused* to exercise throughout his ministry.

- *Economic power:* Jesus' messiahship was not to be based on his ability to provide for the material wants and needs of the people (symbolized by turning stones into bread). Rather, he came to provide for the spiritual hunger of the people by proclaiming the word of God, which offers true life.
- *Magical power:* Nor was Jesus' messiahship to be based on magic and works of wonder that would somehow capture the imagination of the people and almost force them to believe in him (symbolized by throwing himself off the top of the Temple and surviving). Jesus responded to the devil's temptation by saying that God does not reveal divine power through trickery and magic.

Jesus resisted the temptations of economic power, magical power, and political power.

Photo: The Mount of Temptation, the site popularly believed to be the place where Jesus was tempted

(Wonder-working would constantly be an expectation of the crowds throughout Jesus' ministry, as we will see in our later discussion of his miracles.)

- *Political power:* Finally, Jesus' messiahship was not to be based on political power (symbolized by the temptation to worship the devil and control all the kingdoms of the world). Jesus said that God alone was to be worshiped and that the Reign of God in the world would take place in the hearts of the people, not in political domination of them.

All three of the temptations we see Jesus confronting—and defeating—in the desert represent the kind of temptations he would have to deal with throughout his ministry.

We must remember that the Gospels were written to guide the early church and its members. The writers, in addition to relaying information about Jesus' ministry, were warning Christians to resist the temptation to find their own meaning and purpose in life through economic security or through personal or political power over others. **6**

For Review

- Describe the significance of John the Baptist in the story of Jesus. What religious ritual is associated with John the Baptist?
- Why was the early church uncomfortable with Jesus' accepting baptism? How did Matthew respond to the church's concern?
- What two chief lessons did Jesus learn from his baptism?
- What does the story of the three temptations in the desert tell us about Jesus' understanding of his messiahship?

6
For each of the three temptations Jesus experienced in the desert, write a brief explanation of how a similar temptation might be experienced by a young person in today's society.

Jesus' forty days in the desert were a time of intense, prayerful preparation for his ministry.
Photo: **The mountains of the Desert of Judah**

Wandering Preacher, Unique Teacher

Like the Rabbis of His Day

Following his baptism, Jesus became a wandering preacher and religious teacher. It was common for the Jewish rabbis, or teachers of the Law (sometimes called scribes), to roam from place to place teaching. Often the rabbis were accompanied by a band of disciples, young men who freely chose to follow and study under them. It was common for the rabbis to teach in the synagogues and, less often, wherever people were willing to gather to listen to them—on mountainsides, in fields, or along the roadsides. So even though Jesus was probably not a rabbi in an official or legal sense, in many ways his ministry appears similar to a rabbi's.

Unlike the Rabbis of His Day

Several factors in the content of the message Jesus proclaimed, in the way he shared it, and in his relationship to his disciples clearly set him apart from the other teachers of his day.

Jesus proclaimed the Kingdom of God. Jesus proclaimed in both his words and his actions the coming of a "new Kingdom of God." The notion of such a Kingdom was a central one for the Jewish people of his day, so it was not surprising in itself that Jesus would speak of it. But his sense of the Kingdom was truly different.

Jesus claimed a special role. Jesus not only proclaimed the coming of a new Kingdom, but he also claimed for himself a special role as the one who would personally establish and embody it, not only announce it.

Jesus taught with unique authority. Jesus amazed the crowds not only with the content of his message but with the attitude he possessed while sharing it. As we read in Matthew's Gospel, "the crowds were astonished at his teaching, for he taught them as one having authority, and not as their scribes" (7:28–29).

The rabbis at the time of Jesus were called to study the Hebrew Scriptures and the teaching of other rabbis thoroughly. Whenever they taught they were expected to back up what they were saying with direct quotes from the Scriptures or statements from other respected rabbis.

Jesus, on the other hand, claimed himself as the sole judge of the truth of what he taught. At times he would even say, for example, "'You have heard that it was said to your ancestors, . . . But I say to you'" (see Matthew 5:21–48). This was a clear break from the common practice, and it both impressed and alienated many people who listened to him preach.

Jesus used parables and performed miracles. Finally, Jesus differed dramatically from other teachers of his time in his use of parables and in the miracles he performed.

Jesus and His Disciples: A Unique Relationship

The Meaning of Discipleship

As has been mentioned, it was typical for a rabbi to attract disciples who would study under him. The disciples would learn from the rabbi in a process of lengthy discussion, memorization through word games, and so on. The goal was for the disciples to learn perfectly the teachings of the rabbi, to the point of being able to repeat his teachings

The Apostle Peter

So Much Like Us

The Gospels' portrait of the Apostle Peter—also called Simon or Simon Peter—is one of the most thorough, intriguing, and enlightening character studies available in the entire Bible. He is mentioned more than any other disciple. Among Roman Catholics, Peter is of primary significance because of the eventual leadership role he played in the early community of faith, a role that leads Catholics to identify him as the first pope. But Peter's great calling is not always evident in the Gospels' portrait of him. In fact, the portrait of Peter that we have from the Gospels at times seems to be just the opposite of a leader!

Peter is a wonderfully appealing person to read about because he is so much like us—at our best and at our weakest. He makes mistakes and requires forgiveness. He is often bold, even hotheaded, and then cowardly. He can seem terribly bright, then incredibly ignorant. He, more than any other person in the Gospels, exemplifies the claim that the Apostles were ordinary people who, because of their association with Jesus, were capable of extraordinary things.

Selected Gospel Passages on Peter

The following are a number of key Gospel passages on Peter. They are organized, to the extent possible, in chronological order. You are encouraged to read some if not all of these passages to gain a rich sense of Peter's personality and an appreciation of how much he was like us.

Luke 5:1–11
Jesus recruits Peter after an almost too successful fishing trip.

Matthew 14:22–33
Peter learns a lesson about humility while taking an unexpected swim.

Mark 9:2–8
Peter sees Jesus in a new "light."

Matthew 16:13–23
Peter shows deep faith in Jesus and proves for just a moment that he is ready for more responsibility—until he questions Jesus' ability to understand what the future holds and gets reprimanded by Jesus for his limited understanding.

Luke 22:31–34
Jesus sees through Peter's "cocky" self-confidence.

John 13:4–9
After initially rejecting a quick foot-washing by Jesus, Peter volunteers for a total bath.

Matthew 26:36–41
A sleepy Peter keeps nodding off when Jesus most needs him.

Mark 14:66–72
Peter, as predicted by Jesus, fails a major test, not just once but three times.

John 21:1–19
After a breakfast barbecue on the beach with the Risen Jesus, Peter makes up for his earlier failures by passing another test . . . again, three times.

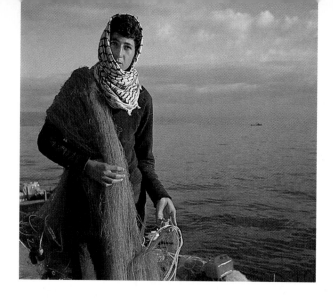

word for word. Once they had done this, the disciples would leave the rabbi and become independent rabbis themselves.

With Jesus and his disciples, however, the relationship was different.

- First of all, Jesus' disciples did not choose him; rather, he called them (see Mark 1:16–20; Luke 5:1–11).
- Second, unlike other rabbis, Jesus did not simply share with his disciples a body of teachings that they were expected to memorize word for word. According to the common practice, one who had mastered all of the teachings of a rabbi would in turn be recognized as a rabbi himself and could claim some personal authority on that basis. But Jesus told his disciples that they were not to take the title *rabbi,* because their only basis of authority came from their relationship with him (see Matthew 23:8–10).
- Third, the disciples of Jesus were not only expected to watch and learn from Jesus, but they were actually called to share in his mission of proclaiming the Kingdom (see Luke 9:1–6).

The special role of the first disciples of Jesus lends insight into what it means to be a disciple of his *today.* Jesus calls each Christian to a personal, lasting relationship of love with God, and Jesus also sends his followers out to share in his mission of proclaiming the Kingdom.

The Twelve Apostles

Many people responded to Jesus' message and followed him, and all of these people might qualify as his disciples. But the Gospels are clear that Jesus carefully selected special men who were to play a central and significant role during his ministry and in the future. These were the *Apostles,* most frequently referred to in the Gospels as "the Twelve." (Their names are recorded in Matthew 10:2–4; Mark 3:16–19; and Luke 6:13–16.) Curiously, the Twelve are not mentioned in John's Gospel at all, perhaps because John wished to focus more specifically on Jesus himself as the one called to manifest Yahweh's presence and power.

The Twelve echoed the twelve tribes of Israel. It is significant that the Evangelists portrayed Jesus as choosing exactly twelve Apostles and that the early community of faith would work to maintain that number after the death of one of them (see Acts of the Apostles 1:15–26). Think back to the earlier discussion of the history of the Jews. You will recall that the Israelites at one time consisted of twelve tribes, each descending from one of the twelve sons of Jacob. It seems certain that the early Christian community recognized exactly twelve Apostles to suggest that they would be the foundation of a new community of faith, a new Israel, what we today recognize as the Christian church.

What was so special about the Apostles? The Apostles were, of course, disciples of Jesus. But they were selected by him to be his constant companions, traveling with him from place to place and becoming thoroughly instructed in the truths he shared. The word **apostle** comes from a Greek

Some of the Apostles were ordinary fishermen.
Photo: A fisherman on the shore of the Sea of Galilee

word meaning "to send forth." Jesus apparently commissioned these men to go out and carry on his Good News about the Kingdom of God. In a special way the Twelve shared Jesus' power, and after his death and resurrection they continued, in his name, to preach, to heal, and to make disciples through baptism (Matthew 28:16–20).

Ordinary People with an Extraordinary Calling

What sort of people did Jesus seek for this mission as Apostles? Some were simple fishermen. One was a hated tax collector. Two were such hotheads that Jesus called them "sons of thunder." One would eventually betray him. One was a leader who could show signs of great insight but could also demonstrate outright cowardice. The Gospels often portray these men as dull, baffled, unable to understand what Jesus is telling them. At times they seem to hunger for great power. Eventually they desert Jesus out of fear. In the end, though, all of them but Judas reconcile with Jesus after his resurrection, and most if not all of these go on to die as heroes in the early church. In short, the Apostles were ordinary people, but because of their association with Jesus, they were capable of extraordinary things. **7**

For Review

- In what ways was Jesus the teacher both similar to and different from the rabbis of his day?
- Briefly describe Jesus' relationship with his disciples called the Apostles.
- What connection can be made between the twelve Apostles and the early history of the Jews?

The Proclamation of the Kingdom

Central to Jesus' identity, his life, his mission and message, and all of his words and actions is the notion of the Kingdom of God. Jesus' history as a Jew inspired the notion of the Kingdom. His prayer and life experiences led him to identify himself as the proclaimer and possessor of the Kingdom. His parables pointed to and described the Kingdom, and his miracles were signs of its presence in the people's midst. Therefore, we have to understand what Jesus meant by the Kingdom of God if we are to understand him. The next chapter of this course will take a look at the Kingdom.

7
According to the Gospels, the Apostles came from ordinary walks of life. Write a brief description of twelve people Jesus might choose as Apostles today. Consider questions such as these:

Would the twelve people all be men? What occupations would they come from? In terms of personality traits, would they be similar to one another or a mix?

Photo: **A row of olive trees on a hillside in Bethlehem against a glorious sunset**

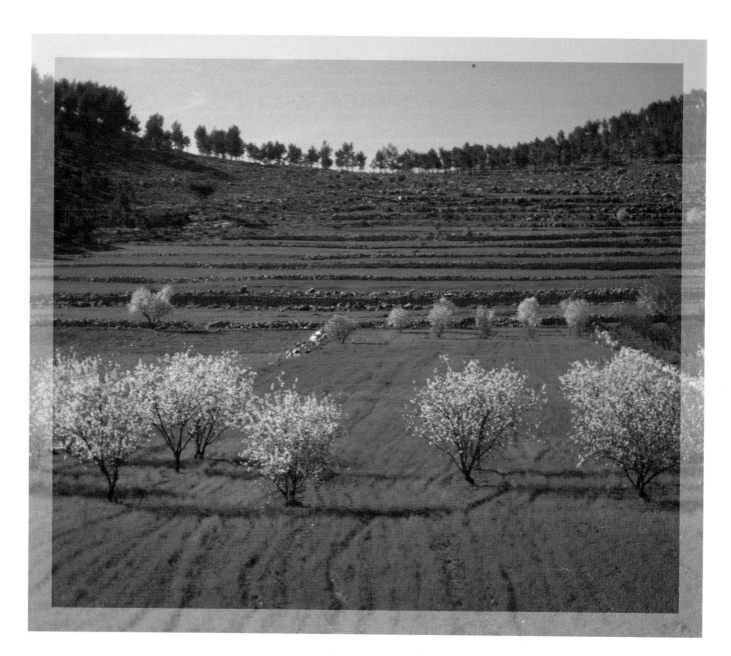

6

The Kingdom of God:
Proclaiming the Dream of Jesus

ONE of the scribes . . . asked [Jesus], "Which commandment is the first of all?" Jesus answered, "The first is, 'Hear, O Israel: The Lord our God, the Lord is one; you shall love the Lord your God with all your heart, and with all your soul, and with all your mind, and with all your strength.' The second is this, 'You shall love your neighbor as yourself.' There is no other commandment greater than these." Then the scribe said to him, "You are right, Teacher; you have truly said that 'he is one, and besides him there is no other'; and 'to love him with all the heart, and with all the understanding, and with all the strength,' and 'to love one's neighbor as oneself,'—this is much more important than all whole burnt offerings and sacrifices." When Jesus saw that [the scribe] answered wisely, he said to [the scribe], "You are not far from the kingdom of God." (Mark 12:28–34)

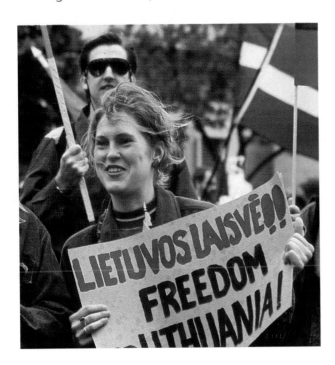

Dreams: Future Hopes Grounded in the Past and the Present

The Human Need to Hope

All religions—indeed, all people—reflect a human need to hope for a future that is in some way better than the present. Sometimes such hoping is expressed in a vision of a future society in which all the idealistic dreams of the particular religion are fulfilled. We might call such an idealized picture of the future a religion's *Dream,* with a capital *D.*

A particular religion's Dream will vary depending on what the believers ground their hopes in. For example, a given religion might focus on the military defeat of its enemies. Its Dream would be of a future in which the members of the religion dominate their world with political and military power.

Another religion might be based on the conviction that all its members can experience a deep personal sense of peace. This religion might offer as its Dream a picture of what society would look like if all people attained such inner tranquility.

Jesus, too, had a strong vision of an ideal future, and he dedicated his life to making that future a reality. Jesus referred to his vision as the **Kingdom of God.** Many of his teachings and stories revealed his understanding of the Kingdom. His miracles were expressions of the fact that God was inaugurating the Kingdom through Jesus himself. Jesus' vision came to serve as the driving force for all who would follow him. A full understanding of Jesus—and, therefore, of all Christianity—requires an understanding of the Dream that Jesus proclaimed. The purpose of this chapter is to help you understand that Dream. **1**

Photo, facing page: Almond trees blossom in the Judaean hills.
Photo, above: Young Lithuanians demonstrate for their Dream— freedom of their republic from what was then the Soviet Union.

1
Think of a time when you were so committed to achieving a certain goal that you regularly made sacrifices to attain it. As you read the rest of this section, jot down your thoughts on how your experience might be similar to Jesus' commitment to his Dream, the Kingdom of God.

Everyone Has a Dream

To gain some sense of the nature and purpose of a Dream, try to recall as vividly as you can your first day as a student in your present school. Try to regain a sense of how you felt about the following things:

- going to school in an unfamiliar building
- meeting many new people your own age and older—some friendly, some not
- encountering teachers who were more demanding than those you had had earlier
- taking more difficult courses
- running into much stiffer competition academically, athletically, even socially

Now, try to imagine in as much detail as possible what the week of your graduation from high school will be like if everything turns out exactly as you now hope and dream it will.

- Imagine how many close friendships you will have developed by that time.
- Envision the class spirit that will have developed, even among those students who have not become good friends with one another.
- See in your mind how all the various groups in your class will relate to one another.
- Consider the ideal relationship that will have formed between the faculty and the students.
- Imagine what the senior graduation parties will be like.
- Picture yourself going through the graduation ceremony, no doubt with a real mix of feelings.

The vision you have created of your final days of high school is your personal Dream. Though perhaps idealized and seemingly beyond reach, this Dream is grounded in your past experience in the school and reflects as well your present hopes. And what is important is that you do have it within

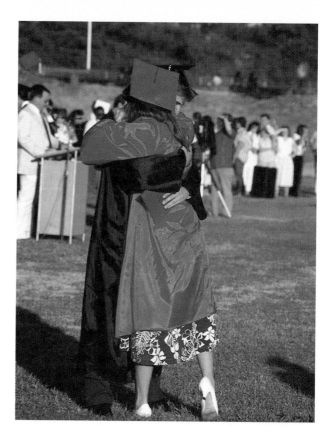

your power to influence, at least to some degree, whether anything remotely like your Dream will become a reality. That is precisely the power of a Dream: it can focus our energies, guide our choices, influence our friendships, even lead us closer to personal happiness.

Jesus, like us, rooted his Dream in his own history, his life experiences, and his hopes for the future. And he directed his entire life toward making his Dream of the Kingdom of God come true, living every moment as if the Dream were already within reach.

For Review

- Define *Dream*, spelled with a capital *D*.
- What is the name given to Jesus' Dream?

Photo: **Your idealized vision of the week of your high school graduation can be thought of as your personal Dream.**

The Kingdom of God Is Like a Party

Jesus frequently used stories and figures of speech to describe the Kingdom of God. He apparently realized that what he was trying to describe as a reality—his great Dream—was far beyond what anyone might imagine. He needed a special kind of language to express that reality. For example, he compared the Kingdom of God to many things:

- a mustard seed, which "'is the smallest of all the seeds, but when it has grown . . . is the greatest of shrubs and becomes a tree'" (see Matthew 13:31–32)
- someone who sowed good wheat seed in a field, only to have an enemy plant weeds among the wheat (see Matthew 13:24–30)
- a treasure hidden in a field, or a merchant searching for fine pearls, or a fishing net thrown into the sea (see Matthew 13:44–49)

If we today were going to follow Jesus' example and describe the Kingdom of God through a figure of speech, we might say that the Kingdom is like a great party. Many times, seemingly well planned parties fizzle and fail even though the setting is fine, the food is wonderful, and good entertainment has been provided. On the other hand, some parties are memorable even though they "just happen" with little or no preparation. Somehow, the right chemistry is present and makes the parties successful. But what makes up that "chemistry"?

- First, the most important ingredient in any party is the mix of people involved. And curiously, the greater the mix, the more memorable the party. If everyone at the party is "best friends" or alike, the party can get bogged down. As the saying goes, "variety is the spice of life," even when it comes to people.
- Second, fancy food might be impressive to look at if not to eat, but a party seems to go better when everyone can contribute something, however simple. A party at which everyone brings their favorite topping for a homemade pizza is more fun than one where a pizza is delivered to the door and eaten in ten minutes.
- Third, people have to feel comfortable at a party—relaxed, not pressured to

live up to others' expectations. The worst parties occur when people feel like they have to watch their every move for fear of embarrassment. Good parties happen when people can be themselves and accept others.

- Finally, the good party has a host who is less concerned with his or her own "performance" and more concerned with the guests' being at ease and enjoying themselves.

So how might Jesus sum up this "parable" of the Kingdom of God? Maybe like this: The Kingdom of God is like a good party—with a lot of different kinds of people being themselves and sharing their unique gifts because the host (Jesus?) has created a warm, accepting place for all of them to gather.

Photo: **Some parties are memorable because they have the right recipe: a variety of people, an involvement of everyone, a sense that people can be themselves and still be accepted, and a concern that everyone has a good time.**

The Kingdom of God Proclaimed

The word *kingdom* can sometimes get in the way of our understanding what Jesus meant when he preached about the Kingdom of God. For us, the *Kingdom* of God can automatically imply a place or region. When discussing Jesus' teachings, a better reference might be the *Reign* of God or the *Rule* of God over all of the created world. With this qualification in mind, let's explore what God's Reign or Rule over the world meant to Jesus and, therefore, what it should mean to Christians. 2

The Focus of the Synoptic Gospels

Just as we ultimately turn to the Gospels for an understanding of Jesus, so too we must turn to them for an understanding of the Kingdom of God. In fact, we must look primarily to the synoptic Gospels. Significantly, John's Gospel never explicitly mentions the theme of the Kingdom. John seems to suggest that Jesus himself already embodied the Dream that the synoptic authors describe as primarily a future kingdom. Matthew, Mark, and Luke, then, tell us most directly about Jesus' understanding of the Kingdom of God, and a key part of their message concerns what Jesus did *not* see as the Kingdom.

What Jesus Did Not See as the Kingdom

The Jewish Notion of the Kingdom of God

The basic notion of the Kingdom of God was part of the Jewish worldview with which Jesus was raised. The Jews accepted, for example, that Yahweh was the king over all creation. Many of the Hebrew religious hymns, which we call *psalms*, celebrated the kingship of God. For example:

The LORD is king, he is robed in majesty;
   the LORD is robed, he is [encircled] with strength.
He has established the world; it shall never be
   moved;
   your throne is established from of old;
   you are from everlasting.

(Psalm 93:1–2)

So God's kingship was recognized first in the wonders of creation. Some rabbis taught as well that the Kingdom of God was present in the Law, in the Torah. They felt that the Law was God's instrument for ruling people.

It was also clear to the Jews that the Kingdom of God had not yet been fully established, because so much evil obviously still existed in the world. They recognized that this was due in large part to their own failure to cooperate with Yahweh, their failure to follow God's will completely.

For the Jews, Yahweh was the ruler over all creation, and they praised God for the beauty of the natural world.
Photo: The Tel Dan Reserve in upper Galilee

2
Respond in writing to the following question: *If you did not know anything about Jesus and Christianity, what might you think the term* Kingdom of God *referred to?*

New Insights into Old Ideas

Jesus certainly accepted much of the Jewish understanding of the Kingdom of God, but he also went beyond it and brought new insights into the older ideas. In some cases he actually contradicted expectations about the Kingdom that were held by the Jews of his day.

As discussed earlier, the Jews believed that the Kingdom of God would be established through a savior. In the centuries following King David's military conquests, the people's expectation of a savior became bound up with the notion of a new national, political kingship. And by the time of Jesus' ministry, after nearly a hundred years of Roman domination, many Jews expected the Kingdom to begin with a military takeover of the country and the expulsion of the Romans. This overthrow was to be led by the Messiah, who was by then expected to be a military leader, a warrior. Jesus' understanding of the Kingdom and of his messiahship proved to be far different from what his people commonly understood.

Ideas That Jesus Rejected

From the story about Jesus' temptation in the desert—and from all his teachings and actions—it is clear that Jesus rejected specific ideas in the Jewish understanding of the Kingdom. He was certainly not trying to begin a new political reign over his people. In the Gospels, people try to make Jesus a king or political ruler, and he firmly rejects the notion.

Jesus' stand on nonviolence eliminated the possibility of a military takeover of any kind. It is also clear from the Gospels that he did not have in mind a geographical state or nation when he spoke of the Kingdom. Jesus' Kingdom would have no boundaries, no borders separating one nation from another.

Nor was Jesus' concept of the Kingdom of God simply a new philosophy or a new plan for social reform. But if the Kingdom was none of these things, what was it?

For Review

- Briefly explain the Jewish notion of God as a king.
- Why did the ancient Jews believe the Messiah would be a great warrior who would establish the Kingdom through military conquest?
- What ideas about the Kingdom of God did Jesus clearly reject?

Illustration: **Jesus rejected specific ideas common to the ancient Jews regarding the Kingdom, such as the notion that the Messiah would be a political ruler or a member of royalty.**

Jesus' Understanding of God

Jesus' vision of the Kingdom of God was closely tied to his understanding of God, which differed dramatically from the understanding of God commonly held by the Jewish people.

God as Father

The Traditional Jewish Understanding

Jesus was thoroughly Jewish, so his understanding of the Kingdom of God necessarily flowed out of Jewish history, the Hebrew Scriptures, Jewish worship, and of course, his own personal prayer and reflection on all of these. That personal prayer and reflection led him to a unique and remarkable recognition of God as his "Father." The notion of God as Father was not entirely new to Jesus. The Hebrew Scriptures occasionally used this term for Yahweh. But as noted earlier, the Jews held Yahweh in such awe and reverence that they would not even consider using Yahweh's name in prayer and worship. Instead they said "the Lord," "the Most High," or "the Holy One." Calling Yahweh "Father" was definitely out of the question.

Jesus' Teachings

Jesus shattered Jewish belief and practice and took the incredible position of referring to God as "'Abba, Father'" (Mark 14:36). *Abba* is an Aramaic word that means something far more intimate than just "father." It was the word used by little Jewish children for their fathers; it had the sense of "da-da," which is uttered so easily by infants. The term *abba* was also used by adults as an affectionate term for their father, much as adults of today may continue to call their father "Dad" or "Daddy." In other words, Jesus was saying that people

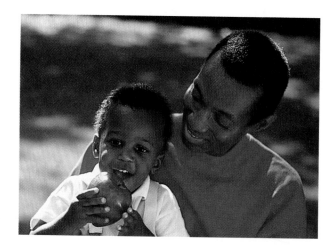

not only could call God by name but could even refer to God with an equivalent of our word *Dad* or *Daddy!* No Jew would have ever dared such intimacy, and it must have shocked many to hear Jesus speak of God with such a sense of childlike affection. **3**

A God Who Loves Without Condition

The Traditional Jewish Understanding

Some Christians unfairly stereotype the Jewish Yahweh as "a God of fear and justice" and Jesus' God as "a God of love." Actually, the Jewish notion of a loving God was very strong. But because the Jewish reverence for God was so great that the people could not even utter the divine name, they often experienced God as distant and removed.

One way the Jews expressed their feeling of distance from God was by referring to God as "the heavens." This explains an interesting expression that Matthew uses in his discussion of the Kingdom of God. Remember, Matthew was writing to a Jewish audience, and he was sensitive to their

---

Photo: **Jesus taught people that they could refer to God not only by name but even with the word** *Abba*—**an equivalent of our word** *Dad* **or** *Daddy.*

3
Slowly say the Lord's Prayer to yourself. Then repeat the prayer, substituting the words *"My Daddy"* for *"Our Father."* In a paragraph, describe any

feelings or insight you had from this exercise.

Images of God: Limited by Our Language

Our language poses a problem in discussing Jesus' understanding of God. Jesus found the need to speak of God with a new vocabulary, a new set of words and terms. Many people today sense a similar need because of exclusive, sexist language that has commonly been used in talking about God. For example, masculine pronouns are frequently used in reference to God—words like *him, himself,* and *he.* A similar situation is the word *Kingdom,* which has a strongly masculine connotation regarding God's Rule over the world. This language problem is based on past cultural understandings (many of which were deeply affected by sexism), Jesus' own notion of God's fatherhood, and the Gospels' constant use of masculine images.

The fact is that God is neither masculine nor feminine in the common sense of those terms. God is spirit and does not have a sexual identity in the same way that people or other creatures do. It is helpful, therefore, while acknowledging the special significance of the title *Father* for God, to use additional names, such as *Mother, Creator, Gracious One,* and so on.

Somehow the whole community of Christians must arrive at an acceptable solution to this language problem. A sincere attempt has been made to avoid exclusively male references to God in this book, but it must be acknowledged that the problem is a difficult one. An apology is offered for the limitations in dealing with it in this course.

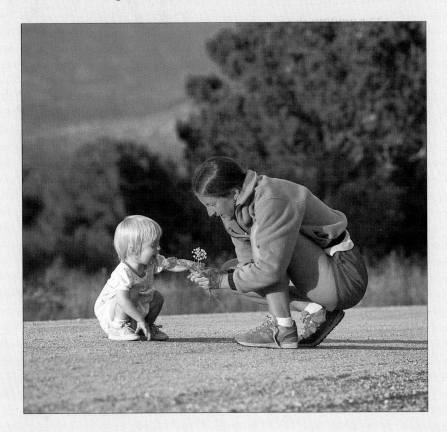

Photo: **We can think of God as Mother as well as Father.**

God who is influence

God can [?]

he alone had with God. But he also teaches people to pray to "our Father." Jesus saw God as a passionately caring parent whose love is tireless, healing, unlimited, and unreserved. God offers that love to sinners as well as to the just, to rich and poor people alike, to women and men, to slaves and free people. To the people of Jesus' time, this was a radically new vision, a vision of a God in whom they could place their complete trust. This trust is beautifully expressed in a passage from Matthew that has been treasured by Christians throughout the ages:

"Look at the birds of the air; they neither sow nor reap nor gather into barns, and yet your heavenly Father feeds them. Are you not of more value than they? And can any of you by worrying add a single hour to your span of life? And why do you worry about clothing? Consider the lilies of the field, how they grow; they neither toil nor spin, yet I tell you, even Solomon in all his glory was not clothed like one of these. . . .

So do not worry about tomorrow, for tomorrow will bring worries of its own. Today's trouble is enough for today." (Matthew 6:26–34) **4**

The Kingdom that Jesus announced, therefore, was in fact a new understanding of a relationship that God had always offered. In his teachings about the Kingdom of God, Jesus was sharing new insights into the nature of God.

feelings and religious practices and convictions. Therefore, instead of writing "the kingdom of God," Matthew wrote "the kingdom of heaven." The God of the ancient Jewish people was full of mystery, as demonstrated by the Holy of Holies in the Temple, that sacred place reserved for Yahweh alone.

Jesus' Teachings

Out of his own experience of a profoundly intimate relationship with God, Jesus taught about God's relationship with all people—and indeed with all of creation. That conviction of God's intimate union with people was a primary part of Jesus' vision of the Kingdom of God. Jesus experienced the nourishing love of God in a deeply personal sense. In the Gospels, Jesus refers often to "my Father," indicating a special relationship that

For Review

- With what Aramaic word did Jesus address God? Why did this shock the people of Jesus' time?

Illustration: **Referring to the beautiful wildflowers growing in the fields of Galilee, Jesus said, "Consider the lilies . . . even Solomon in all his glory was not clothed like one of these."**

4
Referring to Matthew 6:26–34, as quoted above, select one line that you think would be particularly significant for young people today. Write a short explanation of your choice.

Jesus' Understanding of the Command to Love

According to Jesus, the ability to recognize and fully participate in the Reign of God requires a *conversion*, a change of heart, a turning from selfishness to openness to God and the call to love. When this conversion happens, the Kingdom of God takes root in the heart of the believer. Jesus' initial call, therefore, is to repentance, to a change in the way we live. Jesus said, "'The time is fulfilled, and the kingdom of God has come near; repent, and believe in the good news'" (Mark 1:15).

Not Just "Me and God"

The Reign of God proclaimed by Jesus was not simply a "me and God" situation, a one-to-one relationship between God and an individual person. Rather, Jesus clearly understood the Kingdom as being communal in nature, implying a new relationship not only between God and individuals but *among* individuals. That is, Jesus saw the Kingdom as the rule or reign of God's love over the very hearts of people and, consequently, as a new social order based on people's unconditional love for one another. This meant that an entirely new era in history had begun, a time characterized by peace, joy, freedom, and love.

The Jewish Roots of the Command to Love

Jesus' concept of love for others—like his concepts of the Kingdom and God as Father—was not so much an entirely new notion as an expansion of a notion already held by the Jews. The Jews had such a deep sense of communal love, of concern for the poor, and of generosity that these attitudes had become their identifying traits to the other cultures that surrounded them.

The Ten Commandments, the cornerstone of the Jewish Law, included seven commandments directly related to relationships between people. The giving of *alms*, or contributions, to the poor was *required*, not merely suggested, by the Jewish Law. And in a touching example of Jewish generosity, the Law forbade the harvesting of corn on the outer edges of the fields, so that poor people would have easy access to it. The rabbis even went beyond the basic Law and insisted on attitudes of kindness and gentleness. Over time, however, there developed among the Jews two main problems that conflicted with the command to love others. These were the problems of nationalism and legalism.

Nationalism

The first problem that developed among the Jews was an excessive sense of *nationalism*. The Jewish sense of separation from all other cultures led some Jews to believe that "love your neighbor" referred to Jewish neighbors only. Some Jews—

Jewish Law not only suggested but required the giving of alms (charity) to the poor.
Photo: A beggar receives alms in Israel today.

though certainly not all—even believed that they were called to love their neighbor but *hate* their enemy. (Jesus refers to this belief in Matthew 5:43: "'You have heard that it was said, "You shall love your neighbor and hate your enemy."'" But Jesus knows that such a command is never actually stated in the Hebrew Scriptures or in the writings of the rabbis.)

Legalism

Another problem among the Jews was *legalism*. This was particularly true among the Pharisees.

The Jews looked upon the Law as a great gift from Yahweh, a sign of God's love for them. And certainly, some laws are necessary if a society is to maintain any reasonable kind of order. However, over time, minute rules and regulations had developed in Jewish society, not only guiding but dominating virtually every aspect of life. The combination of the Torah (the written version of the Law contained in the Hebrew Scriptures) and the oral teachings of the rabbis, which grew up over the years, led to an extensive system of religious laws. The Torah alone listed over six hundred such laws, governing everything from the Sabbath rest to ritual cleanliness, food and meal preparation, circumcision, and so on. In other words, a basic and decent moral foundation had become overly legalistic and was no longer just guiding the people but actually oppressing them. As you will learn later in this course, Saint Paul would have much to say about legalism and the Law in light of Jesus' life and message. 5

Love Without Limits

Jesus went beyond the limitations of the Law, shattering any sense of narrow nationalism as well as breaking down the barriers of legalism. A particularly marvelous Gospel passage captures this well: In Luke 10:25–37, Jesus asks a lawyer to explain what the Law requires for eternal life. The lawyer responds, as every good Jew would, with the dual commandment to love God and neighbor, and Jesus approves. But then the lawyer presses the issue by asking, "'And who is my neighbor?'" Jesus responds with the thought-provoking story of the good Samaritan. Remember how deeply the mainline Jews despised the Samaritans. By telling the story of the good Samaritan in the context of the command to love, Jesus is clearly telling his listeners that they are called beyond the limits of their own Judaism to love *all* people, even their enemies. 6

The Gospel of Matthew teaches the same lesson:

"But I say to you, Love your enemies and pray for those who persecute you, so that you may be children of your Father in heaven; for he makes his sun rise on the evil and on the good, and sends rain on the righteous and on the unrighteous. For if you love those who love you, what reward do you have? Do not even the tax collectors do the same? And if you greet only your brothers and sisters, what more are you doing than others? Do not even the Gentiles do the same? Be perfect, therefore, as your heavenly Father is perfect." (5:44–48)

Jesus' call to love enemies was unique to him, with no parallel in either the Hebrew Scriptures or the writings of the rabbis.

Love Expressed in Deeds

Jesus did not actually use the word *love* all that much. He spoke more often of the results or expressions of love: service to others, compassion,

---

5
In writing, respond to the following question and support your response with an example. *Do Christians have the same tendency toward legalism that the Jews of Jesus' time had?*

6
Rewrite the story of the good Samaritan (Luke 10:25–37) as you believe Jesus would tell it today if he were addressing your class or school.

forgiveness, and reconciliation. For a powerful summary of Jesus' teaching on the law of love, we need only read his familiar story of the last judgment in the Gospel of Matthew: Jesus says that at the end of time, "'the Son of Man'" will offer "'the kingdom prepared . . . [since] the foundation of the world'" to all those who responded to his needs when he was hungry, thirsty, lonely, naked, ill, imprisoned (25:31–36). The story continues:

"Then the righteous will answer him, 'Lord, when was it that we saw you hungry and gave you food, or thirsty and gave you something to drink? And when was it that we saw you a stranger and welcomed you, or naked and gave you clothing? And when was it that we saw you sick or in prison and visited you?'

And the king [Son of Man] will answer them, 'Truly I tell you, just as you did it to one of the least of these who are members of my family, you did it to me.'" (25:37–40)

According to Jesus, faith in God cannot be lived out apart from service to people in need.

Jesus also claimed that the call to love is a call to unlimited forgiveness, and that God's willingness to forgive people is very much related to their willingness to forgive one another (Matthew 6:14–15). In the Lord's Prayer, Christians pray, "Forgive us our trespasses, *as we forgive those who trespass against us.*" Perhaps if people were more conscious of what they were saying, those words would not come out so easily!

Illustration: **In Jesus' Dream of the Kingdom of God, barriers of prejudice and nationalism would no longer divide people. All persons—poor and rich, male and female, Jew and Gentile, slave and free, oppressed and oppressor, young and old, prestigious and outcast—would be able to sit down together in peace and joy at the banquet of God's love.**

The Roman Catholic Church and the Kingdom of God

At times in its long history, Roman Catholic church members have understood the church and the Kingdom of God to be one and the same. In recent years, however, the leaders of Catholicism have been careful to distinguish between the church itself and the Kingdom. The Kingdom of God is realized whenever and wherever the power of God's love is manifest, whenever and wherever the will of God is fulfilled. Because of that, the Kingdom is a reality much "bigger" than the church. For instance, Catholics today believe that other, non-Christian religions can also bring about the Kingdom of God to the degree that their members live in dedication to service, compassion, forgiveness, and reconciliation.

At the same time, the church cannot be understood apart from Jesus' vision of the Kingdom of God. The mission of the members of the church is to live in such a way that the Dream of Jesus is proved possible. The church is called to be a community transformed by the Spirit of God into a people of faith, hope, love, freedom, and truth. When it exhibits such characteristics, the church proclaims in word and action that Jesus' vision of the Kingdom is not a pipe dream, not a "pie in the sky," but a reality within reach of people who dare to share that Dream.

Jesus' Teachings on Love: A Source of Challenge

Jesus did not believe that the Law, in itself, was bad. Rather, he recognized that the many spin-offs and additions to it, created by the rabbis and others, had actually crippled the believers' ability to respond to one another with compassion and love. Jesus' challenge to certain dimensions of the Law—for example, the Sabbath laws (Mark 2:23–28) and the laws on ritual cleanliness (Mark 7:14–23)—could not help but alienate many who based their lives on the Law.

The key to comprehending Jesus' teaching about the Kingdom of God, therefore, is in understanding his conviction about the passionate, unrestricted, unconditional love of God—and the power of that love to release and free people to love one another unconditionally, without restrictions. The Reign of God becomes real when God reigns over the hearts of people, and God reigns over the hearts of people when people are in tune with God's will. It has been said that "the will of God is the good of people." This means that when people conform their lives to God's will, there will be peace, joy, and love for all—that is, the Kingdom of God will be fully realized. 7

For Review

- According to Jesus, what is the meaning of the word *conversion?*
- What does it mean to say that Jesus understood the Kingdom of God as being communal in nature?
- Name and briefly describe the two problems that developed among the Jews and conflicted with their following the command to love one another.
- When will, or does, Jesus' Dream of the Kingdom of God become realized?

7
In a paragraph, react to the following statement: *True Christianity can never be understood as a "me and God" religion.*

The Reign of God and "the Reign of Sin"

Jesus' understanding of the Reign of God also touches upon one of the most difficult realities of life: the presence of sin and evil in the world. In praying the Lord's Prayer, Christians ask God to "lead us not into temptation, but deliver us from evil." As the Lord's Prayer is found in the Gospel of Matthew, it reads, "'And do not bring us to the time of trial, but rescue us from the evil one'" (6:13). In one sense or another, all religions acknowledge the experience of sin and evil in life and offer some response to it.

Sometimes the source of evil is personified, or given almost human characteristics. In those cases,

evil may be represented as a devil or as Satan. At times, Jesus uses such images in the Gospels, reflecting the common beliefs of the Jews of his day. As a faithful Jew, Jesus would have been very familiar with the Book of Genesis and its story of Adam and Eve in the garden (see Genesis, chapter 3). This story was the attempt by Jesus' people to explain the presence of evil in the world, while acknowledging that all that had come from God was good. The point of the story is that people are responsible for evil and its effects, because people choose to reject God, not the other way around. Several hundred years after the death of Jesus, the church named this historic rupture between God and people *original sin,* the effects of which have been passed down through the ages from generation to generation.

The effects of the sinful actions of individual people accumulate over time into communal sin, which affects us all. War and poverty, whose victims are innocent, are examples of communal sin.

Photo: **Egyptian children scavenge for food and supplies from a pile of trash. Millions of children around the world live in this kind of extreme poverty.**

The chief points to recognize here are that sin and evil do exist in the world and that the conflict between good and evil takes place both in the hearts of individual people and in their relationships with one another.

Sin: Both Personal and Communal

Sin can be defined, understood, and experienced in several ways. Catholics commonly think of sin as personal, freely chosen actions that have negative effects on the sinners as individuals and on their relationships with others. But sin can also be understood as a social evil that affects all people simply because we live in community with one another. That is, we can say that the effects of the sinful actions of individual people accumulate over time into communal sin, which affects all who are born into it. This kind of sin is reflected in the isolation, alienation, and loneliness that afflict so many people today. Examples of communal sin and its effects are war, poverty, and the destruction of the environment.

Evil That Is Not Caused by Sin

Another evil—different from the moral evil associated with and brought about by sin, different from the evil that is chosen—often challenges Christians' basic conviction about the goodness of God. This kind of evil finds expression most readily in the suffering, pain, and often untimely deaths brought about by natural but powerfully destructive occurrences (such as hurricanes and earthquakes) and also by sickness and diseases such as cancer. Such occurrences are not evil in a moral sense but are nonetheless great tragedies for human beings.

There is no simple explanation for, or response to, such tragedies. The ancient Jews thought that even this kind of evil was a sign of personal sin. They believed, for example, that someone suffering from a disease was in some way being punished by God. Jesus did not accept such an explanation. Yet if the message of Jesus was to be truly heard as Good News, he clearly had to say something about both sin and evil, and especially about the power of God in him to ultimately overcome sin and evil. **8**

God Is Ultimately Victorious

Throughout the Gospels we see Jesus encountering the power of personal and communal sin as well as other forms of evil. The constant message of the Gospels is that God in Jesus ultimately does conquer evil in all its manifestations. This does not mean, however, that Jesus did not feel the effects of sin during his lifetime. On the contrary, in his acceptance of the cross he demonstrated his willingness to submit to the effects of sin and evil in their most brutal forms. But God conquered even death by raising Jesus to life in the Resurrection. That is precisely what the Good News is all about—that God is ultimately victorious, that love is stronger than hate, that good always wins out over evil, and that life, not death, has the last say.

For Review

- Define *sin*, both personal and communal.
- In what sense are sin and evil different realities? What kind of evil is not caused by sin?

8

Write a brief essay about a time in your life when you struggled to understand an evil situation for which no single person seemed responsible.

The Kingdom of God: Right Now, but Not Yet

In reading the Gospels, we encounter repeated tension, if not complete contradiction, between various claims made about the Kingdom of God. For example, at one point it seems that the Kingdom is very close to us—right around the corner, so to speak (Mark 1:15). At another point it seems that the Kingdom is something to be achieved only at the end of time (Matthew 25:31–46). On one occasion Jesus states that "'the kingdom of God is among you'" (Luke 17:21), but on another occasion he tells people to pray for it to come (Matthew 6:10). Three important realizations can be gained from these apparent contradictions:

1. **Jesus embodied the Kingdom of God.** Jesus believed that the Kingdom was being revealed in his own life and work.

2. **Jesus' followers fully recognized the Kingdom only after Jesus' resurrection.** God's Reign, as expressed in the life and message of Jesus, was fully recognized by the early community of faith only after Jesus' death, his resurrection, and the sending of the Holy Spirit at Pentecost. This was when the full meaning of Jesus' words and actions became clear to his followers and they began, with the guidance of the Spirit, to understand him and his message in a different light. The entire Gospel presentation of Jesus' life and ministry was shaped by this recognition.

3. **Complete acceptance of the Kingdom is required for its fulfillment.** One possible explanation for the tension between the "right now" and the "not yet" of the Kingdom is that the power of

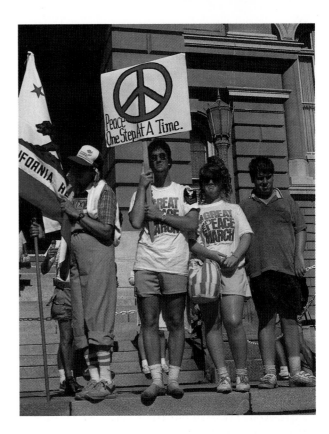

God was fully present in Jesus and then released to all humanity through Jesus' death, his resurrection, and the gift of the Spirit. Therefore, the Kingdom of God *is* close at hand—it is already here in the sense that all the power we need to overcome sin is available to us. But God has chosen to give people freedom, and we individually and collectively have not yet fully accepted the responsibility of making the Kingdom real by living compassionate and forgiving lives. Until people do accept the challenge to love as Jesus did, the Kingdom in its richest sense will not be fully realized. **9**

For Review

• What does it mean to say that the Kingdom of God is "right now, but not yet"?

■

Photo: **To bring about the Kingdom of God, we must accept the challenge to love as Jesus did—patiently and hopefully.**

9
Read the material in the shaded box titled "The Kingdom of God Is Among You," which appears on page 134. Write a paragraph explaining how the examples in the box illustrate the "right now, but not yet" quality of the Kingdom of God. Add an example or two from your own experience.

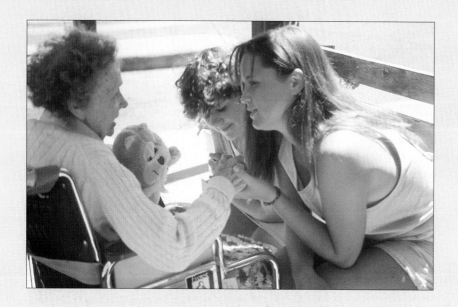

The Kingdom of God Is Among You

Jesus' Dream of the Kingdom of God is made a reality whenever people are compassionate, concerned, and willing to extend themselves in service to others. Jesus' teaching on the last judgment in Matthew, chapter 25, shows the many ways in which such compassion can be lived out. If we really think about Jesus' words, we can see how the Kingdom of God is made real by the actions of young people today:

"'I was hungry and you gave me food, I was thirsty and you gave me something to drink'" (verse 35).

- Glenn contributes the cost of one fast-food meal a week to an agency that works with poor people.
- One day each month Jackie volunteers to work at the local soup kitchen.
- Sharon makes a special effort to thank her parents for the meals they provide.

"'I was a stranger and you welcomed me'" (verse 35).

- Rochelle occasionally eats lunch in the cafeteria with a student who seems left out and lonely.
- Ben, a junior, volunteers to help make incoming ninth graders feel more welcome in his school.
- During a volleyball game, Debbie invites Bruce to play, even though he has little ability for the game.

"'I was naked and you gave me clothing'" (verse 36).

- Jolene decides to buy a less expensive pair of jeans than she would like and gives the money she saves to a special cause.
- Bret stops one of his friends who is ridiculing a student who cannot afford popular clothes.

"'I was sick and you took care of me'" (verse 36).

- Janet's mother suffers from migraine headaches. Janet avoids using her stereo and keeps the volume on the television very low at those times.
- Craig's friend is out of school with the flu for almost a week. Craig makes copies of all his own class notes and offers to tutor his friend when he feels better.
- Linda volunteers to tend the neighbor's yard while the neighbor's broken leg heals.

God's Kingdom exists whenever people are compassionate, concerned, and willing to serve others.

Photo: **Young people bring happiness and friendship to a woman in a nursing home.**

Jesus' Special Stories

Ultimately we must confront the sense of mystery that accompanies the coming of the Kingdom of God. The Gospels' language about the Kingdom is so diverse that it is impossible to describe the Kingdom precisely. For example, it may come suddenly, like the unexpected return of a traveler (Mark 13:33–37), or slowly and secretly, like yeast working in bread dough (Matthew 13:33). All of the Gospels' variety of language is an expression of a truly wonderful reality: What God can do for people is far greater than anything we can imagine or understand. The vision of the Kingdom—that is, the Dream of Jesus—is magnificent beyond our understanding, yet somehow simple enough that all can respond to its challenge and invitation.

This complex nature of the Kingdom explains, at least to some degree, Jesus' unique use of *parables*—stories that allow us to catch a glimpse of something that is too big for words. Chapter 7 discusses these special stories told by Jesus.

We cannot fully understand the magnificence of the Dream of Jesus. Still, we can imagine a peaceful, loving world and work toward it.

Photo: **The Waterton-Glacier International Peace Park in Montana and Alberta, Canada, is dedicated to the hope that the world's nations can live in peace.**

7

Jesus Speaks:
Sayings and Stories
of the Kingdom

AGAIN [Jesus] began to teach beside the sea. . . . He began to teach them many things in parables, and in his teaching he said to them: "Listen! A sower went out to sow. And as he sowed, some seed fell on the path, and the birds came and ate it up. Other seed fell on rocky ground, where it did not have much soil, and it sprang up quickly, since it had no depth of soil. And when the sun rose, it was scorched; and since it had no root, it withered away. Other seed fell among thorns, and the thorns grew up and choked it, and it yielded no grain. Other seed fell into good soil and brought forth grain, growing up and increasing and yielding thirty and sixty and a hundredfold." And he said, "Let anyone with ears to hear listen!" . . .

With many such parables he spoke the word to them, as they were able to hear it; he did not speak to them except in parables, but he explained everything in private to his disciples. (Mark 4:1–34)

Unlocking Jesus' Words

Previous chapters in this course briefly discussed Jesus' public life in terms of his role as a teacher. The title *teacher* is a common one for Jesus in the Gospels, appearing at least thirty times in direct reference to him. Other related titles used for Jesus in the Gospels are *master* and *rabbi*. Different translations of the Gospels use these three terms almost interchangeably.

Jesus' style as a teacher, which differed from the traditional style of the rabbis, has also been mentioned in this course.

- Jesus relied on himself alone as the judge of the truths he shared, rather than depending on the teachings of other rabbis to support his ideas.
- Jesus called his disciples into a lifelong relationship with him and then commissioned them to

Photo, facing page: **The Mountain of the Beatitudes, with a view of the north end of the Sea of Galilee; popular tradition says Jesus preached there.**

Illustrations: **Jesus taught in parables: "Other seed fell on rocky ground. . . . Other seed fell among thorns. . . ."**

disciples, for example, he simply walks up to them and says, "'Come after me, and I will make you fishers of men'" (Mark 1:17, NAB). And at once they leave their nets and follow him. It is difficult to understand how Jesus could get such an immediate response with so little explanation of what he was calling the disciples to.

On another occasion, Jesus says:

"If any of you put a stumbling block before one of these little ones who believe in me, it would be better for you if a great millstone were hung around your neck and you were thrown into the sea. If your hand causes you to stumble, cut it off; it is better for you to enter life maimed than to have two hands and to go to . . . the unquenchable fire." (Mark 9:42–43)

Clearly, Jesus could talk tough when he wanted to!

To understand the words, sayings, and stories of Jesus, we must keep in mind the vehicle by which they come to us: the Gospels. The Gospels are the early faith community's reflections upon and expressions of Jesus' life and message as understood in light of his resurrection. In other words, we do not find Jesus' everyday, casual conversation in the Gospels. We have, rather, his most significant thoughts and ideas—expressed through the words of those who heard him. In most cases, these words were passed on orally for many years before finally being recorded in the Gospels.

share in his ministry of spreading the Good News.

- Jesus referred to Yahweh as "Abba," an intimate name for God that did not appear in the Hebrew Scriptures or in the writings of the rabbis.

This chapter pursues Jesus' role as a teacher a bit further, looking at his words and sayings and, in particular, reflecting on his special form of storytelling: the parables.

Do We Know
What Jesus Really Said?

The Gospels:
Not Records of Everyday Conversation

Readers of the Gospels are often struck by the fact that many of the words of Jesus seem stark, blunt, sometimes even cruel. When calling his first

Jesus' Words:
Reflections of a Unique Message

In one sense, we do not know what Jesus actually said, at least not with the exactness of a tape recording. Scholars do agree, however, that Jesus' use of two words was clearly unique to him:

- The reference to God as "Abba" originated with Jesus.

Illustration: **"Other seed fell into good soil . . . yielding . . . a hundredfold."**

- Jesus also demonstrated an unusual use of the word *amen* in his teachings. In Jesus' day, the word *amen* was normally used much as it is today—as a statement of agreement or affirmation at the conclusion of a prayer. Jesus, however, *began* many of his teachings with the word, saying, "Amen, amen, I say to you . . ." and then making a statement of some kind. Used in this way, the word was a confirmation of Jesus' own teaching, a manner of giving weight to what he was saying. This use of the word *amen* was unheard of in Jesus' time.

So whenever we see *amen* or *Abba* in the Gospels, we are probably reading something at least close to Jesus' original words. But beyond these relatively rare occasions, we cannot be quite sure which words of Jesus are his own and which are interpretations by the early faith community.

Jesus' Words . . . and Then Some

As stated at the beginning of this course, the omission of some factual material from the Gospels does not mean that we cannot find truth in them. Rather, what we find in the Gospels is *more* than just some words Jesus said; we also find the *meaning* his words had for his followers. And because Christians believe that the Gospels were written with the guidance of the Holy Spirit, they also firmly hold that the words and sayings of Jesus as recorded in the Gospels convey the truths Jesus taught to his original followers. **1**

A Jew Speaking to Fellow Jews

Another key to understanding Jesus' words is to remember that Jesus was thoroughly Jewish, as were most of his followers. He naturally spoke to them with their imagery and speech patterns, and with-

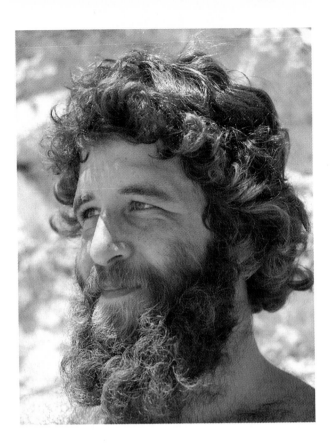

in the context of how they experienced and understood the world.

Engaging the Whole Person

Our own culture has been heavily influenced by the Greek way of thinking. That is, we expect ideas and arguments to be arranged in an orderly manner, and we expect logical proofs for things. But this way of thinking and talking was not common among the Jews of Jesus' day.

For the ancient Jews, the art of speaking was not so much a matter of convincing people through logical formulas, but rather one of establishing contact with the *total* person—with the listener's emotions and feelings as well as their intellect. Thus, the Jewish manner of speaking was far more poetic than our own, filled with a heavy use of symbolism, figures of speech, exaggeration, and so

---

1
In a paragraph, react to the following statement: *If we cannot be sure that Jesus actually said the things that the Gospels say he did, we have no reason to trust in any of what the Gospels tell us.*

Photo: **Establishing contact with the *total* person—the listener's emotions and feelings as well as intellect—was part of the art of speaking among the ancient Jews.**

on. For example, Jesus said, "'If your hand causes you to stumble, cut it off'" (Mark 9:43). Surely Jesus did not mean this literally but was using exaggeration to make a point as strongly as possible.

Supporting Statements with the Scriptures

In the Jewish tradition, a master of public speaking also filled his presentations with imagery from the Hebrew Scriptures. Virtually every statement had to be supported with the word of God as preserved in the Hebrew Bible.

Jesus demonstrated a thorough familiarity with the sacred writings, and his teachings were filled with references to them. In fact, some of his most striking statements were actually biblical quotes. For example, most of us are familiar with his statement that we are called to "turn the other cheek" if someone strikes us. But this statement by Jesus was actually based on one already contained in the Book of Lamentations (3:30), of the Hebrew Scriptures. Jesus was following a common practice when he taught in this way, though he often gave his own special "twist" or insight when doing so.

For Review

- Do the Gospels give us Jesus' actual words? Explain your answer.
- What two words do scholars agree were uniquely used by Jesus? What was unique about Jesus' use of these words?
- In what ways did Jesus follow the traditional Jewish format of public speaking? Why did he speak in these ways?

Jesus' teaching was filled with references to the Hebrew Scriptures, and he often taught in the synagogues.

Photo: The ruins of a second-century synagogue in the town of Capernaum, where Jesus based his ministry

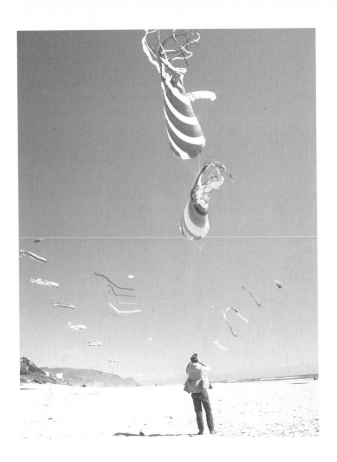

Jesus' Sayings and Stories in the Gospels

Jesus' teaching and preaching included a variety of styles of speech, but most common were these four: direct pronouncements, short sayings, instructions for disciples, and—perhaps most significant—parables.

Pronouncement Stories

Setups for a Punch Line

The Gospel writers situated Jesus' pronouncements within stories. A story acted as a setup for a *pronouncement,* much like a story is told today to get to a punch line. Jesus' "punch lines" contained the main lessons he wanted to get across. Scholars suggest that although the pronouncements themselves may have originated with Jesus, the stories preceding them were composed by the Evangelists to meet the needs of their audiences. This would be one explanation of why a pronouncement by Jesus sometimes appears with different stories in different Gospels.

Examples of Pronouncement Stories

Pronouncement stories were popular in ancient cultures and were often told about famous teachers. The stories commonly described a scene of tension—for example, the opponents of the teacher posing a difficult question. The teacher, in heroic fashion, would respond with an insightful proverb or statement, demonstrating wisdom superior to that of the opponents. Here are two examples of pronouncement stories used by the Gospel writers:

Picking corn on the Sabbath: In Mark 2:23–28, Jesus and his disciples are seen walking through cornfields, or grain fields, on the Sabbath. As they walk along, the disciples begin picking the corn— a direct violation of the laws restricting work on the Sabbath. The Pharisees confront Jesus on this, and he responds with a story about David and his followers. The scene closes with Jesus saying, "'The sabbath was made for humankind, and not humankind for the sabbath.'" The point of the entire episode is to get to that "clincher," a direct and powerfully simple statement about the relationship of the Law to the needs of people. (This pronouncement story has parallels in Matthew 12:1–8 and Luke 6:1–5.) **2**

Responding to a scribe: Another pronouncement story (Mark 12:28–34) can be found at the opening of chapter 6 of this course. There, a scribe

---

■
"The sabbath was made for humankind, and not humankind for the sabbath."
Photo: **In the Christian vision, Sundays are for renewal and relaxation.**

2
Create a modern pronouncement story that leads to this "punch line": *People were not made for Sunday Mass; Sunday Mass was made for people.*

asks Jesus which of the commandments is most important, and then the scribe affirms Jesus' answer. The central point of the entire story is Jesus' closing statement—that the scribe demonstrates by his understanding that he is "'not far from the kingdom of God.'"

Short Sayings

"Words to the Wise"

The Jews were very fond of *proverbs,* short statements that were "words to the wise." These were offered without any story leading up to them. For

example, in the Gospel of Mark, Jesus offers this series of short but highly thought-provoking statements:

"If any want to become my followers, let them deny themselves and take up their cross and follow me. For those who want to save their life will lose it, and those who lose their life for my sake, and for the sake of the gospel, will save it. For what will it profit them to gain the whole world and forfeit their life? Indeed, what can they give in return for their life? Those who are ashamed of me and of my words in this adulterous and sinful generation, of them the Son of Man will

---

Illustration: "Blessed are the poor in spirit, for theirs is the kingdom of heaven." (Matthew 5:3)

The Beatitudes

The Beatitudes, found in Matthew's Sermon on the Mount (5:3–12), are among the most familiar and popular passages of the Christian Scriptures. (Luke's Gospel has a shorter and somewhat different version of the Beatitudes, offered as part of "the Sermon on the Plain." See Luke 6:20–23.)

Lessons to Live By

Both Matthew's and Luke's versions of the Beatitudes convey three main lessons:

1. The Kingdom's fulfillment is yet to come. The Beatitudes point to the future, when the Kingdom of God will be fully realized. They describe a time of promise when the deepest desires and needs of the people will be fulfilled.

2. The Kingdom is in our midst. While the Beatitudes point to the future, they also teach that the Kingdom is even now being proclaimed and inaugurated by Jesus. That is, Jesus himself embodies the Kingdom, and he wants his followers to live in response to an already-present reality.

3. Participation in the Kingdom requires a life of love. The Beatitudes paint a portrait of a life of loving service to others. In doing so, they call Jesus' followers to live out certain values and attitudes now, knowing that only later will they be rewarded ("Blessed *are* those . . . for they *will* . . . "). Christians are called to hunger and thirst for justice, to be merciful, to be peacemakers, to suffer persecution for others, especially the poor.

Why Say Yes to the Call of the Beatitudes?

One must pose the obvious question: Why risk a life of service and persecution with only the promise of some *future* fulfillment? One of the most basic principles of Christian morality is this call by Jesus to live right now *as if the Kingdom of God were a fully present reality*. In living this way, Christians help make the Kingdom real. Jesus, of course, stands as the model of one who lived the Beatitudes to the full.

---

also be ashamed when he comes in the glory of his Father with the holy angels." (8:34–38)

Hardly any scene is set, no story introduces the statements—the stark and challenging words of Jesus stand alone. We can imagine the impact his words would have had on his hearers.

A Classic Example: Matthew's Sermon on the Mount

Matthew, in writing his Gospel, used an interesting method for presenting the short sayings of Jesus. That is, he put them together in a sort of collection. He developed a scene in which Jesus instructs his disciples on a hill, offering them a series of proverbs (see Matthew, chapters 5 through 7). We have come to call this scene "the Sermon on the Mount." Surely it is one of the most popular sections of the Gospels, and one of the most frequently quoted.

An example of the use of short sayings in our day would be the posters of meaningful sayings that have become popular. These posters usually combine beautiful photography with short, insightful statements that catch our attention and cause us to think. 3

3

Looking at the Book of Proverbs (in the Hebrew Scriptures), pick a chapter from 10 to 20 and then any proverb that catches your attention within that chapter. Copy the proverb onto paper and write down its chapter and verse numbers. Then briefly explain why the proverb caught your attention.

The Lord's Prayer

The prayer that Jesus taught us, the *Lord's Prayer,* may be the most fundamental statement of faith a Christian can utter. Certainly, no prayer is more familiar to Christians. Taking a closer look at the prayer as given in the Gospels can offer some new insights into it and its meaning.

A formula for prayer: The Lord's Prayer appears in two Gospels—Matthew's (6:9–13) and Luke's (11:2–4)—and it is the only "formula" for prayer attributed to Jesus himself. Most scholars agree, however, that the prayer consists of statements or concepts taught by Jesus that were later gathered into a formalized prayer by the early faith community.

Different settings, different purposes: Luke shows Jesus teaching the Lord's Prayer in response to a request from his disciples, who have been watching him pray. Matthew places the prayer as part of a comparison between the prayer of Christians and the prayer of pagans. Because Luke's Gospel is considered to have been written before

Matthew's, Luke's setting is considered the original one. As frequently happened in the writing of the Gospels, Matthew most likely adapted Luke's version to fit his own purposes.

Different communities, different concerns: Each Gospel version of the Lord's Prayer reflects characteristics of the community in which

the version was used. Matthew's version is longer than Luke's, perhaps because Matthew added phrases to make his version more useful for communal prayer. And Matthew's Jewish audience would have been uncomfortable with Luke's addressing God as "Father"; therefore Matthew says "Our Father" and stresses God's existence "in heaven."

Photo: **In the Lord's Prayer, Christians ask God as their Father to take care of their human needs.**

Themes about the Kingdom: Though the two Gospel versions of the Lord's Prayer differ slightly, they share several basic themes. These shared themes are best understood in light of Jesus' teachings about the Kingdom of God.

- The phrase "hallowed be your name" emphasizes the power and significance of God's name. The phrase means, "may all people recognize your name as holy and above all other names."
- The sentence "Your kingdom come" reflects the Kingdom as a future reality that is now only fully realized in the life of God. The Kingdom will be established on earth when the will of God is recognized and followed by people. Therefore, Christians are called to live now as if the Kingdom of God were already fully present, because when they do so, they make the Kingdom real.
- The second half of the Lord's Prayer (beginning with "Give us this day") reflects the desire of the early Christians to live in such a way that God's holiness would be reflected in their behavior. The Kingdom demands that Christians express their love for God in their actions toward their sisters and brothers.
- The early church often interpreted the words "daily bread" as referring to the Eucharist. Today, "daily bread" is most often seen as referring to the fulfillment of the ongoing needs of Christians. The prayer is a petition for God to take care of all human needs—personal and communal, physical and spiritual.
- Both Matthew's and Luke's versions of the Lord's Prayer make a strong connection between God's forgiveness of people and people's willingness to forgive one another. When taken seriously, this can be a difficult prayer for Christians to utter. The hope is that God is far more willing and able to forgive us than we are to forgive one another! In any case, the Lord's Prayer makes it painfully clear that a believer's relationship with God

cannot be understood or lived out apart from the believer's relationships with other people.

Just as we can fully understand Jesus and his proclamation of the Kingdom only in light of his Jewish roots, Christians can fully appreciate the Lord's Prayer only when they see it and pray it with the mind-set and conviction of the early Christians.

Photo: "Hallowed be your name" means "may all people recognize your name as holy."

Instructions for Disciples

Some of Jesus' teachings are recorded in the Gospels as instructions for those who would be his followers, his disciples. At times, these passages incorporate other forms of teaching, such as the short sayings and the pronouncement stories.

The Lord's Prayer

One example of Jesus' instructions for disciples would be his words on prayer. Both Matthew and Luke include a section on Jesus' teaching about prayer, each section containing a version of the Lord's Prayer, or the Our Father (see Matthew 6:5–15 and Luke 11:1–13). A comparison of the two versions of the prayer reveals some interesting points: For example, in Matthew's version, it appears that words and phrases have been added to Luke's original version in order to make the prayer more useful for communal worship. Some scholars suggest that the Lord's Prayer is really a summary of the entire Gospel message of Jesus, and it may have been the early church's attempt to summarize his major teachings.

Matthew, Chapter 10

Matthew, chapter 10, presents another example of Jesus' telling his followers what they can expect of discipleship. This Gospel chapter includes a number of statements that Christians may well wish to skip over altogether:

- "'You will be hated by all because of my name'" (verse 22).
- "'Whoever denies me before others, I also will deny before my Father in heaven'" (verse 33).
- "'I have not come to bring peace, but a sword'" (verse 34).

Not easy reading! Fortunately, doom and foreboding is not all that Jesus offers. He also says:

- "'Cure the sick, raise the dead, cleanse the lepers, cast out demons. You received without payment; give without payment'" (verse 8).
- "'Whatever town or village you enter, find out who in it is worthy, and stay there until you leave. As you enter the house, greet it'" (verses 11–12).
- "'Are not two sparrows sold for a penny? Yet not one of them will fall to the ground apart from your Father. And even the hairs of your head are all counted. So do not be afraid; you are of more value than many sparrows'" (verses 29–31).

The Jewish affection for short, thought-provoking statements is evident throughout chapter 10 of Matthew.

Parables

The parables form a central part of the synoptic Gospels. The word *parable* comes from a Greek word meaning "comparison." The term has been used to refer to a variety of Jesus' sayings, stories, riddles, and so on, but it is probably most precise to reserve it for his special stories about the Kingdom of God.

A parable usually builds from a literary device called a *simile*. In a simile, two very different things are compared to one another in order to illustrate a point. The word *like* often—though not always—joins the two parts of the comparison. For example, Jesus would say, "The kingdom of heaven is like . . ." and then compare it to a sower in a

Photo: "Are not two sparrows sold for a penny? Yet not one of them will fall to the ground apart from your Father. . . . So do not be afraid; you are of more value than many sparrows."

146

Focus on John: In a Different Voice

The Gospel of John uses different styles of speech than those found in the synoptic Gospels. One example that has already been noted in this course is John's use of highly symbolic, poetic language. Here are some other literary devices that characterize John's Gospel:

Long discourses: John's Gospel does not contain the rapid-fire, one-after-another miracle stories, the lists of short sayings, and so on, that characterize much of the synoptics. Rather, John offers long, unified stories and *discourses,* which are extended presentations by Jesus. For examples of discourses, see the "bread of life" discourse (John 6:22–59) and the Last Supper discourse (John 14:1–31).

Allegories: John does not use similes like those found in the parables in the synoptic Gospels. Instead, he uses the literary form called *allegory.* A simile is a relatively simple literary device comparing one thing to another, and the meaning of a simile should not be overanalyzed. An allegory, on the other hand, is complex, and virtually everything in it has significance. Examples of the use of allegory by John are the "good shepherd" passage (10:1–18) and the passage about the vine and the branches (15:1–11).

"I am" sayings: A distinctive feature of John's Gospel is the use of what are called "I am" sayings. These sayings are somewhat like similes in that they compare Jesus to another reality.

Recall that the name for God revered by the Jews was *Yahweh* and that the translation of the name is "I am who am." In John's Gospel, Jesus often begins his teachings with the words "I am." Scholars tell us that John intended for such references to show a direct relationship between Jesus and Yahweh. That is, the "I am" sayings signal Jesus' divinity as the Son of God.

Seven "I am" sayings appear in the Gospel of John. They are the following:

- "'I am the bread of life'" (6:35–40).
- "'I am the light of the world'" (8:12).
- "'I am the gate'" (10:7–10).
- "'I am the good shepherd'" (10:11–18).
- "'I am the resurrection and the life'" (11:17–27).
- "'I am the way, and the truth, and the life'" (14:1–7).
- "'I am the true vine'" (15:1–11).

field, a mustard seed, or the yeast in bread (see Matthew 13:24–33). In concluding the Sermon on the Mount, Matthew offers a parable that sums up the purpose of the entire sermon:

"Everyone then who hears these words of mine and acts on them will be *like* a wise man who built his house on rock. The rain fell, the floods came, and the winds blew and beat on that house, but it did not fall, because it had been founded on rock." (7:24–25, emphasis added)

Let's take a closer look at the use of parables in the Gospels.

For Review

- Identify and briefly define the four main styles of speech that Jesus used in his teaching.
- Explain Matthew's organization of the Sermon on the Mount.

A Closer Look at the Parables

The Technique Behind the Parables

The use of parables is one of the most significant characteristics of Jesus' teaching style. He had a way of connecting his points to the everyday experiences of his listeners, so that his teaching would be clear to them and easily remembered.

Based on Everyday Life

The basic story elements in Jesus' parables grew out of the land, culture, and family life of his people: farming and shepherding, children playing and adults working at their trades and crafts. Naturally, some of the settings and story elements can seem strange to the modern reader. As may be quite evident by now, knowing something about the land and daily life of the Jewish people of Jesus' time is essential to grasping the meaning of Jesus' teachings. Yet it was precisely because Jesus drew from the common experiences of his listeners that his teachings—and especially his parables—were powerful. When we read the parables today, it is often helpful to find parallels between our experiences and those of the people Jesus was directly addressing. That is, we can translate the parables into familiar language. 4

Filled with Surprises

In developing a parable, Jesus would take a common occurrence of the day and add a surprising twist to it, such as a surprise ending. These surprises would keep his listeners alert, or catch them off-guard. The idea was to make people think, to stop them in their tracks and get them to reflect on the lessons he was trying to teach. Here are two examples of Jesus' technique:

The parable of the lost sheep: The parable of the lost sheep is found in Matthew 18:12–14 and in Luke 15:4–7. In the story, a shepherd leaves ninety-nine sheep in search of one that is lost, and then rejoices at great length over finding the lost one. Jesus' listeners would have been taken aback by this, because no ordinary shepherd would have considered risking the entire flock for the sake of one sheep. 5

The parable of the prodigal son: In the popular parable of the prodigal son (Luke 15:11–32), a father's younger son leaves home to go off and spend his inheritance in a wild spree, while the older son remains loyal to the father and continues to fulfill his responsibilities. When the younger son runs out of money, he returns home begging for mercy. What does the father do? He does not start comparing the younger boy with the older one, who remained loyal. Nor does he *reluctantly* agree to take back the wayward son. Instead the father

---

4
For each of these three areas—your daily life, your family life, and your culture—list five to ten elements that could serve as the basis for a modern parable.

5
Rewrite Luke's version of the parable of the lost sheep (15:4–7) to make it into a modern parable.

■
Photo: **No ordinary shepherd would have considered risking the entire flock for the sake of one sheep.**

A Modern Parable: "The House"

More than anything else in the whole world, a man wanted to possess a house of his own. Not just any house, but a house that everyone would marvel at. So he worked long hours and hard days over many years until at last he acquired the house of his dreams.

Alas, once he set foot in his house, he was never seen again. He dared not leave his prize for fear that thieves would steal or vandals ruin what he had labored so hard to possess.

Moral: Whatever you possess, possesses you.

(Aurelio, *Fables for God's People,* page 7)

throws a magnificent party for the one who was such a disappointment to him. (Anyone listening to this parable has to be awfully sympathetic with the older son's anger about the situation!)

With both of these parables, Jesus was teaching his followers about God's boundless and forgiving love for those who have gone astray. God's love is so profound that it literally seems to defy common sense!

Themes of the Parables

Chapter 6 of this course addressed the central significance of the Kingdom of God in Jesus' message.

Not surprisingly, many of Jesus' sayings and stories either relate directly to his proclamation of God's Kingdom or flow out of his own awareness of the complex nature of the Kingdom.

Although it is hard to arrive at a clear-cut breakdown of all the parables, the following organization of the parables into four main themes or purposes is helpful. **6**

1. Descriptions of the King

Some parables describe the King of the Kingdom, namely God. That is, these parables deal primarily with God's nature, qualities, attitudes in dealing with people, and so on.

6
As you read, select one example from each of the four categories of parable themes and spell out, in your own words, the main point Jesus was trying to make.

The parable of the lost sheep: As noted earlier, the parable of the lost sheep (Matthew 18:12–14 and Luke 15:4–7) demonstrates God's gracious love. God takes the initiative and seeks out those who stray.

The parables of the lost coin and the prodigal son: The stories of the lost coin and the prodigal son (Luke 15:8–32) illustrate that God will do almost anything to find us and then will rejoice when we are finally found.

The parable of the laborers in the vineyard: In the parable of the laborers in the vineyard (Matthew 20:1–16), a landowner apparently pays some laborers more than they deserve. Jesus' point, however, is to illustrate the almost overwhelming generosity of God, the fact that God operates out of a completely different "economic system" than the one used by people.

All four of these parables reflect that wonderful image of the Father presented by Jesus—the image of a God whom people can call "Abba."

2. "Kingdom" Responses

Some of the parables emphasize how we should act if we hope to "enter the Kingdom."

The parable of the Pharisee and the tax collector: The parable of the Pharisee and the tax collector (Luke 18:9–14) tells us that we should adopt the basic attitude of humility if we are going to participate in the Kingdom. The Pharisee is self-righteous, congratulating himself on his strict religious practices, while the tax collector feels deep sadness for his sinfulness. Jesus says the tax collector is the more righteous of the two because the tax collector recognizes, as all people must, that the need for repentance in life is real.

The parable of the rich fool: In the parable of the rich fool (Luke 12:16–21), we find a man who is self-satisfied because he has grown huge amounts of grain. He plans to build large barns in which to store his harvest. God, however, interrupts the man's planning and says to him, """You fool! This very night your life is being demanded of you. And the things you have prepared, whose will they be?""" This parable illustrates the need to rely on God's graciousness rather than solely on our own resources.

The parable of the talents: In the parable of the talents (Matthew 25:14–30), a man gives each of his three servants a different number of *talents,* or weights of silver. He then leaves the servants to their own resources as to how they will manage

In the parable of the rich fool, a
man plans to build large barns in
which to store his harvest.
Photo: A grain silo in Israel

the silver. Two of the servants work to turn a profit with their talents, but one servant fearfully hides his, afraid that he will lose it. Upon returning, the master angrily rebukes this servant for not doing something beneficial with what he has been given. The lesson to Jesus' listeners—and to us—is to make good use of the gifts and talents we have been given, in order to further the Kingdom.

3. Relationships with Our Neighbors

Other parables address people's relationships with one another and the world at large.

The parable of the unforgiving servant: In the parable of the unforgiving servant (Matthew 18:21–35), a servant begs his master to relieve him of a debt. The master, moved with pity, completely cancels the debt, only to find later that the servant went out and had a fellow servant thrown into prison for not paying a debt owed to *him*. In great anger the master has the unforgiving servant tortured. The lesson of the parable is that we must truly forgive one another from our heart if we expect to be forgiven.

The parable of the good Samaritan: The popular parable of the good Samaritan (Luke 10:25–37) has already been mentioned a few times in this course. Though the lesson of the parable may be clear enough to us today, it was shockingly clear to Jesus' listeners: If people want to be part of the Kingdom of God, they must open their heart to *everyone,* even the outcasts of society.

4. The Fulfillment of the Kingdom

Finally, some of the parables refer to the future coming of God's Kingdom in its fullness.

The parable of the wedding banquet: In one parable (Matthew 22:1–14), a king is preparing a banquet for his son's wedding. The king sends his servants out to invite selected guests, all of whom reject the invitation. Some of the invited guests even go so far as to kill the servants who deliver the invitation. The furious king has the murderers killed and then sends other servants out to invite anyone they can find. The parable symbolically tells the story of the Jews, who were the first people invited to God's Kingdom. Some of them not only rejected the invitation but actually killed God's servant, Jesus. The "heavenly banquet"—the Kingdom—was then offered to everyone, Jews and Gentiles alike.

The parable of the weeds among the wheat and the parable of the ten bridesmaids: In the parable of the weeds among the wheat (Matthew 13:24–30), Jesus says that the weeds must be allowed to grow together with the wheat, and they

Illustration: **In the parable of the talents, one servant fearfully hides his talent, or weight of silver.**

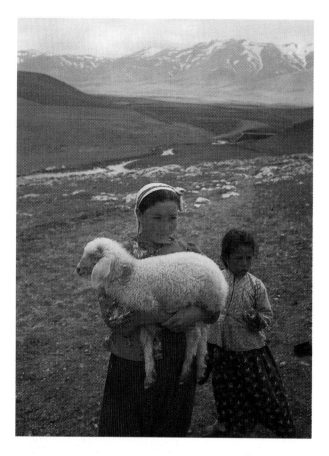

will be separated from the wheat at the harvest. In the parable of the ten bridesmaids (Matthew 25:1–13), some foolish bridesmaids get locked out of the wedding banquet because they were unprepared for the arrival of the bridegroom. Both of these parables point to the *end time,* or the future day of judgment by God.

Multiple Uses of the Parables

Occasionally a parable is used to teach different lessons in different Gospels, oftentimes by changing the setting in which Jesus tells the parable. Take the parable of the lost sheep, for example.

Matthew puts the parable in the context of Jesus' answer to the disciples' question, "'Who is the greatest in the kingdom of heaven?'" (18:1). Jesus uses the parable to illustrate his response that those who become like little children are most important in God's Kingdom. After telling the parable, Jesus says, "'So it is not the will of your Father in heaven that one of these little ones should be lost'" (18:14).

In the Gospel of Luke, Jesus tells the parable of the lost sheep to teach a group of tax collectors and sinners about God's mercy. Jesus concludes the parable by saying, "'I tell you, there will be more joy in heaven over one sinner who repents than over ninety-nine righteous persons who need no repentance'" (15:7).

These seemingly contradictory situations for telling the parable can be explained as follows:

- It is quite possible that Jesus used the same story more than once to illustrate different points and that the Gospel authors simply differed in which version of the story they selected.
- An individual Gospel author may have changed the setting of the parable to better illustrate the point *he* wished to make to his readers.

Of course, minor differences in how Jesus' parables are used do not deny the truths or lessons of the parables themselves. If anything, the multiple use of the parables demonstrates how rich these marvelous stories truly are.

Understanding the Parables Today

The parables challenge us, as modern readers, to let them speak to our own life situations. And insofar as they give us a picture of the Kingdom, they also challenge us to accept it—that is, to accept the will of God. We, as individuals and as communities of

Photo: **One version of the parable of the lost sheep teaches that those who become like children are most important in God's kingdom, and that God wills that not one of them should be lost.**

faith, are called to identify with the lost sheep, with the wicked tenants, with the good Samaritan, and so on, just as Jesus' original listeners were. How can we meet these challenges? Here are a few suggestions that can make the reading of the parables more enjoyable and enlightening for us:

1. Look for the central messages of the parables. The details in some of the parables can make the stories more interesting perhaps, but we should not try to read too much into them. The messages of Jesus are often far more direct and to the point than we might expect or recognize.

2. Look for the questions posed in the parables. Jesus sometimes asks his listeners to offer their own response to a parable, before he gives his intended message. For example, following the parable of the good Samaritan, Jesus asks his listeners, "'Which of these three [men], do you think, was a neighbor to the man who fell into the hands of the robbers?'" (Luke 10:36). Whenever such questions are posed directly or indirectly in the parables, we should pause and attempt to answer them ourselves.

3. Compare our answers with those recorded in the Gospels. Many times the sayings and interpretations that conclude the parables reflect the early faith community's answers to Jesus' questions. It is possible, in other words, that Jesus may not have actually answered some of his own questions or interpreted the parables for the people. Instead, he probably encouraged them to figure out as many insights as they could on their own. As we read the parables, then, we should compare the answers we would give with those given by the early church and recorded in the Gospels. This sets up a kind of dialog between ourselves and the Gospel writers—precisely the kind of exchange that can make the Gospels come alive for us today. **7**

For Review

- Why did Jesus often conclude his parables with a surprise ending?
- List and describe the four main themes by which we can categorize Jesus' parables. What is the common thread that runs through all of these themes?
- Why might a parable be used, or even modified, to teach different lessons in different Gospels?
- List three suggestions that can make the parables more enjoyable and enlightening for us.

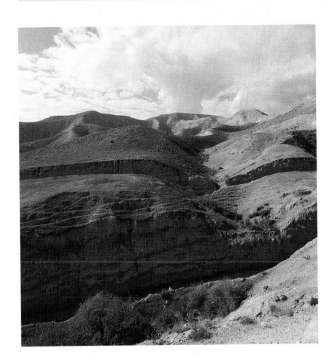

7
Browse through any one of the synoptic Gospels and note all the occasions when Jesus asks a question. Write down each question (and its chapter and verse numbers) and try to answer it before reading the answer recorded in the Gospel. Write down the Gospel's answer if it is different from your own.

Photo: Jericho Road, from Jerusalem to Jericho, was a barren place to be attacked by robbers and left to die. One of the most familiar Gospel stories is the parable of the good Samaritan.

Jesus' Parables in the Synoptic Gospels

	Matthew	Mark	Luke
The house built on rock	7:24–27		
The sower	13:1–23	4:1–20	8:4–15
The weeds among the wheat	13:24–30		
The mustard seed	13:31–32	4:30–32	13:18–19
The hidden treasure and the pearls	13:44–46		
The unforgiving servant	18:23–35		
The good Samaritan			10:25–37
The rich fool			12:16–21
The great feast			14:15–24
The lost sheep	18:12–14		15:4–7
The lost coin			15:8–10
The prodigal son			15:11–32
The unjust servant			16:1–13
The rich man and Lazarus			16:19–31
The unjust judge			18:1–8
The Pharisee and the tax collector			18:9–14
The laborers in the vineyard	20:1–16		
The wicked tenants	21:33–46	12:1–12	20:9–19
The wedding banquet	22:1–14		
The faithful servant	24:45–51		
The ten bridesmaids	25:1–13		
The talents or sums of money	25:14–30		19:11–27

Putting Jesus' Words into Actions

When trapped by a contradiction between what they profess to believe and the way they actually live, some people fall back on the old saying, "Don't do what I do. Do what I say." A somewhat-related proverb states a similar point: "What you do speaks so loudly that I can't hear what you are saying."

In the case of Jesus, however, there were no contradictions between what he said and the way he acted. All that he said and did revealed his tremendous vision of the Reign of God over all creation and in the hearts of people. This chapter discussed the words and sayings of Jesus. But because Jesus spoke and acted, no study of him and his message can be complete without discussing some of his most challenging and perhaps confusing actions: his miracles. These marvelous actions of Jesus are the topic of the next chapter.

Photo: **Unusual rock formations on the northwest shores of the Sea of Galilee**

8

Jesus Heals:
Signs of the Kingdom

WHEN John [the Baptist] heard in prison what the Messiah was doing, he sent word by his [own] disciples and said to [Jesus], "Are you the one who is to come, or are we to wait for another?" Jesus answered them, "Go and tell John what you hear and see: the blind receive their sight, the lame walk, the lepers are cleansed, the deaf hear, the dead are raised, and the poor have good news brought to them. And blessed is anyone who takes no offense at me." (Matthew 11:2–6)

Jesus' Marvelous Deeds: As Important as His Words

Chapter 6 explored Jesus' Dream of the Kingdom of God—his vision of the will of God, who releases the power of unlimited love over all creation and in the hearts of people. Chapter 7 looked at the words of Jesus, especially his parables, as teachings

about the Kingdom of God. That discussion concluded with a pivotal point: Words not backed up with actions are most often hypocritical, if not meaningless.

When we read about Jesus in the Gospels today, how do we know that he was not suffering from delusions, that he was not insane or perhaps just plain lying when he spoke of the Kingdom? As some have stated it, Jesus was one of three things: a lunatic, the greatest con artist in history, or precisely who he claimed to be—"the One sent by God." What makes his words worthy of our trust?

One significant factor is Jesus' actions. His actions—particularly his **miracles,** or signs—were as important to his ministry as his teachings. 1

A Variety of Signs

The Gospels are filled with a variety of "works of wonder" by Jesus.

- *Healing miracles:* Many times Jesus is shown relieving the suffering of people afflicted with fever, paralysis, deafness, dumbness, blindness, or leprosy. (*Leprosy* was a general name for many kinds of skin disease in Jesus' day.)
- *Exorcisms:* Dramatic accounts portray Jesus as driving evil spirits or demons out of people.
- *Restorations of life:* Three stories tell of Jesus' raising people from the dead.
- *Nature miracles:* Frequently the Gospels demonstrate Jesus' apparent control over the forces of nature: he walks on water, calms a storm, feeds thousands with just a few loaves and fish, and so on.

The miracles of Jesus are of special significance because they demonstrate that the power of God was truly manifested in Jesus. Without some concrete demonstration of Jesus' power over sin and evil, his words would lack credibility.

In Luke 7:11–17, Jesus raises a widow's son from the dead on the road approaching the city of Nain.
Photo, facing page: The road leading to Nain in Galilee.

Jesus controls the forces of nature in Gospel stories such as the calming of a storm at sea.
Photo, above: A storm on the Sea of Galilee

1
In a paragraph, react to this statement: *Jesus was one of three things: a lunatic, a con artist, or precisely who he claimed to be.*

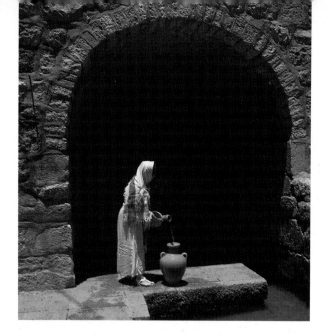

The Meaning of the Miracles

This chapter will take a close look at the meaning of Jesus' miracles. The discussion will focus on these three interrelated questions:

1. What did the *Gospel writers* intend to teach about Jesus and his Kingdom through the miracle stories?
2. What did *Jesus* intend to reveal through his miracles?
3. How are *we* to understand Jesus' miracles today? The last question may be the most critical of the three. No feature of Jesus' life and ministry is more debated, confusing, or subject to interpretation than his miracles. And unless we come to a credible, contemporary understanding of Jesus' miracles, we may not be able to "hear" what the Gospel writers—and Jesus—were trying to teach.

For Review

- Identify and describe the kinds of miracles found in the Gospels.
- Why are Jesus' miracles of special significance?

Focus on John: Signs of God in Jesus

Chapter 7 noted that the synoptic Gospels include parables as a major part of the teaching style of Jesus, but the Gospel of John excludes the use of parables altogether, instead using allegories to explore the message of Jesus. Likewise, John's use of miracle accounts differs from what we see in the synoptics. The following points are the most significant differences:

1. John includes just seven miracles in his Gospel, far fewer than in the Gospels of Matthew, Mark, or Luke. However, John describes those seven miracles in much greater detail than the synoptics describe theirs. For example, John often follows the story of a miracle with a lengthy discussion about its deeper meaning among those who witnessed it.

2. In the synoptic Gospels, the miracle stories are often presented in groups, one right after another. This can make the miracle stories seem set off from the main part of the Gospels, like they were just "popped in" to fill gaps in the overall story. John's Gospel has

In chapter 9 of John's Gospel, Jesus cures a blind man by anointing his eyes with clay and having him wash in the pool of Siloam.

Photo: A woman draws water at the pool of Siloam, at the edge of Jerusalem.

a more structured flow than the synoptics do, so the miracle stories are more directly woven into John's portrait of Jesus.

3. Four of the seven miracles in John's Gospel do not appear at all in the synoptic Gospels. John's miracle stories are listed below. Those that are unique to his Gospel appear in bold type.

- **Changing water to wine at Cana (2:1–12)**
- Restoring health to the royal official's son (4:46–54)
- **Curing on the Sabbath (5:1–18)**
- Multiplying the loaves (6:1–15)
- Walking on the water (6:16–21)
- **Healing the man born blind (9:1–12)**
- **Raising Lazarus (11:1–44)**

John, chapter 21, includes a miracle about a great catch of fish, but that chapter is not considered an original part of the Gospel.

4. The synoptic Gospels refer to Jesus' miracles as "acts of power" intended to demonstrate that the Kingdom of God is being established in

Jesus. John's Gospel centers, instead, on Jesus himself as the Son of God, the One in and through whom the Father is fully revealed. Jesus' miracles are referred to as "signs" that through Jesus, God's creative and transformative power is present in all aspects of life.

5. The synoptic accounts focus on the miracles themselves, whereas John's accounts focus on the *symbolic meaning* of the miracles. Physical miracles in John's Gospel symbolize deeper spiritual truths and realities. For example:
- The health restored to the royal official's son is a sign of the Spirit that will be

given through the death and resurrection of Jesus (5:21–24).
- The primary intent in curing the man born blind is not the matter of giving physical *sight*. Rather, it is the matter of giving spiritual *insight* into the real identity of Jesus (9:35–41).
- The raising of Lazarus illustrates not only God's power over life and death but also Jesus' own identity as "'the resurrection and the life'" (11:25–26).

The miracle stories in the Gospel of John can be a rich source of prayer and reflection for Christians.

Photo: **The miracle stories in John's Gospel, as signs of God's transformative power, can be rich sources of prayer and reflection.**

Why Are the Miracles So Challenging?

Perhaps no image of Jesus both captures our imagination and challenges our mind more than that of Jesus as "the miracle worker." Our imagination is caught up with scenes of power and awe—people raised to life with a simple word, blindness cured with a touch, sickness and disease rendered powerless in the presence of Jesus. These same scenes have moved millions of people to faith throughout the history of Christianity. Yet the notion of miracles often presents the logical and scientific mind of today with serious, disturbing questions rather than faith-strengthening signs of hope. Why might this be so?

Miracles in the Modern World

As mentioned in chapter 7, the way we view the world today is drastically different from the way the Jews viewed it in Jesus' day. We expect and need proof, evidence, and logical explanations for virtually everything we encounter.

The Typical Responses

Two extreme responses to Jesus' miracles are typical of our time, given our contemporary expectations: people "either take 'em or leave 'em."

Take 'em: Some of today's Christians simply accept all of the Gospel miracles at face value. And in doing so, they feel forced to reject many of our modern scientific and biblical findings. These people are often referred to as *fundamentalists*, and they opt for a *literal interpretation* of the Bible. That is, they do not accept any part of the Scriptures as symbolic or open to various interpretations.

Leave 'em: At the other extreme, many people—both Christians and non-Christians—reject any possibility of the miracles. Miracles are, by definition, phenomena that go beyond the laws of nature and point directly to the hand of God as their cause. Those who deny Jesus' miracles consider these Gospel accounts as the illusions of a backward people or as fables of some kind.

Another Option

Today's Christians can and should hold a middle ground between the two extreme positions on Jesus' miracles. It is not right or necessary, for example, to lump all of the miracle accounts together and treat them the same way, giving one as much factual validity or significance as another.

Illustration: **In the miracle accounts, sickness and disease are rendered powerless in the presence of Jesus.**

But if we get too bound up with whether an individual event occurred exactly the way the Gospels describe it, we risk completely missing the truth that the story can reveal to us. Certainly all of these marvelous stories have something true and valid to teach us about Jesus and his proclamation of the Kingdom. **2**

Jesus Did Work Some Miracles

The Christian who takes the middle ground on the issue of miracles can be sure that Jesus did, in fact, work *some* wonders. Much evidence, and even common sense, upholds this. Consider the following points about Jesus' miracles:

Supported by historical records: Some non-Christian historians of ancient times referred to Jesus as a "wonder-worker." So it is evident from historical records that Jesus greatly impressed the crowds with his actions.

Not denied by the Pharisees: Even the Pharisees in the Gospels do not deny that Jesus worked many wonders. Instead, the Pharisees charge him with doing so through the power of the devil (see Matthew 12:24 and Luke 11:15). Biblical scholars claim that this charge by the Pharisees would have been too unusual, too unexpected, to be included in the Gospels if it were not based on an actual incident.

Affirmed by eyewitnesses: An undeniable historical fact is that many eyewitnesses to the works of Jesus—many of whom were still alive when the Gospels were written—believed so firmly in him and his message that they became committed followers. Many even freely chose to die rather than deny faith in him. Such devotion certainly lends

great weight to the claims made about Jesus by the Gospel writers. Also, if the Gospel claims had not been based on actual happenings, serious objections would likely have been raised by the eyewitnesses themselves.

Jesus seems to have worked many wonders. The task of sorting out which miracle events occurred just as the Gospels describe them continues to be a major challenge to biblical scholars, and it is certainly beyond the scope of this course. Again, the major concern of this chapter is to understand the meaning of the miracles.

A Persistent Problem

One significant problem is unavoidable in trying to understand the meaning of Jesus' miracles. It is a difficulty even for those who accept a literal interpretation of the Gospels. This persistent problem centers around the fact that the Gospels themselves seem to disagree with one another about the same events. Some miracle accounts show definite

---

2
Draw a horizontal line. At the far left end of the line write, "All of the Miracles Exactly as Described." At the far right end of the line, write, "None of the Miracles." Mark on the line where

you think *most young people* stand in terms of believing in the Gospel miracles. Then mark where *you* stand. Follow up with a brief explanation of your responses.

In Matthew 8:14–15, Jesus enters Peter's house and cures Peter's mother-in-law of a fever.
Photo: The ruins of a house in Capernaum, believed to be the home of Peter

signs that each Evangelist offered his own imaginative details. For instance, the miracles tend to intensify, magnify, and even multiply from one Gospel to the next, from the earliest one (Mark's) to the later ones. Consider these examples:

- The Gospel of Mark says that Jesus "cured *many* who were sick" (1:34), while the Gospel of Matthew says that Jesus "cured *all* who were sick" (8:16).
- In Mark's Gospel, a man named Jairus approaches Jesus and pleads, "'My daughter is at the point of death'" (5:23). In a parallel scene in Matthew's Gospel, Jairus says, "'My daughter has just died'" (9:18).
- The healing of one blind man in Mark's Gospel (10:46–52) becomes the healing of two in Matthew's Gospel (20:29–34).

It is conceivable as well that a tendency to exaggerate existed in the early community of faith *before* the Gospels were written. There was plenty of time for such embellishment to occur between Jesus' death in the year 30 C.E. to the writing of Mark's Gospel around the year 70.

The possibility of exaggeration and elaboration in the miracle stories raises two questions: On what basis can we approach and judge the truth of the miracles? How are we to understand them if they cannot always be understood as historical events reported with complete accuracy by the Evangelists? The remainder of this chapter will offer several possible answers to these questions.

For Review

- What is the fundamentalist response to the Gospel miracles?
- Why should Christians avoid extreme positions regarding the historical accuracy of the miracle accounts?
- Briefly summarize the evidence given to uphold the conviction that Jesus did work some miracles.
- What persistent problem regarding the miracles exists even for those who accept them all literally?

Cana, in Galilee, is the scene of a wedding where Jesus changed water into wine (John 2:1–11).
Photo: **The city of Cana today**

Jesus' Miracles in the Synoptic Gospels

	Matthew	Mark	Luke
Cleansing of a leper	8:1–4	1:40–45	5:12–16
Healing of a centurion's servant	8:5–13		7:1–10
Curing of Peter's mother-in-law	8:14–15	1:29–31	4:38–39
Calming of a storm	8:23–27	4:35–41	8:22–25
Healing of the Gadarene demoniac(s)	8:28–34	5:1–20	8:26–39
Healing of a paralytic	9:1–8	2:1–12	5:17–26
Jairus's daughter and the woman with a hemorrhage	9:18–26	5:21–43	8:40–56
Healing of two blind men	9:27–31		
The man with a withered hand	12:9–14	3:1–6	6:6–11
First miracle of the loaves	14:13–21	6:30–44	9:10–17
Raising of the widow's son			7:11–17
Walking on the water	14:22–33	6:45–52	
Curing of the Canaanite woman's daughter	15:21–28	7:24–30	
Healing of a deaf man		7:31–37	
Second miracle of the loaves	15:32–39	8:1–10	
The blind man of Bethsaida		8:22–26	
Healing of a boy with a demon	17:14–20	9:14–29	9:37–42
Cleansing of ten lepers			17:11–19
Healing blindness at Jericho	20:29–34	10:46–52	18:35–43
The barren fig tree 3	21:18–22		

3
Read any one of the miracle stories listed above. Write down any problems you can think of that would be associated with interpreting the story in a strictly literal way.

The Jews and Miracles

A Different View

One way to understand the miracle stories is to recognize that what we today mean by *miracle* is not what the people of Jesus' day meant by *miracle*.

Now Versus Then

People in our modern Western culture tend to view everything from a scientific perspective. That is why miracles are commonly defined as exceptions to the laws of nature. People in our culture also tend to view God as remote and not particularly involved in the day-to-day happenings of life.

The Jews of Jesus' day, however, viewed the world primarily from the perspective of their faith in Yahweh. To them, miracles were evidence of the presence and power of God. And because the Jews believed that God was *always* present and powerful, miracles were seen not as exceptions to, but actually as the law of, nature. In other words, though the Jews were naturally awed by works of wonder, they were not terribly surprised by them. They expected God to work that way.

God's Power over Evil

In the ancient Jewish view, everything was an expression of either God's creative power or the power of evil in the world. The rain and the breeze were the direct results of God's activity—the rain was released through the floodgates that Yahweh opened, and the breeze was Yahweh's breath passing over the earth. On the other hand, all illness—from blindness to leprosy to death itself—was the result of evil. Any cure, therefore, was an *exorcism,* because it "cast out," or conquered, evil.

More Miracles and Miracle Workers

Given the ancient Jewish view of the world, it is not surprising that the people recognized various events as miracles more readily than we do, even though we might be looking at similar events. We look for logical explanations for everything. The Jews already had their explanation for things they could not understand: those things were the activities of their God, Yahweh, who was demonstrating total control over the universe.

Not only were there more events identified as miracles in Jesus' day, but there were also many more *miracle workers,* persons who appeared to have strange powers over people and events. We know from sources other than the Gospels, for example, that other rabbis at the time of Jesus were also considered to be wonder-workers, able to cure people of their afflictions. Miracle workers were also commonly found in the Greek culture of the time. 4

Seeing the Hand of God Today

Today's Christians do not have to hold the ancient Jewish view of the world in order to see the active presence of God in history. Likewise, a commitment to science need not blind Christians to

---

Ancient Jews believed the breeze was Yahweh's breath passing over the earth.
Photo: **A wheatfield in Galilee**

4
List at least ten of your everyday experiences that the Jews of Jesus' day might have considered miracles.

A Modern Miracle: Turning Tragedy into Opportunity

Tony was quiet-spoken and somewhat shy during high school. The friendships he formed were few but deep. He was a gifted baseball player and even dreamed of a pro career. But the summer after he graduated from high school, his life radically changed.

Tony landed a summer job working for a company that manufactured steel products. His job was to run a machine that flattened steel beams into sheets a quarter of an inch thick. One day while working on the machine, Tony became distracted for a moment. Before anyone knew what was happening, the sleeve of Tony's shirt got caught in the machine, pulling his right hand into the machine up to the wrist.

The hours that followed were filled with terrifying sounds and images: Tony's scream of pain and shock, co-workers frantically trying to help, the wailing of the ambulance siren, eight hours of emergency surgery, Tony's family gathered in tears and prayer.

The chief surgeon finally brought news to the family. "After more than twenty years of surgery," he said, "I think I just experienced my first miracle." He went on to say that he thought they had saved most of Tony's hand—though he would never have normal use of it. Now everything depended on how Tony would react to the accident and the long therapy that lay ahead.

The recovery and therapy lasted for nearly three years. Skin was grafted from Tony's legs to slowly build up the tissue on the injured hand. Then the long, painful physical therapy began. It incorporated experimental hypnosis that allowed Tony to ignore the pain while exercising what remained of his fingers, all of which had been lost beyond the first joint.

Tony started attending a college some thirty miles from home, driving there in a car equipped with push-button transmission to accommodate his disability. He was attracted to business as a field, knowing that his dream of an athletic career had been shattered. Despite his basically shy personality, he knew that sales and marketing held out the best hope for him, and he worked on becoming more outgoing. He graduated with honors.

Once in the business world, Tony became a top salesman for a paper manufacturer, eventually becoming the national sales manager. He had learned to hold a pen and write with the stubs that remained on his injured hand. His customers learned with time that he knew the paper industry well, and they admired his business abilities. But most of them would admit that at least initially, they were most impressed by Tony's courage in warmly extending his partially amputated hand for a firm handshake—quite an achievement for a once-shy young man who had dreamed of a baseball career.

the marvels of the universe. In fact, science can provide tremendous insight into the creative power of God.

Some scientists, for example, study the origins of the world or the expanse of the universe and come to a strong conviction that a loving God was the source of it all. Surgeons occasionally claim to experience a miracle in the operating room when a patient survives against all odds. Or we ourselves might spy a single flower blooming in a garden and be overwhelmed with the wonder of creation. Such encounters can give us a hint of the worldview that dominated the minds and hearts of the Jews. Sacred Mystery is present behind or within all

of our life experiences. Realizing this helps us in relating to the worldview of the ancient Jews. **5**

A Different World

Another way to understand Jesus' miracles is to remember the rather gruesome aspects of the world that Jesus encountered, a world very different from the one most of us experience.

Common Scenes

The people of Jesus' day had no hospitals and no institutions for those who were mentally disturbed or insane. Medicine was primitive. It was common

---

■
Illustration: **In Jesus' day, blind and crippled persons could be seen begging at the gates of the cities.**

5
Write either a pro or a con reaction to this statement: *It is much more difficult to believe in God today than it was during Jesus' time.*

to see blind and crippled beggars along the road-ways and at the gates of the cities. People with dis-eases like leprosy were forced to roam in bands throughout the countryside, because they were forbidden to enter the cities. Insane people were chained in caves, and their screams could be heard through the days and nights. And not surprisingly, all of these ill people were banned from worship-ing in the Temple.

Cruelty or Fear?

Our tendency might be to condemn the ancient Jewish society for its cruel treatment of the physi-cally and mentally ill, but we must remember *why* the society acted as it did. All sickness, insanity, and disease was seen as the direct manifestation of the power of evil. Logically, then, healthy people were terrified of those who were sick, fearful of be-ing contaminated by them. In other words, sheer terror, not cruelty, motivated people to reject and banish those who were in need.

Some Jews even felt that sickness was a punish-ment from God for personal sins or the sins of one's ancestors. This was a terribly difficult belief for those who held it, however, because it was clear that good people seemed to suffer as much, some-times even more, than apparent sinners. (Jesus talks about this in Luke 13:1–5, assuring his listen-ers that those who suffer accidents and other mis-fortunes do not do so because of their sins.)

The Reign of God: No More Evil

If, as most Jews believed, all illness and other hu-man suffering was the result of the power of evil in the world, then common sense indicated that the Reign of God would not be truly present until all these manifestations of evil were overcome. It was precisely this belief about God's Reign that the Gospel writers sought to address in telling about Jesus' life and ministry, especially his miracles.

- Through Jesus, God was destroying evil in all its forms and expressions.
- Because God was using Jesus in this way, Jesus was truly the Messiah, the One sent by God to establish the new Kingdom that the Jews had been waiting and praying for.

Now as Then

Though we today need not adopt every aspect of the ancient Jewish understanding of evil, that understanding does have some truth to teach us about reality. Just as we might see the goodness of God operative in the wonders of creation, we can also understand much of the pain and suffering in the world as a result of the power of sin and evil. And whenever good conquers evil—whether in world affairs or in our own relationships—we, like the ancient Jews, can recognize the hand of God at work. In other words, Jesus' vision of the Kingdom of God can be as real to us today as it was to his first followers two thousand years ago. **6**

For Review

- How do the differences between the modern Western worldview and that of the ancient Jews help to explain the ancient Jews' under-standing of miracles?
- Why would the ancient Jews have viewed any cure of illness as an exorcism?
- Why should we hesitate to condemn the ancient Jews for their treatment of physically and mentally ill people?
- What did the Gospel writers try to say about Jesus through the miracle stories?

6
Major catastrophes—earth-quakes, tornadoes, floods, and even diseases like AIDS—are viewed by some as being directly caused by God for a specific reason, such as punishment of the victims. Write a short re-sponse to this view.

Understanding Jesus' Miracles Today

Despite the validity of seeing wonders in everyday life, some of the events that are considered miracles in the Gospels do not have to be seen as such during our time. We understand, for example, the incredible power of the human mind to effect change in the body. We talk about *psychosomatic illnesses,* which seem to disappear when patients' attitudes change. And we know of the remarkable power of suggestion that is demonstrated through hypnosis. These phenomena may account for some of the exorcisms recorded in the Gospels, in which emotionally distraught people are calmed by the strength of Jesus' character.

Other accounts of Jesus' cures may be explained in part as exaggeration by the Evangelists. Exaggeration was characteristic of the writers in Jesus' culture, who made strong and true points by stretching the historical facts a bit.

But these insights do not explain *all* of the miracles of Jesus. Nor do they negate Christianity's solid tradition of accepting miracles throughout its history—a history that Christians believe has been guided by the Holy Spirit, the Spirit of Truth. Ultimately, when trying to understand the meaning of Jesus' miracles, we are dealing with both a faith question and a faith answer.

A Faith Question and a Faith Answer

What Do the Miracles Mean?

Christians are not expected to blindly accept irrational claims. Rather, they are asked to recognize and accept the real significance of the miracles—their religious meaning—in light of faith in Jesus. In other words, yes-or-no questions about the historical reality of the miracles are not of prime concern. The question to be repeatedly posed is this: What do the miracles *mean?* And this question can be answered only from the perspective of faith.

Faith: The First Requirement

The requirement of faith for accepting Jesus' miracles was as necessary for the people who actually witnessed these events as it is for us today. Over and over again the Gospels mention that Jesus required belief in him and faith in God before he would cure one who was ill. In fact, Jesus could not cure those in his home region:

They said, "Where did this man get all this? What is this wisdom that has been given to him? What deeds of power are being done by his hands! . . ." And they took offense at him. . . . And he could do no deed of power there, except that he laid his hands on a few sick people and cured them. And he was amazed at [the prevailing attitude of] unbelief. (Mark 6:2–6)

The Father's Business

Recall from the earlier discussion of Jesus' temptation in the desert that Jesus refused to try to impress people with his power. He was not in show business. Rather, he was wholeheartedly involved in the "business" of his Father—that is, the task of revealing God's nature and relationship with people by revealing and establishing the Kingdom.

Miracles and the Kingdom

The key to understanding the miracles of Jesus is grasping their relationship to his proclamation of

A Modern Miracle: From Death to New Life

Reverend Ann Holcomb had been pastor of Our Savior's Lutheran Church for only six weeks when the tragic news spread through the community: at thirty-five, she had been diagnosed with incurable cancer. Many members of the congregation expected her to move back to her former parish, where closer friends could help her through the inevitable pain and loneliness she faced. But Pastor Ann said, "God has called me to this parish at this time. I want to dedicate my life to service as your pastor. It looks like I might serve you only by facing my own death with you."

Over the next months, the transformation of the congregation was remarkable. People who hardly knew one another became deeply bonded by their concern for Pastor Ann. Worship services became the center of parish life as people gathered in sincere prayer. Especially touching were those services when Pastor Ann, seated in a wheelchair, would join the community, with an oxygen tank nearby to help her breathe as the cancer slowly sapped her body of strength. She even managed to distribute diplomas at the eighth-grade graduation.

As Pastor Ann's condition worsened, tension developed among members of the congregation. Some of them gathered weekly to pray for a miraculous cure of Pastor Ann's cancer. Others claimed that praying for such a cure was almost superstitious and would only lead to great disappointment—even a loss of faith for some people—when Pastor Ann inevitably died.

Pastor Ann had the perfect response to both sides: "I firmly believe that God has a miracle in store for me," she told the people. "God may decide to heal my body of this cancer. Or God may choose to work a greater miracle and call me into everlasting, resurrected life. I'm ready for either one."

A year from her installation as pastor, Ann Holcomb died in her own parsonage bedroom, remaining to the end among the people she had promised to serve. Her funeral service drew an overflowing crowd. Parishioners may have experienced a more profound depth of faith in her dying than if she had lived. Many commented that Pastor Ann had been absolutely right: God *had* worked a miracle. The miracle for Pastor Ann was resurrected life. But another miracle had taken place—in the hearts of the members of Our Savior's Lutheran Church. **7**

the Kingdom of God. At the core of that proclamation—and therefore at the core of the miracles—are these realities:

- God's promise of unconditional love
- God's commitment to the poor and outcasts of society
- God's complete control over the power of sin and evil
- God's offer of complete reconciliation

The Force of Love

Jesus did not just speak of his Father's love. He lived out that love in his actions. Love, not a desire to impress the crowds, made Jesus heal people and work wonders. The Gospels are clear on this: Quite simply, Jesus healed because people needed to be healed. He healed out of profound compassion. In Mark 1:41, for example, he is moved with pity for a leper who begs to be cured. In Luke 7:13, sorrow

---

7
Write a response to this opinion: *Miracles that take place in people's hearts are as significant as dramatic, physical cures.*

touches Jesus when he meets the widow of Nain, whose son has died.

Special Signs

Kindness was not Jesus' only motive for working wonders, however. In the synoptic Gospels, the most common word used for miracles and cures is *power*. In John's Gospel, the word used most often for these works is *sign*. Jesus' miracles, therefore, were signs intended to show God's power over all creation and, in a special way, over the forces of sin and evil. **8**

The healing miracles: In the Gospels, we see Jesus relieving people of their physical suffering and even bringing some people back from the dead. Wherever evil and its effects are most directly and dramatically evident in the lives of people—in their suffering, their pain, their death—Jesus heals and restores fullness of life.

The casting out of demons: The extent of God's power is the chief lesson of the exorcisms, in which Jesus casts out evil spirits. The Evangelists are showing us that God, in and through Jesus, can confront the power of sin in its most direct forms and conquer it.

The forgiveness of sins: Many of Jesus' miracles reflect a far deeper and more important level of healing than the "mere" healing of the body. For in the context of his miracles, Jesus frequently mentions that the physical healing of individuals is directly linked to their acknowledgment of their sin and Jesus' forgiveness of it. Matthew's Gospel, for instance, tells of some scribes who attack Jesus for claiming the authority to forgive the sins of a paralyzed man. Jesus responds to them by showing them that his authority comes from God:

"Why do you think evil in your hearts? For which is easier, to say, 'Your sins are forgiven,' or to say, 'Stand up and walk'? But so that you may know that the Son of Man has authority on earth to forgive sins"—he then said to the paralytic—"Stand up, take your bed and go to your home." And [the man] stood up and went to his home. When the crowds saw it, they were filled with awe, and they glorified God, who had given such authority to human beings. (9:4–8)

The nature miracles: The so-called nature miracles reveal the same basic message that the other miracles do: God's Reign over all creation is present in this man, Jesus, and is being revealed to the world through him.

- Just as Yahweh drew order out of chaos in the creation of the world (Genesis 1:1–2), so God in Jesus now overcomes all chaos in the world.
- Just as Yahweh parted the waters of the sea to allow the safe passage of the Israelites (Exodus 14:15–31), so God in Jesus calms a storm and walks on water.

8
Read another miracle story listed in the shaded box "Jesus' Miracles in the Synoptic Gospels," on page 163. Using the list of Kingdom realities above as a guide, write an essay on the connections between the miracle story and Jesus' proclamation of the Kingdom of God.

Illustration: **Just as Yahweh offered manna to the Israelites as they roamed in the desert, so Jesus multiplied the loaves and fish to feed the multitudes.**

• Just as Yahweh offered the special food *manna* to his people as they roamed in the desert (Exodus 16:12–35), so God through Jesus multiplies the loaves and fish to feed the multitudes.

For Christians, all miracles are signs of the healing and redeeming power of God's love, a loving power present in and revealed by Jesus. No wonder those who walked with Jesus, who watched him touch people, were convinced that he truly was a man of extraordinary power and force! **9**

The Gospel Understanding of Jesus the Miracle Worker

To be consistent with the image of Jesus portrayed in the Gospels, we must certainly avoid viewing him as some kind of biblical superman or magician. Jesus constantly refused any such designation or image. He worked miracles almost reluctantly and, curiously, often instructed those he had cured to tell no one what he had done for them (see, for example, Mark 1:44). Jesus even became angry with those who actually expected miracles as proof of his power (see Mark 8:12). Why? Because he did not want his miracles to cloud or confuse the far greater and more important reality—that "the Kingdom of God is among you!"

Liberator of the Heart

Once people have faith in Jesus and his message, a real miracle has already begun in their heart. The physical cure they experience becomes an expression of an interior reality, a conversion, a change of heart. The cure of their body represents a deeper, more profound change within them. Therefore, they are liberated not only from lameness but also, for example, from legalism. They are liberated not only from a crippling deformity but also from a closed mind. They are liberated not only from physical blindness but also from the inability to recognize the needs of their neighbors. Ultimately, Jesus liberates people *from* sin and death *to* goodness and life.

A Man Full of God

One author has beautifully summarized the meaning of the miracles Jesus performed during his ministry:

We find in the miracle stories, as in other parts of the Gospel heritage, that steady testimony to absolute wholeness and utter genuineness of Jesus of Nazareth. He was a man so close to his God that God's own creative power flowed out of him in healing waves. He was a man so dedicated to God's work that his own fascinating power seemed to embarrass him; at times it seemed to get in the way of his message. But, most of all, Jesus was a man so charged with God's own compassion and love that any cry of pain or confusion drew from him an instant response of healing and restoration. (Senior, *Jesus,* page 131). **10**

For Review

- Why can the meaning of the miracles be answered only from a faith perspective?
- What is the key to understanding the miracles of Jesus? What realities are at the core of the miracles?
- Name two things that motivated Jesus to perform miracles.
- What happens once people have faith in Jesus and his message? Give an example to illustrate your answer.

9
Write about an incident in your life (or in the life of someone you know) that could be considered a modern miracle, a sign of God's loving power.

10
Write a short essay comparing what you thought about Jesus' miracles before you studied this chapter with what you understand about them now.

A Modern Miracle:
From Frightened Stutterer to Popular Speaker

Up until the eighth grade, Tom was an average kid—a decent student, a fair athlete, generally outgoing and popular. Oh, he made his share of poor decisions, like most kids do. In the seventh grade, for instance, he stole some beer from his dad for a party with his friends. But most people thought Tom would turn out okay. Then things changed.

In the eighth grade, Tom developed a speech problem. For some reason he became very self-conscious when asked to speak or read in front of the class, and he would begin to stutter and stammer. The rest of the class laughed. The teacher thought all Tom needed was practice, so he began asking Tom to read aloud on a regular basis. The problem, however, only grew worse, and Tom became more and more embarrassed and withdrawn.

After graduation from the eighth grade, Tom went to a Catholic senior high school. There he tried to hide his problem by making new friends, staying away from anyone from grade school who knew about his stuttering. He never achieved his potential in the classroom because he avoided any situation in which he would have had to read aloud or speak to everyone. He also began to drink regularly, often arranging beer parties as a way to gain some "respect" from his friends. Several times while arranging his almost weekly parties, Tom was caught in the act—either by his parents or by other adults, and on a couple of occasions by the police. His reputation as a troublemaker grew.

One day, near the end of Tom's sophomore year, the principal of the high school called Tom to his office. Once again the police had contacted the school about Tom. The principal told him that he was going to be expelled from school if he didn't shape up. Tom wouldn't show it, but he was scared.

That same day, Tom was approached by a teacher who had heard about the trouble he was in. Rather than criticizing or threatening Tom, the teacher stunned him by asking him to join a Christian youth group. Tom, much to his own surprise, accepted the invitation. That was the start of an amazing transformation.

Tom became an active member of the youth group. By the end of his senior year, he decided to try out the religious life by joining the Christian Brothers (the order of brothers who taught at his high school). He stayed only five months or so with the brothers, but while he was with them, he confronted and began to deal with his speech problem for the first time since it had begun five years earlier. After he left the religious life, Tom became involved in church youth programs as a volunteer leader. Later, after completing college, he decided to make youth ministry his occupation. He wanted to help other young people who, like himself, needed someone to turn to at difficult times in their life. Perhaps most amazingly, Tom became known for his public speaking, and he was often asked to make presentations at youth retreats and conferences.

Eventually Tom was hired by a publisher of materials for religious education and youth ministry. The book you now hold in your hand was written by him. In fact, three days before this little story was written, Tom Zanzig gave a talk at a youth convention attended by 2,300 high school students. Nobody who had seen him stuttering in front of his eighth-grade class some twenty years before would have believed it!

The other two "modern miracles" relayed in this chapter are also the experiences of real people, both known well by the author, Tom Zanzig. Their stories have been altered a bit to respect their privacy. A common thread ties all of these stories together: they are about people who responded in trust to God's goodness and power, which Jesus proclaimed and the Evangelists wrote about nearly two thousand years ago.

There are many miracles in each person's life. Some are dramatic, like those relayed here. Others are so ordinary that they might easily be missed. Jesus teaches us that in order to see any of them, we need the eyes of faith.

On the Way to the Cross

It is difficult to comprehend how someone as dedicated to works of love and compassion as Jesus could become a source of great conflict, an object of hatred and fear. Yet surely no single event in the story of Jesus is more etched into the hearts, minds, and emotions of Christians than his agonizing execution on the cross. How can we make sense of the horribly brutal death of such a good man? The next chapter will seek an answer.

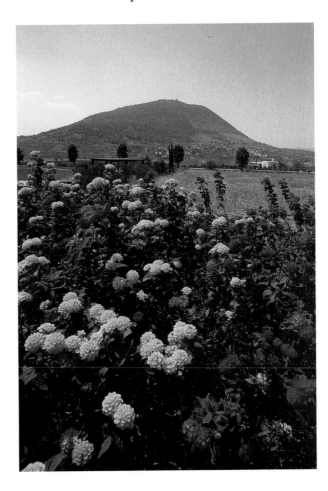

In the synoptic Gospels, after Jesus predicts his passion and death, Peter, James, and John go with him to the top of a mountain and witness Jesus' appearance transformed in glory. This Transfiguration affirms for believers that Jesus in his earthly existence truly is the Son of God, and that glory follows the passion.

Photo: Mount Tabor, the site traditionally suggested as the scene of the Transfiguration

9

The Cross:
The End or a Beginning?

THEY went to a place called Gethsemane; and [Jesus] said to his disciples, "Sit here while I pray." He took with him Peter and James and John, and began to be distressed and agitated. And [he] said to them, "I am deeply grieved, even to death; remain here, and keep awake." And going a little farther, he threw himself on the ground and prayed that, if it were possible, the hour might pass from him. He said, "Abba, Father, for you all things are possible; remove this cup from me; yet, not what I want, but what you want." He came and found [Peter, James, and John] sleeping; and he said to Peter, "Simon, are you asleep? Could you not keep awake one hour? Keep awake and pray that you may not come into the time of trial; the spirit indeed is willing, but the flesh is weak." And again he went away and prayed, saying the same words. And once more he came and found them sleeping, for their eyes were very heavy; and they did not know what to say to him. He came a third time and said to them, "Are you still sleeping and taking your rest? Enough! The hour has come; the Son of Man is betrayed into the hands of sinners. Get up, let us be going. See, my betrayer is at hand." (Mark 14:32–42)

The Road to the Cross

"'Enough! The hour has come.'" With those simple but chilling words, the drama that was Jesus' earthly life moved toward its horrifying climax. It was probably the year 30 C.E. Jesus was a man of some thirty-five years, and his life was about to end abruptly and violently. He had preached for no more than three years, and perhaps less than one. He had proclaimed good news about a kingdom of love, joy, peace, and harmony. But it had all led to this—the road to the cross.

This chapter will take a close look at the events that immediately preceded and surrounded Jesus' death on the cross.

- What actually happened and why?
- Did Jesus know he was going to die when he made his last fateful journey to Jerusalem?
- And—for Christians especially—what does it all mean?

A Man of Peace, a Source of Conflict

Certainly Jesus was committed to peace, and we are right to remember most strongly his acts of love and compassion. But we must remember as well that he seemed to cause conflict and tension wherever he went. His words were often challenging, even threatening, to his listeners. His behavior often shocked those who witnessed it, for it ran contrary to many of the accepted practices of the time. Consider the following:

- On virtually every important issue of his day—marriage, authority, the role and meaning of the Law, the Temple and worship—Jesus' opinion conflicted with that of most people, particularly with the people in positions of power.

After the Last Supper, Jesus and his disciples left Jerusalem, descended into the Kidron Valley, and walked up to the Garden of Gethsemane on the slopes of the Mount of Olives.

Photo, facing page: **The Mount of Olives and the Kidron Valley**

Jesus spent the end of his life in Jerusalem.
Photo, above: A scale model of Jerusalem as it likely appeared in the time of Jesus

So in many ways, Jesus' violent end was the price he paid for living a life of love and commitment to the One who sent him. For Jesus, to have lived otherwise would have been not only a betrayal of his Father but also a betrayal of his own Dream, his own vision and values. For Christians, the historical event of Jesus' death is significant—but not just because a man was willing to die for his beliefs. As will be discussed shortly, Jesus' death has a larger, more profound meaning. **1**

The Nature of the Passion Accounts

In preparation for the discussion of the events surrounding Jesus' death, take some time now to read at least one, but preferably all, of the synoptic accounts of the passion of Jesus: Matthew, chapters 26 and 27; Mark, chapters 14 and 15; and Luke, chapters 22 and 23.

Next, turn to John's account of the last days of Jesus, which begins with chapter 13 and runs through chapter 19. The description of Jesus' arrest, trial, and execution in John's Gospel (chapters 18–19) is quite similar to the descriptions found in the synoptic Gospels. However, John precedes these events with an extended discussion of Jesus' last meal with his disciples. This discussion includes what are referred to as Jesus' "Last Supper discourses" (chapters 14–17). Reading these discourses will prove valuable later, when looking at the meaning of the Last Supper. **2**

Central Events in the Gospels

As we might expect, the arrest, trial, and crucifixion of Jesus are the most extensively reported events in the Gospels. (Even the non-Christian historians mentioned earlier in this book reported that Jesus died by crucifixion.) The Gospels seem

- Jesus made the outcasts of society—women, poor people, tax collectors, those who were physically sick or emotionally disturbed—the very cornerstone of his message about God's Kingdom.
- Jesus claimed for himself a position of authority above that of both the religious and the political powers of his day.

All of this and much more brought Jesus to a direct and unavoidable confrontation with the Jewish and Roman authorities. He was a very real religious and political threat to the way things were, to religious tradition and political stability.

Photo: Oscar Romero, archbishop of San Salvador, was assassinated in 1980 because of his commitment to the Gospel and his outspoken advocacy for El Salvador's poor people.

1
Write a short piece about a time in your life (or in the life of someone you know) when doing good became a source of conflict and tension.

2
Draw four columns and label each one with the name of one of the Gospels. As you read the four accounts of the Passion, take brief notes on the progress of events and compare accounts.

keyed to these events, as if everything in the Gospels is intended to prepare the reader for Jesus' execution. Even the writing style of the Passion accounts is much different from that of the Gospels' typical stories and short sayings. For instance, we find many more details in these accounts than in other parts of the Gospels. This is so for several reasons, including these:

- The **death** and **resurrection** of Jesus are at the heart of the Christian story. His **crucifixion** had to be very carefully explained to the members of the early community of faith.
- What happened to Jesus was totally contrary to what the people had been expecting for their Messiah. Their desire for a great deal of information about these events would have been natural and intense.
- The Evangelists were writing to and for the early followers of the Risen Jesus. These people themselves would confront almost immediate persecution for their faith in him. The reminder that Jesus had suffered persecution and death would be a constant consolation to them.

The Passion accounts were probably among the first stories about Jesus to take on a consistent form. They may well have been part of the worship of the early faith community even before they were committed to writing.

Reconciling the Differences

We find a lot of detail in the Passion accounts, but we also find signs of editorial work by the Evangelists. Naturally, the Evangelists were trying to provide theological insights into the meaning of the Crucifixion. Matthew's Gospel, for example, is the only Gospel that mentions the eruption of graves at the point of Jesus' death (27:52–53). This may well be a case of symbolic imagery that was

added to the basic account of the Passion. Also, the Gospel accounts differ—sometimes a great deal—on a number of other points. By concentrating on what most or all of the Gospel accounts have in common, we can arrive at a reasonably clear idea of the historical facts surrounding the arrest, trial, and crucifixion of Jesus.

For Review

- Why is the image of Jesus as a man of peace, love, and compassion not a complete one?
- What are the literary characteristics of the Passion accounts in the Gospels?
- Why did the Evangelists use a style different from their typical stories and sayings to tell the story of Jesus' death?

Photo: **The road to Jerusalem from the Mount of Olives**

Jesus' Final Days

The Last Supper

All three synoptic Gospels give an account of what has come to be known as the **Last Supper.** Interestingly, the earliest recorded account of the actual institution of the Eucharist—that is, the blessing of the bread and cup—is found in Paul's first letter to the Corinthians (11:23–26). For some reflections and insights on John's version of the Last Supper, see "Focus on John: The Last Supper," on page 180. The attention in the following discussion will be on the three synoptic accounts.

A New Covenant Is Made

As the synoptic Gospels relate, on the evening before he was crucified, Jesus hosted a meal for his disciples, in a room loaned to them by a friend in Jerusalem. He followed the normal Jewish custom of his day, giving thanks to God for the meal. But then he took the bread, handed it to his disciples,

and said, "'This is my body, which is given for you. Do this in remembrance of me'" (Luke 22:19). Likewise, after they had eaten, he took the cup, saying, "'This cup that is poured out for you is the new covenant in my blood'" (Luke 22:20).

According to the Gospels, the Last Supper took place near the time when the Jewish people were celebrating Passover, one of their greatest religious feasts. Recall that during this feast, the people remembered how Yahweh had delivered them from slavery in Egypt many years before and how, in gratitude, the people of Israel had pledged their loyalty to Yahweh. Ever since that time they had been known as "the People of the Covenant." Thus, when Jesus identified his actions as representing a "new covenant," he was linking those actions to a reality that was at the heart of Jewish history. **3**

"Do This in Remembrance of Me"

Jesus' words and actions at the Last Supper were packed with meaning. The synoptic Gospels suggest these main two points:

- Jesus had his approaching death in mind as he gathered his disciples for that meal.
- Jesus made a real connection between the meal itself and his death on the cross.

When Jesus stood up to do his customary duty as host in saying the blessing over the cup and bread, he startled his disciples by saying that the cup and bread were to be recognized as signs of his own death. At the time, the disciples did not understand what he was talking about. They believed that he had come to Jerusalem to assume his role as king, not to die!

Only later—after Jesus' death and resurrection— did the early community of faith recall that meal and begin to use the words and gestures of Jesus as

---

Illustration: **After the meal, Jesus took the bread and cup and gave them to his disciples as signs of his own life poured out for them.**

3
Using an encyclopedia or other sources, write a short essay on the origins and major characteristics of the Passover meal.

a continuing reminder of his death. Nearly two thousand years later, Christians all over the world gather in their communities, solemnly repeating those words and gestures—still recalling in this special way the life, death, and resurrection of Jesus. Christians continue to "do this in remembrance" of him.

Is Jesus Really There?

It is significant that the various Christian churches today have differing convictions about the way in which the Risen Jesus is present in the consecrated bread and wine of the Eucharist. On the one hand, some Christians believe that the blessing of the bread and wine today is done *only* in memory of what Jesus did nearly two thousand years ago. That is, the blessed bread and cup are but symbols of Jesus' risen presence within the community. On the other hand, Roman Catholics are firm in their conviction that the Risen Jesus is truly and fully present in the consecrated bread and wine of the Eucharist. How this is so, is a profound matter of faith, and it is better discussed in a course on the Eucharist or the sacraments.

Illustration: **In John's account of the Last Supper, Jesus washes the feet of his disciples to show that loving service of others is at the heart of his message.**

Focus on John: The Last Supper

John's account of the last meal Jesus shared with his disciples is so rich in imagery, so poetic in expression, and so deeply touching in its portrayal of the human Jesus that it has been an especially popular source of prayer and reflection for millions of Christians. Here are a few of the major features that distinguish John's account from the synoptic accounts:

The Lamb of God: The synoptic writers agree that Jesus celebrated the Last Supper as a Passover meal, but John situates the meal on the day *before* that religious feast. It seems obvious, nevertheless, that John did want to link Jesus' death with the Passover.

Recall that a major part of the Passover ritual was the slaughter of lambs in the Temple; the meat of the lambs was then consumed during the Passover meal. The lambs were slaughtered in memory of the Exodus, the time of the original Passover, when the Israelites were brought out of slavery. In his account, John links Jesus' death with the killing of the paschal lambs. That way, Christians can see Jesus as the new paschal lamb, "the Lamb of God, who takes away the sins of the world" through his death on the cross.

The washing of the disciples' feet: Very significantly, John does not include the institution of the Eucharist in his description of the Last Supper. Instead, John has Jesus perform a ritual not found in any of the synoptic Gospels. Jesus washes the feet of the disciples as a sign of the centrality of his message about service to others (13:1–17). The connection John seeks to make is this: Christians can fully celebrate the Eucharist only when committed to loving service to others.

The Last Supper discourses: As noted earlier, John includes a series of Last Supper discourses by Jesus, which are among the most profound passages in the Christian Scriptures. Here we discover such memorable statements as the following:

- "'I give you a new commandment, that you love one another. Just as I have loved you, you also should love one another'" (13:34).
- "'I am the way, and the truth, and the life. No one comes to the Father except through me'" (14:6).
- "'Abide in me as I abide in you. . . . I am the vine, you are the branches. Those who abide in me and I in them bear much fruit, because apart from me you can do nothing'" (15:4–5).
- "'No one has greater love than this, to lay down one's life for one's friends. . . . I do not call you servants any longer, . . . I have called you friends'" (15:13–15).
- "'Very truly, I tell you, if you ask anything of the Father in my name, he will give it to you. . . . Ask and you will receive, so that your joy may be complete'" (16:23–24).

"Thy Will Be Done": The Agony in the Garden

At some time or another, each of us has felt the terrible ache of loneliness, the feeling that no one understands or cares about us. Perhaps it is because we all have felt this pain that the image of Jesus in the garden of Gethsemane can touch us so deeply.

We might try to somehow soften the pain of Jesus at Gethsemane with thoughts of how, as the Son of God, he could heroically accept the pain of his impending death, sure in the knowledge that his resurrection awaited him. But the Gospels are clear on this: Jesus' agony in the garden was a time of sheer human terror and darkness. He knew the time was fast approaching when all the conflicts surrounding him would build to a breaking point.

Jesus Could Read the Signs of the Times

Toward the end of his life, did Jesus have a premonition or expectation that he was about to die? We do not have to imagine some interior revelation by God on this, some mysterious inner voice that permitted Jesus to foresee the future. For Jesus could read the signs of the times. That is, he could look at what was happening around him and put all the pieces together.

The building hostility: Jesus was definitely aware of the building hostility of all the people who opposed him, which included nearly every faction of Judaism—Pharisees, Sadducees, Zealots. In a rare situation indeed, all of the leaders who normally conflicted with one another were united against Jesus.

The situation in Jerusalem: Jesus had freely chosen to go to Jerusalem. He probably realized that great tension, if not violence, would result

from his presence there. Scholars dispute the historical accuracy of the Gospel accounts of Jesus' triumphant entry into Jerusalem (remembered today on Passion Sunday, or Palm Sunday). However, it is reasonable to assume that Jesus' arrival in the holy city did cause some sort of stir. And Jesus would have been aware that the authorities—both Jewish and Roman—would not tolerate such emotionally charged happenings during the already intense season of Passover.

The fate of a prophet: Jesus probably recognized himself as a true prophet of Israel, as one led by the Spirit. He knew the history of his people and the way they had treated their prophets. Because Israel had repeatedly rejected the prophets, Jesus would have had a growing expectation of his own rejection as well. At one point earlier in his ministry, he had cried out over the city of David,

---

■
Jesus encountered the hostility of the scribes and Pharisees, most likely as he taught in the porticoes, or covered walkways, of the Temple.

Photo: **A scale model of the Temple with its porticoes that surround the Court of the Gentiles**

Judas: Betrayer of Jesus?

During the Last Supper, Jesus predicted that one of his disciples was about to betray him. The disciples were shocked at the thought and vigorously denied the possibility. But among them sat one man whose story is probably far more ambiguous, and perhaps touching, than we are normally inclined to believe. The man was Judas.

The widely accepted understanding of Judas has been that he was a greedy, weak man who "sold out"—betrayed Jesus for thirty pieces of silver. But perhaps it is not quite that easy to assess Judas's motives.

Matthew, for instance, is the only synoptic writer who even bothers to mention the payment of silver. Matthew also says that Judas, even before the official condemnation of Jesus, is filled with remorse when he realizes that Jesus will probably be executed. Judas throws the money down before the chief priests and elders and then goes out and hangs himself in despair (27:3–5). It is difficult to mesh the stereotyped image of the greedy Judas with Matthew's image of a man filled with sadness, despair, and apparent surprise at what is happening to Jesus.

Some scholars propose that Judas was actually trying to force Jesus to respond to the official charges of the chief priests and others. These scholars contend that Judas figured Jesus would do so by revealing his power and assuming the role of king. In other words, maybe Judas did not expect or intend Jesus' execution at all, but rather was trying to pressure Jesus into the expected role of Messiah. This is all guesswork, of course, but perhaps it will keep us from too quickly or too harshly judging Judas—or anyone else, for that matter.

"'Jerusalem, Jerusalem, you who kill the prophets and stone those sent to you . . .'" (Matthew 23:37, NAB). Jesus would have seen at least the possibility, if not the likelihood, of his having to suffer and even die for his proclamation of the Kingdom.

The faithful love of Yahweh: Throughout their history, the Jews had recognized a strong link between death and victory, between hope and despair. Their experience as a people had led them to realize that often Yahweh was most with them in times of despair—that somehow the greater their suffering, the more vividly was Yahweh's love revealed to them. Jesus was certainly aware of this tradition and must have drawn strength from it.

He Could Have Run Away

In the face of all the evidence pointing to the possibility of a violent death, Jesus could have run away. This would seem to have been the most human thing to do. Yet Jesus stayed—not because he knew that God would raise him from the dead, but

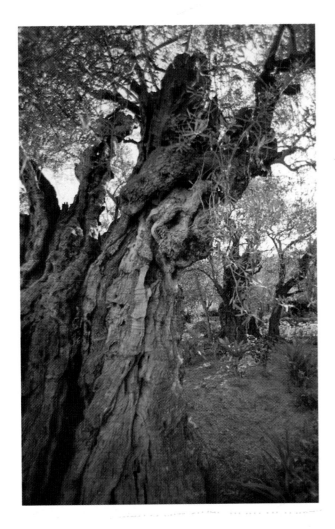

somehow fooled by circumstances; or as someone who would have sacrificed his convictions by running away, had he known what was coming; or even as someone who knew with absolute certainty that he would be raised from the dead in three days.

The account of Jesus' agony at Gethsemane is a dramatic departure from other stories of martyrs that were popular among the Jews during and before the time of Jesus. In those stories, as in many of our modern TV shows and movies, the martyr faced death with courage and firm resignation, hardly showing a sign of fear. Jesus, however, was no such fictional character, no actor playing out a dramatic role. He was totally immersed in our human experience and, like us, felt loneliness and fear. But he found—as do many of his followers—consolation, strength, ultimate hope, in the one he called "Abba," his Father. And it was in his commitment to his Father's will that Jesus found the courage to accept what was to come. **4**

For Review

- With what historical Jewish event is the Last Supper linked? What two main points do the synoptic Gospels make about Jesus' words and actions at the Last Supper?
- What is the Roman Catholic conviction regarding the presence of Jesus in the Eucharist?
- Explain the meaning of this statement: *Jesus could read the signs of the times regarding his death.*
- Why is Jesus' free acceptance of his death central to all of Christian theology?

because he was firmly committed to doing the will of the One who sent him: "'Abba, Father, for you all things are possible; remove this cup [death] from me; *yet, not what I want, but what you want'*" (Mark 14:36, emphasis added).

Jesus' free acceptance of his death is central to all of Christian theology. The entire Good News crumbles if Jesus is seen as a dreamer who was

Photo: **An ancient olive tree in the Garden of Gethsemane**

4
Compose a personal letter to Jesus as you imagine him facing his last days. Base your words on your own experiences of loneliness and fear.

Jesus' Final Hours

Appearing Before the Great Sanhedrin

At the Great Sanhedrin, the Jewish aristocracy met as a "court of inquiry" to determine what charge to level against Jesus in the trial to be held before the Romans. Although the Jewish leaders clearly wanted Jesus dead, they did not have the authority to carry out the death penalty while they were under Roman control.

The Fateful Question

During Jesus' confrontation with the Sanhedrin, Caiaphas, the high priest, asked the question that—along with Jesus' answer—would eventually lead to Jesus' execution. Caiaphas, becoming frustrated with Jesus' refusal to answer the questions of the other priests, asked Jesus directly, "'Are you the Messiah, the Son of the Blessed One [God]?'" (Mark 14:61). Jesus answered,

> "I am; and
> 'you will see the Son of Man
> seated at the right hand of the Power,'
> and 'coming with the clouds of heaven.'"
>
> (Mark 14:62)

In this scene, Jesus not only accepts the title *Messiah* (*Christ*) from Caiaphas, but even expands that to say that he is uniquely in touch with divinity, with God. Jesus' response draws an immediate charge of blasphemy from the high priest, Caiaphas (Mark 14:63–65). (For parallel scenes of Jesus before the Sanhedrin, see Matthew 26:57–68 and Luke 22:66–71.)

A Charge That Would Stick

Blasphemy means "showing a lack of reverence toward God" or, more specifically in Jesus' case, "claiming for oneself a dignity due to God alone." It was not Jesus' claim of being the Messiah that gave rise to the furor among the Jewish leaders. Other men had made that claim before him, and others would make it after his death. According to the Gospel accounts, what totally shocked and appalled the members of the Sanhedrin was Jesus' apparent claim—which he expressed through the striking imagery of the Hebrew Scriptures—that he himself was somehow divine. By making such a claim, Jesus had gone too far. He had taken the final step toward virtually guaranteeing that he would be executed.

Appearing Before Pontius Pilate

To carry out the death penalty against Jesus, the Jewish leadership needed the help of the Romans.

The Antonia Fortress, just outside the Temple area, housed Roman troops. Jesus' trial before Pontius Pilate probably took place in its central courtyard.

Photo: A scale model of the Antonia Fortress

However, the Roman procurator Pontius Pilate could not accept the charge of blasphemy as a sufficient reason for execution. Blasphemy was a religious offense, not a political one that in any way threatened the Roman state. The Jewish priests and elders then offered several alternative charges against Jesus: inciting the people to revolt against their Jewish leaders, opposing the payment of taxes to Caesar, and claiming to be the Messiah or a king (see Luke 23:2). Pilate was unmoved by those charges. **5**

Pilate: Looking for a Way Out

Luke's Gospel includes a scene that is not contained in either of the other synoptic Gospels or in the Gospel of John: In front of Pilate, the Jewish leaders persist in their angry accusations about Jesus. Eventually Pilate learns that Jesus is a Galilean, and this gives Pilate an opening. The Jesus matter can thus be turned over to Herod Antipas, tetrarch of Galilee.

Recall from chapter 3 of this course that Herod Antipas, son of Herod the Great, had been given authority over the region of Galilee after Herod the Great's death. The fact that Jesus was a Galilean, combined with the coincidence that Herod Antipas was in Jerusalem at the time the charges were brought against Jesus, gave Pilate a possible way out of his dilemma. He could avoid both the responsibility of condemning Jesus, whom he knew was innocent of anything deserving death, and the risk of further infuriating the Jews during the already emotionally intense time of Passover.

The problem was that Herod Antipas did not want to condemn Jesus either. Instead, according to Luke, "when Herod saw Jesus, he was very glad, for he had been wanting to see him for a long time, because he had heard about him and was hoping to see him perform some sign" (Luke 23:8). When Jesus refused to respond to this expectation, an angry Herod Antipas sent him back to Pilate.

"I Am Innocent . . ."

As the angry cries of the Jewish leaders intensified, Pilate was left with only one more option. In accordance with the common practice of the Romans to release a Jewish prisoner during major religious feasts, he offered the Jewish leaders a choice: he could release either Jesus or another "notorious prisoner," who was named—perhaps coincidentally—Barabbas, meaning "son of the father."

The Jewish leaders were adamant about what they wanted—that Jesus be crucified. Pilate realized that the situation was hopeless. In a gesture described only in Matthew's Gospel, Pilate washed his hands in front of the crowds and said, "'I am innocent of this man's blood; see to it yourselves'" (27:24). The "official" Roman charge against Jesus was that he had incited a revolt among the Jews.

Pilate's simple washing of his hands, of course, could not truly cleanse him of the guilt he was to share for the execution of Jesus. Some have tried to minimize his role in the trial, and there is a reasonable chance that the authors of the Gospels did so in an attempt to identify the Jewish leaders as the people chiefly responsible for Jesus' death. But the evidence is that Pilate, under pressure from an angry mob, condemned to death by crucifixion a man he knew to be innocent. **6**

Being Scourged and Crucified

In the Gospels—after all the building tension and conflict, the touching and tragic encounter at Gethsemane, the hurried but complex inquiry and

---

5
Imagine yourself as the prosecuting attorney at the trial of Jesus. Write a brief summary of the charges you would bring against him to prove he deserved execution.

6
In writing, briefly express the degree to which you think each of the following were responsible for Jesus' death: *Judas, the Jewish leaders, Caiaphas, Pontius Pilate.* Give reasons for your answers.

eventual trial—the execution of Jesus is described quickly and with near-frightening starkness.

"King of the Jews"

Before he was crucified, Jesus was first ridiculed by Roman soldiers for his claim to kingship, and he was given a soldier's scarlet cloak as a mocking tribute. A "crown" formed from a thorny plant was pressed onto his head. He was then the object of *scourging*, a beating often given prior to a crucifixion. During the scourging, Jesus was whipped with leather straps that had either bone or metal chips attached to them. Scourging was terribly brutal, many times leading to the death of prisoners as their flesh was literally torn from their body. Jesus survived.

Then Jesus was given a crossbeam to carry—not an entire cross, as so many paintings have depicted it. He was led to a small hill or mound called Golgotha, meaning "the Skull," perhaps because of its shape. There he was placed on his back, with his arms stretched across the crossbeam he had been carrying. Through his wrists he was nailed to the crossbeam, which was then lifted and attached to an upright beam that stood permanently in the ground. After being elevated, Jesus' body was tied to the cross with ropes around his arms, legs, and stomach, in order to keep his body from tearing free of the nails that held it. The cross also had a small "seat" built into the upright beam, on which the body could rest to ensure longer life and therefore greater suffering.

A small sign was nailed to the beam above Jesus' head, bearing not the official charge for which he was being executed, but rather the mocking title "King of the Jews." And he was left to hang there, between two crucified thieves, until he died.

A Spear in His Side

Crucifixion was the method of execution reserved for non-Roman citizens and slaves. (Capital punishment for Roman citizens was through the more "humane" method of beheading.) Sometimes a man would hang for a week or more on the cross before finally dying from bleeding, choking, inability to breathe, or even more hideous, being attacked by wild dogs during the nights. According to the Gospel accounts, Jesus died in six hours or less, surprising both Pilate and the guards.

According to John's Gospel, it was against the Jewish religious laws to have a body on a cross during the Sabbath, so the Jews asked that the legs of the three crucified men be broken to hasten death. (If a crucified man's legs were broken, he could not hold himself up to breathe.) But by the time the soldiers approached Jesus, he had already died.

Illustration: **Scourging was a terribly brutal punishment, often leading to the death of prisoners as flesh was torn from their bodies.**

186

Only John's account mentions that a soldier then pierced Jesus' side with a spear to guarantee his death before the Sabbath observance (John 19:31–37). Out of this wound, according to John, flowed blood and water. For John, water was a symbol of the Spirit. By adding this detail, he may have intended to show that Jesus' death was the source of a great "outpouring" of the Spirit. Some ancient church theologians suggested that the blood and the water were symbols for the Christian sacraments of the Eucharist (blood) and baptism (water). **7**

Jesus' Last Words

The Gospels provide differing versions of the words Jesus spoke on the cross before his death. Two of his statements, however, are particularly memorable:

"My God, my God . . .": According to both Mark and Matthew, Jesus uttered this statement, which is frequently recalled by believers and debated by scholars: "'My God, my God, why have you forsaken me?'" (Matthew 27:46; see also Mark 15:34). Believers are touched by the statement because it reflects such deep loneliness and anxiety on the part of Jesus as he approaches his death. The debate of scholars centers on whether the words do in fact reflect a sense of deep despair. If the answer is yes, this in turn would seem to suggest that Jesus had a certain lack of faith in his Father's love for him.

Most scholars rightly point out that these words of Jesus are the opening line of Psalm 22. Faithful Jews traditionally memorized psalms in their entirety. By placing the first line of Psalm 22 on the lips of Jesus, the Evangelists were likely suggesting that the *entire* psalm was being recalled by Jesus. Scholars point out that although the psalm *begins* with a cry of distress and anguish, it *ends* with a strong statement of faith in Yahweh. While acknowledging the importance of this interpretation, we should not ignore the fact that the cry of Jesus on the cross reflects his undeniable humanity, which included moments of profound doubt and distress.

"Father, into your hands . . .": Of the three synoptic writers, only Luke specifically mentions Jesus' final words before he died. Matthew and Mark say that Jesus cried out in a loud voice and breathed his last (Matthew 27:50; Mark 15:37). John records Jesus' closing words in this way: "When Jesus had received the wine, he said, 'It is finished.' Then he bowed his head and gave up his spirit"; that is, he died (19:30).

The words that Luke places on Jesus' lips, if not actually spoken by Jesus, no doubt reflect the attitude he carried with him to his death: "'Father, into your hands I commend my spirit'" (23:46). **8**

For Review

- The high priest Caiaphas asked Jesus if he was the Messiah. What was significant about Jesus' answer?
- Why did the Jewish leaders bring their charges against Jesus to the Romans?
- Why did Pontius Pilate not accept the Jews' first charge against Jesus?
- Why do scholars debate the meaning of Jesus' utterance on the cross, "My God, my God, why have you forsaken me?"

7
Create a prayerful meditation on the scourging and crucifixion of Jesus and the meaning of those events for you.

8
Which quotation of Jesus' last words impresses you most—the one provided by John or the one provided by Luke? Explain your choice in a paragraph.

The Power of the Cross

Most of the Gospel stories come alive and take on more meaning for us when we try to identify with the main characters. However, when looking at the story of the crucifixion of Jesus, this seems impossible. How can we possibly identify with Jesus as he faced his horrifying death on the cross?

As the following true story illustrates, we *can* begin to identify with—and certainly draw strength from—Jesus' experience of the cross, including his deep faith and total trust in his Father. The story is a first-person account by the author of this textbook, Tom Zanzig.

A couple of years ago, I was asked to address a group of young people who were attending a weekend youth conference. My task was to prepare the group for the Mass that would close the conference. The day was Palm Sunday, and the themes of the liturgy readings were pain, suffering, death, and the crucified Jesus.

I would much rather have talked about something more joyful than the fact that pain and suffering are a central and necessary part of life and the Gospel. But I stuck to my task, and I was almost brutally honest at times. "If we're lucky," I said, "our pain is periodic and temporary, but for some people it is a permanent state. During painful times, we cannot help but ask, If life is so terribly difficult, how can we believe in a good God? Where do we find our meaning? How do we cope?"

Then I proceeded to tell the gathering of six hundred young people about a recent incident in my life:

I had been going through a particularly difficult time in almost every area of my life. I was so wracked with loneliness that I was rarely able to sleep. Even prayer seemed useless, empty.

About three o'clock one morning, I gave up on sleep and went to the family room. Sitting in my rocking chair, I felt totally alone, overwhelmed by the seeming hopelessness of my situation. I started to weep.

Then, as if a small voice came out of my past, I remembered the words, "Father, into your hands I commend my spirit." I silently said those words, not as an act of faith but out of sheer desperation. Something stirred in me as I said them, so I said them again. "Father, into your hands . . ." Then I started to whisper them over and over, ". . . into your hands . . . into your hands . . ."

Finally, after I'm not sure how long, I got up and went back to bed. That night I fell into the deepest sleep I had had in years. When I awoke the next morning, I knew that I had experienced a fundamental change in my life.

At the youth conference, hearing me share my experience, was a young woman named Susan. Shortly before the conference, Susan had felt so miserable about her life that she

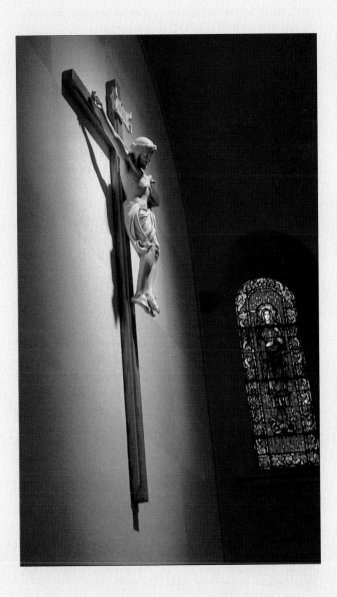

wanted to kill herself. Searching for some way to help, Susan's youth minister talked her into attending the conference, in the hope that she would find a better answer there.

Once at the conference, however, Susan only became more depressed. Everyone else was so happy. They all felt close to God, and she didn't. They all talked about love, and she felt that no one cared for her. They all laughed and sang and danced, while she became more lonely. On the Saturday night of the conference, Susan decided that when she got home, she would end her life.

Then she heard me speak. She was stunned that anyone "who seemed to know a lot of stuff" could feel so lonely and sad. Maybe she wasn't so messed up after all. Maybe life is *supposed* to include some pain and heartache, even though people seem to deny that all the time.

Susan shared all of this with me by phone about a month after the conference—at the urging of her youth minister. She told me that she had started to say that prayer, "Father, into your hands . . . ," and it was keeping her alive.

About a year after I received the call from Susan, I heard from her youth minister that she was attending college and studying to be a youth minister. She wanted to specialize in counseling suicidal adolescents.

Photo: "Father, into your hands I commend my spirit." (Luke 23:46)

Let's look at the common expressions listed above, to see what they can tell us about that meaning.

"Jesus Died for Our Sins"

Perhaps the most popular statement about the death of Jesus—the **cross**—is, "He died for our sins." Unfortunately, this wording is confusing for many of us. It can convey an image of God that is far removed from the one Jesus revealed to the world. Such a statement can give a sense, for instance, that Jesus had to die in our place in order to satisfy an angry God who was demanding a "pound of flesh" in payment for past offenses. This image of God runs directly contrary to Jesus' message—that God is a totally loving and forgiving Father.

"Jesus Conquered Death"

Jesus' death can also be understood as a decisive confrontation between good and evil, between the forces of life and the forces of death. As the next chapter in this course will show, what at first appears to be the death of both Jesus and his Dream of the Kingdom of God is eventually recognized as a total victory by God in Jesus' resurrection. In that sense we can say, "Jesus conquered death."

Understanding the Cross

Throughout the history of the church, the struggle to come to terms with Jesus' death has led to a wide variety of expressions, symbols, and theological interpretations. Certainly the cross has a profound and complex significance for Christians, one that may well be too great for words.

Common Expressions

Jesus' death has been referred to as a "sacrifice," perhaps reflecting the Passover theme mentioned earlier. It is said that Jesus "died for our sins," that he "conquered death," that he "gave his life as a ransom for many." It would be easy but dangerous to settle on any one expression to capture the complex meaning of the cross. In doing so, we would risk seriously misinterpreting the cross's meaning.

Photo, left: **Jesus' death frees us with the incredible power of a love that knows no limits.**

Photo, right: **Steps outside the walls of Jerusalem**

"Jesus Gave His Life as a Ransom for Many"

Another insight into the meaning of Jesus' death can be found in Mark 10:45, where Jesus states that "'the Son of Man came not to be served but to serve, and to give his life [as] a ransom for many.'" When properly understood, this can be a helpful expression for us.

In the Roman world, a *ransom* was the price paid to release a slave, and it was often paid by someone other than the slave. The payment was made in front of a shrine to a local god, to indicate that the slave was becoming the property of that god and could no longer be owned by another person. The idea of ransom can help us understand the cross if we recognize Jesus' death as liberating us from our slavery to sin. His death sets us free by demonstrating the incredibly freeing power of a love that knows no limits. **9**

For Review

- Why would it be dangerous to settle on only one expression for the meaning of the cross?
- The statement that Jesus died for our sins is important, but what confusion can it lead to?

Only in Light of the Resurrection

At this point in the discussion, we are, in a sense, trying to understand the cross too soon. We cannot completely understand the execution of Jesus until we understand what followed it—Jesus' being raised from the dead by his Father.

None of the Gospels end with Jesus' passion and death on the cross. Rather, we see Jesus' total trust in God at the moment of his death—"Father, into your hands I commend my spirit." That trust in God is then proven to be well-founded in light of the Resurrection. Only through the Resurrection can we see the ultimate message of the cross: God loves all people unconditionally. As the Evangelist John would say years after Jesus' death:

> Whoever does not love does not know God, for God is love. God's love was revealed among us in this way: God sent his only Son into the world so that we might live through him. In this is love, not that we loved God but that he loved us and sent his Son to be the atoning sacrifice for our sins [that is, the sacrifice that would take away our sins]. Beloved, since God loved us so much, we also ought to love one another. (1 John 4:8–11)

9
From the three common expressions for the meaning of Jesus' death on the cross, choose the one that has the most meaning for you and write a brief essay explaining why. Or if you wish, write about your own, more personal, interpretation of the cross's meaning.

■
After Jesus' death in Jerusalem, his followers were not expecting the victory that was to come— the Resurrection.
Photo: David's Citadel, seen from outside the walls of Jerusalem

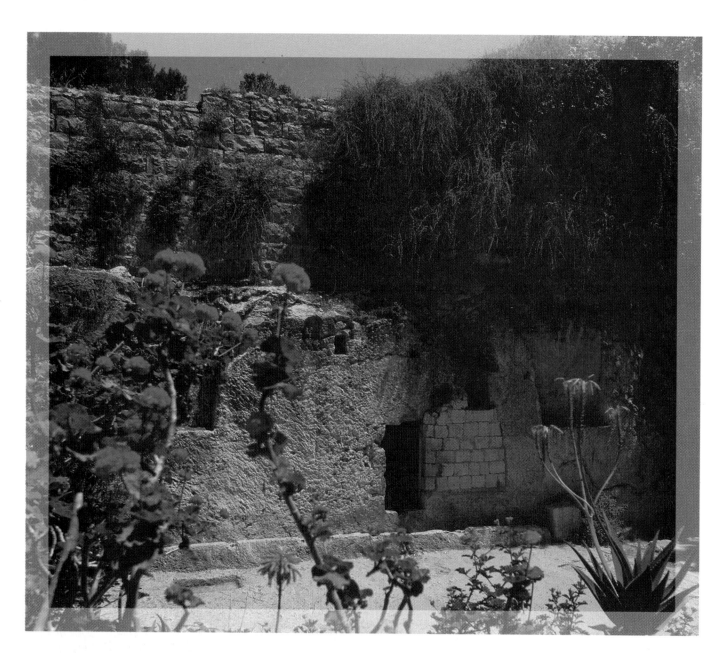

10

The Resurrection:
God Is Victorious! Jesus Is Lord!

WHEN the sabbath was over, Mary Magdalene, and Mary the mother of James, and Salome bought spices, so that they might go and anoint [Jesus' body]. And very early on the first day of the week, when the sun had risen, they went to the tomb. They had been saying to one another, "Who will roll away the stone for us from the entrance to the tomb?" When they looked up, they saw that the stone, which was very large, had already been rolled back. As they entered the tomb, they saw a young man, dressed in a white robe, sitting on the right side; and they were alarmed. But he said to them, "Do not be alarmed; you are looking for Jesus of Nazareth, who was crucified. He has been raised; he is not here. Look, there is the place they laid him. But go, tell his disciples and Peter that he is going ahead of you to Galilee; there you will see him, just as he told you." So they went out and fled from the tomb, for terror and amazement had seized them; and they said nothing to anyone, for they were afraid. (Mark 16:1–8)

The Resurrection of Jesus

The Gospels themselves—indeed, Christianity as a recognized religion—would not even exist were it not for what happened *after* the death of Jesus. The last days of Jesus' earthly life—his arrest, trial, and death by crucifixion—have been recalled and passed on for some two thousand years only because they were followed by an event that gave them meaning. That event, of course, was the Resurrection, Jesus' being raised from the dead by God, his Father on Easter.

Curiously, the Gospel accounts of the resurrection of Jesus are brief compared with those of the final days of Jesus' life. The quotation from Mark's Gospel at the opening of this chapter is typical of the accounts found in the other Gospels—straightforward, offering little detail, with no attempt to further explain what happened. Many of us might like to ask the Evangelists a few of the following questions:

- What did Jesus look like when he was raised from the dead by God?
- Did anyone actually see Jesus come out of the tomb?
- If no one saw him, how do we know that he was really raised? Maybe somebody just stole the body to make people *think* he was raised.
- How can people today be expected to believe something so incredible, something that is almost unbelievable?

All of these are good, reasonable questions. This chapter will attempt to provide some satisfying answers. **1**

What Happened?

Each Gospel tells of the burial and resurrection of Jesus and some of his appearances to his disciples and others after the Resurrection (see Matthew 27:62–66; 28:1–20; Mark 15:42–47; 16:1–20; Luke 23:50–56; 24:1–53; and John 19:38–42; 20:1–31; 21:1–25). Despite the many differences between these accounts, we can arrive at a basic sense of what occurred that remarkable Sunday morning long ago.

Jesus Was Buried in a Tomb

All four Gospel accounts agree that after Jesus died, his body was claimed by a wealthy disciple of Jesus named Joseph of Arimathea. Joseph had asked Pilate for the right to take the body and give it a decent burial. He took the body, wrapped it in a burial cloth called a shroud, and laid it in a tomb

The Resurrection gave meaning to Jesus' whole life and death. *Photo, facing page:* The garden tomb where Jesus was laid, according to some Christians

1
In writing, give any ideas you have in response to the four questions listed above. Write down any questions you have that are not listed on this page.

hewn out of stone. (The full preparation of the body for burial according to Jewish custom had to wait until after the Sabbath, which was already beginning on the evening of the Friday Jesus died.) A large, round, flat stone was then rolled into place at the entrance of the tomb. Matthew's Gospel states that Pontius Pilate assigned Roman soldiers to guard the tomb, to prevent Jesus' disciples from stealing the body. The Jewish leaders were concerned that the disciples would steal the body and then claim that Jesus had risen from the dead as he had predicted he would.

Other Common Points in the Gospel Accounts

After describing Jesus' burial, each Evangelist offers his own version of what happened. However, the accounts do have these points in common:

- Various people go to the tomb and discover that the body of Jesus is no longer there.
- The people who go to the tomb find out—either on their own (in John's Gospel) or through one or more messengers of God (in the synoptic Gospels)—that Jesus is no longer dead but alive, and that he will reveal himself to them again soon.
- The initial reactions of the witnesses are, quite naturally, shock and then fear. But soon they experience Jesus among them in such striking ways that there can be no doubt it is he—alive again, and yet somehow very different from when he walked among them before his death. Jesus has risen, and everything he claimed is proved true by this fact! **2**

Focusing on the Larger Picture

Beyond the common points listed above, a number of differences in the Gospel accounts of the Resurrection are easily recognized with just a quick

reading of those accounts. However, remember this basic lesson about the Gospels: The small details in the accounts are not significant or essential to what is being revealed through them. The truths expressed in and through the accounts far surpass any inconsistency that might be apparent in them.

Evidence for Accepting the Resurrection

Saint Paul, in his first letter to the Corinthians, states, "If Christ has not been raised, then empty . . . is our preaching; empty, too, your faith" (15:14, NAB). No factor in Christian faith is more central, more important, more critical, to our understanding of the Christ of Faith than the Resurrection. Ultimately, recognizing the Risen Christ is

---

2
Imagine yourself as one of the disciples, first hearing the news of Jesus' resurrection. In writing, briefly describe how you, as a disciple, might react to this news.

Illustration: **Considerable historical evidence—including the empty tomb—supports the Christian conviction of Jesus' resurrection.**

a matter of faith. Yet considerable historical evidence supports the Christian conviction of the resurrection of Jesus by his Father.

A Consistent Belief in the Early Church

The Resurrection was a consistent belief in the early church. The letters of Saint Paul, sermons contained in the Acts of the Apostles, and all four Gospels mention it. In the Acts of the Apostles, we see that experiencing the Risen Jesus was even considered a key qualification for being accepted as one of the Apostles (Acts 1:15–22).

The Empty Tomb

The empty tomb also testifies to the reality of the Resurrection. All accounts of the Resurrection agree that the tomb was empty on the morning that the women went to prepare Jesus' body for burial. Surely the Romans would have produced Jesus' corpse if they could have found it. Publicly displaying his dead body would have immediately destroyed any stories of his resurrection that might have been falsely created by his disciples.

But one might ask, Could the disciples have somehow stolen the corpse and then either hidden or destroyed it? The problem with this proposition is that many of the disciples would eventually choose to die as martyrs rather than deny their faith in a resurrected Jesus. Would they have freely died for a hoax, knowing that Jesus had not really risen?

Moreover, the Gospels identify women as major witnesses to the empty tomb. In the ancient Jewish society, women were not accepted as legal witnesses. Therefore, an author seeking to convince an audience of something untrue would never have chosen women as primary witnesses; they were not perceived as credible.

Jesus' Post-Resurrection Appearances

Though no one actually witnessed the Resurrection itself, many claimed to have experienced the Risen Jesus later. While the Gospels disagree on who saw him where and when and under what circumstances, the appearances do follow a common pattern:

- Everyone to whom Jesus appears is downcast, distressed, clearly convinced that he is dead.
- Jesus then takes the initiative and reveals himself to them, usually greeting them with the statement that they should be unafraid and at peace.
- Finally, Jesus often gives a command, such as "'Go therefore and make disciples of all nations'" (Matthew 28:19) or "'Go into all the world and proclaim the good news to the whole creation'" (Mark 16:15). The knowledge of Jesus Risen is not to be kept secret, as a private revelation. Those who know him are clearly called to share that knowledge with others.

Note how the empty tomb and the apparitions of Jesus are consistent with, and thus firm up and solidify, each other. Without the empty tomb, the appearances of Jesus could be regarded as hallucinations, as the fantasies of depressed people. Without the appearances, the empty tomb could be considered a trick.

A Courageous Community

A final piece of evidence can be offered to support the reality of Jesus' resurrection: a thoroughly shattered band of Jesus' followers was transformed into a community of courageous witnesses after the Resurrection. This may be the most important evidence of all. The total conviction with which the disciples proclaimed the Risen Jesus as a sign of joy and hope is undeniable. After all, only such a conviction—and the commitment to share the

On the Road to Emmaus

Luke's Gospel contains a particularly beautiful and insightful story about an appearance by the Risen Jesus to his disciples (24:13–35). Pause and read the story as Luke tells it.

This apparently simple story is one many Christians find truly captivating. Luke manages to sum up the entire Good News of Jesus. But he also provides us with insights into what it means today to be a follower of Jesus, as well as a member of the community that professes faith in him.

In the story, two confused and distressed disciples are joined by the Risen Jesus as they walk along the road to Emmaus. The disciples are so wrapped up in their grief about Jesus' recent crucifixion, however, that they cannot recognize him. Jesus does not force himself upon them, nor does he dramatically reveal his identity. Instead, he just walks with them, sharing their journey and listening to their story. They tell him of Jesus of Nazareth, who proved he was "'a prophet mighty in deed and word before God and all the people'"; of how they had hoped he would be the one to

set Israel free from its oppressors; of how he had been crucified; and of the stories they have just heard about his being alive again.

Jesus listens. "Then beginning with Moses and all the prophets, he [interprets] to them the things about himself in all the scriptures." Still the two disciples do not recognize him, though they will recall later that their hearts burned within them as they listened to him speak.

As the three approach the town of Emmaus, Jesus begins to move ahead. Now it is the disciples' turn to take the initiative, to show at least some degree of openness to what he can offer them. And they do so by requesting that Jesus stay with them. Jesus, of course, accepts their invitation. When they gather that evening for a simple meal, he takes the bread, as he did just a few days earlier, and he blesses it, breaks it, and hands it to them. "Then their eyes [are] opened, and they [recognize] him."

The Emmaus story is about what it means to recognize the Risen Jesus, a task that ultimately confronts all who

would choose to follow him. The word *recognize* is significant, coming from the prefix *re-,* meaning "again," and the Latin word *cognoscere,* meaning "to know." In the act of recognizing, we come to know something or someone again. We rediscover or renew our awareness of a reality we have experienced before.

This is what happened to the disciples at Emmaus. In the act of blessing and breaking bread, Jesus was recognized. Suddenly the disciples rediscovered him, and all the memories of what they had shared before his death flooded back upon them. They came to the powerful realization that Jesus was alive, present with them! The joy and excitement that overwhelmed them was typical in the witnesses to whom Jesus appeared.

The Emmaus story is about recognizing the Risen Jesus in our midst.
Photo: **The road to the site of what is thought to be the village of Emmaus, near Jerusalem**

faith motivated by that conviction—can explain the beginning of the church. 3

Proclamations of Faith

The Gospel accounts of the Resurrection, we must always remember, are not attempts to record in historical detail what occurred the day we call Easter. This does *not* mean that the Resurrection did not happen. On the contrary, the Risen Jesus is the most consistently proclaimed reality in the entire Christian Testament. And the Resurrection is the most pivotal event proclaimed by the Gospels. Only if God actually raised Jesus from the dead is the truth of both Jesus and his message confirmed. Only then is the Gospel proclamation truly Good News, not a lie, a hoax, or a fantasy to be rejected.

As proclamations of faith rather than historical documents, the Gospel accounts and their inconsistent details should not be a stumbling block to believing in Jesus' resurrection. The Resurrection simply was not a historical event in the usual sense. The death of Jesus was historical in that even nonbelievers would have been able to see Jesus crucified. But only people of faith experienced Jesus after his resurrection, and even they sometimes had great difficulty and hesitation. The Risen Jesus could not have been scientifically proven to exist. The Resurrection, in other words, goes beyond history as we know it.

What Was the Risen Jesus Like?

What did the Risen Jesus look like? Exactly how did the disciples experience him? What seems certain yet mysterious in the Gospel accounts is that Jesus was truly transformed through the Resurrection. He was experiencing an utterly new kind of existence. The Risen Jesus was not a person who had been asleep and then suddenly awakened, nor was he a corpse that had somehow come back to life. He was the same Jesus and yet completely different.

Resurrected life is not merely a continuation, after death, of the kind of earthly life we experience. It is, rather, an entirely new way of living, a new relationship in and with God, something completely beyond our imagination. How can we explain this kind of life? The simple answer is, we can't! Nonbelievers have suggested that the authors of the Christian Testament imagined or intentionally created a vision of resurrected life. But it would seem that the Gospel evidence supporting the resurrection of Jesus is too complex and too thorough to have been created by any one author, let alone several authors working independently of one another.

For Review

- According to Matthew's Gospel, why did Pontius Pilate assign Roman soldiers to guard the tomb of Jesus?
- Summarize the common points in the Gospel accounts of Jesus' resurrection.
- List and summarize the four pieces of evidence given to support the reality of Jesus' resurrection.
- Why was the resurrection of Jesus not a historical event in the usual sense?

3
Write your own evaluation of the four pieces of evidence given on pages 194–197 to support the reality of the Resurrection.

After his resurrection, the Gospels record several appearances by Jesus in and around Jerusalem. *Photo:* The village of Silwân (then known as Siloam) in the Kidron Valley at the edge of Jerusalem

What Does the Resurrection Mean?

Let's take a closer look at why the Resurrection is of critical importance to Christian faith.

Affirmation of the Truth of Jesus' Teachings

Of most significance to Christian faith is the fact that the Resurrection demonstrates the truth of Jesus' claims and teachings about God.

- In his claim about God's unconditional love for each of us, Jesus spoke the truth.
- In his promise that we can find fulfillment in loving God and others, Jesus spoke the truth.
- In his rejection of empty religious ritual and his commitment to a prayerful and personal relationship with God, Jesus spoke the truth.
- In his conviction that forgiveness of one another will always be more life-giving and enriching than revenge, Jesus spoke the truth.
- In his call for respect and special affection for the outcasts of society, Jesus spoke the truth.
- In his teaching that the rich must share with the poor, Jesus spoke the truth.
- In his absolute refusal to accept anything that would separate people from one another—social status, sexual or racial discrimination, economic standing, political affiliation, even religious beliefs—Jesus spoke the truth.

All of this is affirmed by the Resurrection.

Jesus Recognized as the Messiah

The Resurrection demonstrates as well that Jesus was and is forever the Messiah, the Christ, not just

a great, good man with a marvelous but unrealistic Dream.

Many people want to give a halfhearted, incomplete assent to Jesus and his message. They are willing to admit that he was a special person, perhaps the greatest in history, and certainly one worth imitating. But the Messiah, the Lord, the Christ? That is going too far, they say.

The resurrection of Jesus, together with the church's constant commitment to belief in the Resurrection as *the* central characteristic of Christian faith, makes a conditional acceptance of Jesus, as merely an extraordinary human being, an unacceptable response for Christians. As bluntly stated earlier in this book, Jesus was one of three things: a

Illustration: **The meaning of the paschal mystery can be found in many facets of everyday life. In nature we see how death precedes and brings forth life.**

lunatic, a con artist, or exactly who he professed to be. The Resurrection points in favor of the last option: Jesus was and is the One sent by God to redeem the world.

Life in Christ

For Christians, the resurrection of Jesus completely transforms the understanding of all human life. Because of the Resurrection, Christians know that happiness and fullness of life are not accomplished merely through rigid religious practices or through some new self-improvement program. Rather, happiness and fullness of life come from a new "center," a new "life force," a new source of power. That new source of power is nothing less than God, the God that is revealed in and through Jesus Christ. "'I live now not with my own life,'" said Saint Paul, "'but with the life of Christ who lives in me'" (Galatians 2:20, JB).

Death to New Life: The Paschal Mystery

A New Passover

Recall that the Evangelist John linked the death of Jesus with the killing of the paschal lambs, which were slaughtered as part of the Passover celebration. John's Gospel refers to Jesus as the "new paschal lamb," "the lamb of God, who takes away the sins of the world." The church's phrase *paschal mystery* builds upon this theme and refers to the profound meaning that the death and resurrection of Jesus can hold for many aspects of human life.

Paschal mystery refers first and foremost to the ways in which Jesus' death and resurrection constitute a "new Passover" for history and for those who believe in Jesus. The Christian Testament speaks of Jesus' death and resurrection as bringing about redemption. That is, Jesus' death and resurrection save all humanity from death and the powers of sin. As discussed earlier, Christians speak of this salvation in many ways—by saying, for example, that Jesus died for our sins, that he gave his life as a ransom for many.

The Paschal Mystery in Everyday Life

To understand the redemptive meaning of the paschal mystery, Christians point to the recurring theme of dying and rising found in everyday experiences.

In nature: Much of nature reflects a repeating cycle of death and rebirth. Reflect, for example, on the plant life that thrives in your yard or in parks

Illustration: **A tree could not bloom brilliantly in spring without its apparent death the previous fall.**

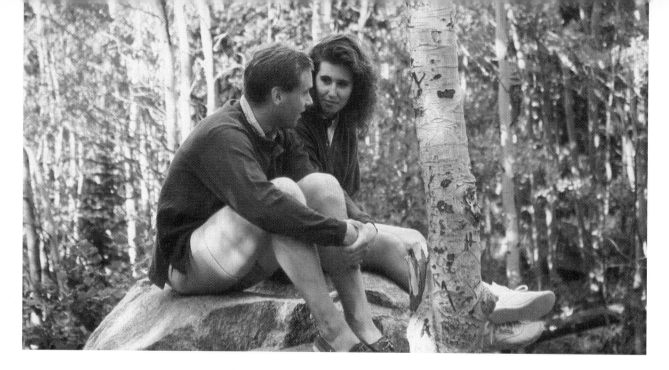

near where you live. Many plants flourish during the summer, wilt and "die" in the fall and winter, only to bloom again each spring. Animals are born, grow to maturity, generate new life, and then die, only to decay and provide nourishment for new life. People too, of course, reflect this pattern on the level of biology.

In pain experiences: The redemptive meaning of the paschal mystery can be witnessed in personal ways as well as in the cycle of nature. Christians believe, for example, that much of the pain encountered in life—whether physical, emotional, intellectual, or spiritual—can serve as an invitation to and opportunity for new growth, when seen with the eyes of faith. When a friend is suffering, an act of love on our part can bring new life to our friend and to ourselves. When a person hurts us through an unkind word or careless action, a gesture of forgiveness from us can renew the relationship and bring it to new depth.

This is not to say that pain and suffering should be sought. Enough of it comes inevitably with life. Through the Resurrection, God lets us know that ultimately, pain and suffering are not what life is about. When responded to with faith, hope, and especially love, pain and suffering can provide the ground from which new life springs. Then the paschal mystery is again made real. 4

From death to resurrection and new life—the paschal mystery seems to permeate all of life for those with "the eyes to see and ears to hear" (see Mark 8:18). Perhaps only when the paschal mystery is lived out in the actions and attitudes of daily life can the full meaning of Jesus' death and resurrection make sense for the Christian. 5

For Review

- What fact about the Resurrection is of most significance to Christian faith?
- Why is viewing Jesus as just an extraordinary man rather than the Christ an unacceptable position for Christians?
- What is the origin and meaning of the term *paschal mystery?*

Photo: **When a friend is suffering, an act of love on our part can bring new life to our friend and to ourselves.**

4
Copy and complete this statement: *In my own life, I see the paschal mystery most clearly reflected in _____ because _____.*

5
Look back at the four reasons that the Resurrection is of critical importance to Christian faith. Choose the reason most significant to you and explain your choice in a paragraph.

Recognizing the Risen Jesus Today

If Only We Could See Him Too

Some people today, as they struggle to decide whether to accept Jesus and Christianity's proclamation about him, make this point: It would be so much easier if only we could experience the Risen Jesus the way his disciples did—or like Doubting Thomas did, placing our hand in the wounds of the Risen Jesus and knowing that in him God has conquered death (see John 20:24–29). Then we could believe also. It was easy for them. How could they *not* believe?

But those who hold the notion that it was easy for the first disciples to believe in the Risen Jesus do not understand the depth of faith of those first disciples. The fact is that the same depth of faith is required of Christians today if they are to "see" Jesus and recognize him as the Christ. Ultimately, nothing *forces* people to believe, nothing compels them to accept Jesus as Redeemer. However, a great deal about Jesus *invites* individuals to freely accept him and his message, which were proved worthy of trust by God's raising him from the dead. **6**

How Do We Encounter Jesus?

Christians throughout time have found and experienced the Risen Jesus in several significant ways. Today's Christians can encounter Jesus in these same ways.

In the Eucharist

Christian faith teaches that Jesus is encountered in a special way in the celebration of the Eucharist, or the Mass. When Jesus took the bread at the Last Supper and said, "'This is my body, which is given for you. Do this in remembrance of me'" (Luke 22:19), he left a concrete and tangible sign to help Christians "see" him anywhere. By celebrating the Eucharist with the believing community, Christians are reminded of a *constant* reality—that the Risen Jesus is with us. They can leave the eucharistic celebration with "new eyes," a renewed capacity to see Jesus present in many other ways in their daily life.

The opposite, however, is also true. Those who make little or no attempt to recall and live out the message of Jesus, who make no effort to reach out in love to others in their daily life, have a difficult time fully experiencing Jesus as present in the Eucharist. The Eucharist is no more "magical" than the Resurrection itself. In both cases, only "those with the eyes to see" will see.

In the Community of Believers

Jesus told his disciples, "'Just as you did [a compassionate deed for] one of the least of these who are members of my family, you did it [for] me'" (Matthew 25:40). Christians discover Jesus in their

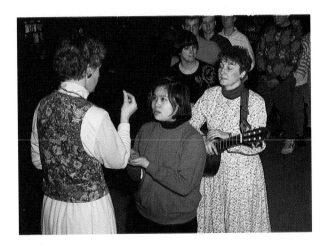

6
Read the story of Doubting Thomas in John 20:24–29. Then imagine yourself as Thomas and write a letter to another disciple who has asked for help in dealing with doubts about Jesus.

Photo: **By celebrating the Eucharist with the believing community, Christians are reminded of a constant reality—that the Risen Jesus is with us.**

loving relationships with one another. Jesus also said, "'Where two or three are gathered in my name, I am there among them'" (Matthew 18:20). Christians discover Jesus within the community of believing Christians, those gathered "in his name," the church. Every loving relationship we experience—especially one in which we love without demanding love in return—is an encounter with the Risen Jesus.

In Remembering and Living Out Jesus' Dream

Memory is a complex and powerful human capacity, and it is especially helpful in understanding how Jesus is with us today.

We can treat some memories as "dead and gone," as events and experiences that no longer influence us. Other memories, however, can be treated just the opposite; they can be "alive and present" and help shape every moment of our life.

We get a hint of the power of memory when a fragrance or a popular song first experienced several years ago creates within us today the emotions associated with the original experience. If this power is true of the memory of aromas and sounds, how much more true it is of the memory of important people in our life. Perhaps we remember a good friend or relative who died when we were much younger. We never truly forget such people. They continue to live within us, sometimes in very real and powerful ways.

In living out the Dream of Jesus, Christians encounter Jesus in very real and powerful ways. They do more than simply recall or remember a past event—that is, the life and ministry of the Jesus of History. They consciously make Jesus, and everything that is associated with him, present again.

Christians remember the Jesus of History, but they encounter and experience the Christ of Faith every day. *7*

The Mark of a True Christian

In summary, then, to fully encounter the Risen Jesus today, Christians must not only gather together and break bread in his memory, but they must live every day in accordance with his Dream of the Kingdom of God. In fact, the key criterion for judging if someone is a Christian is this: whether the person is willing to let her or his life be shaped and led by the power of Jesus' life and message. This openness to a lived faith is of far greater importance than an intellectual grasp of the Resurrection.

The Risen Christ is revealed in and through loving Christians, who say along with Saint Paul, "'I live now not with my own life but with the life of Christ who lives in me.'" After all is said and done, living out one's faith is what it means to discover and know the Risen Jesus and to meet God in and through him. And it is only then that the Gospel becomes what Christians profess it to be—the Good News of salvation in Jesus Christ.

For Review

- Why do some Christians have difficulty experiencing Jesus as present in the Eucharist?
- In what sense can a memory be "alive and present"?
- What is the key criterion for judging if someone is a Christian?

7
In writing, describe an incident from your life that stands out as an encounter with the Risen Jesus.

The Ascension of Jesus

What happened to Jesus after his resurrection and his appearances to the disciples and others? Our immediate inclination is to respond that he "went to heaven." But where and what is heaven? And how did he get from here to there? These are perhaps obvious questions, but they have anything but obvious answers. **8**

What the Scriptures Tell Us

Numerous parts of the Christian Testament refer to Jesus' presence with the Father "in heaven." For example, Jesus is said to be "seated at the right hand of God." However, specific references to the *ascension* of Jesus into the presence of his Father are fewer in number.

- A specific description of the ascension of Jesus as a historical event is made only in Luke's Gospel and in the second part of Luke's work, which is called the Acts of the Apostles.
- Neither Matthew's Gospel nor John's Gospel mentions the Ascension at all, and the brief mention of the event in Mark 16:19 may have been added to Mark's original Gospel.
- Only two brief references to the Ascension can be found in all of the Epistles (1 Timothy 3:16; 1 Peter 3:22).

In his Gospel account of the Ascension, Luke says, "[Jesus] led them out as far as Bethany, and, lifting up his hands, he blessed them. While he was blessing them, he withdrew from them and was carried up into heaven" (24:50–51).

According to the account given in Acts, Jesus promised his disciples, "'You will receive power when the Holy Spirit has come upon you'" (1:8).

When he had said this, as they were watching, he was lifted up, and a cloud took him out of their sight. While he was going and they were gazing up toward heaven, suddenly two men in white robes stood by them. [The men in robes] said, "Men of Galilee, why do you stand looking up toward heaven? This Jesus, who has been taken up from you into heaven, will come in the same way as you saw him go into heaven." (1:9–11).

An Event Beyond Human Comprehension

As was true of the earlier Gospel accounts, contradictions and differences are evident in the various

---

Jesus is said to be with God "in heaven." But where and what is heaven?
Photo: **A twelfth-century artist's conception of Jesus in heaven, entitled "Christ in Majesty"**

8
Write a description of what you hope heaven will be like.

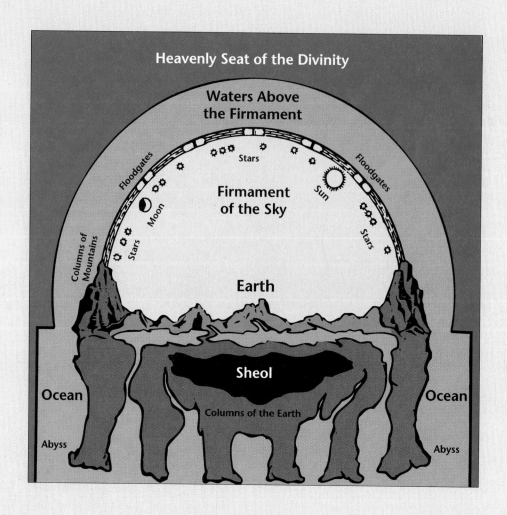

The Worldview of the Ancient Jews

This illustration represents the concept of the universe held by Jews of the first century.

According to this worldview, God resided in the heavens, above the upper waters. The sky, or *firmament,* lay below these upper waters and was visualized as an overturned bowl supported by columns of mountains. The firmament had floodgates that opened to let the upper waters fall to earth in the form of rain or snow. The earth was thought to be a platform that sat upon columns. The lower waters surrounded the columns supporting the earth and the surface of the lower waters formed the oceans. All that lay beneath the earth was called the *abyss,* and therein was the home of the dead, or *Sheol.*

scriptural references to the Ascension. These contradictions and differences are understandable, given the fact that the writers of the Christian story were dealing with an event beyond human comprehension. A happening of this magnitude stretches our ability to express it within the limits of language.

A Problem of Space and Time

We, as humans, cannot escape images of space and time in our speaking, writing, and even thinking. For example, we automatically think of heaven as a place "up there." This notion may have been inherited from the people of Jesus' day, who had a simplistic view of the universe.

The ancient Jews viewed the universe as consisting of several "layers": the earth itself; the firmament above it, which included the sky and the stars; and the abyss, which lay beneath the earth. The people imagined the realm or world of God as existing beyond the sky and the waters above the sky. It was natural for the scriptural authors, therefore, to express their recognition of Jesus as the Risen Messiah through these images of time and space, stating that Jesus was "lifted into the heavens" at a particular time and place.

In spite of our limited understanding of Jesus' ascension, we can get a handle on the *meaning* the scriptural authors intended to express through their description of this event.

Right Here, Right Now

The main lesson that the scriptural authors wished to teach by describing the Ascension was this: Following his resurrection, Jesus passed totally into the presence of God and in doing so, he moved beyond our experience of space and time. What this actually means—strangely enough—is precisely the opposite of what we often *assume* it means. When we speak of the Risen Jesus as "going to his Father," we naturally think in terms of Jesus' being removed from our earthly realm, of his being separated from us. But when we reflect upon where God is (in light of Jesus' teachings about his Father), we realize that it is not right to speak and think of God as "out there" somewhere. The entire message of Jesus hinges on precisely the opposite realization—that the Kingdom of God is among us, that God is not "out there" but rather "right here."

Even small children acknowledge God as "being everywhere." But think of what this implies: If God is totally present, if God is right here and right now, then by "going to the Father," Jesus was actually becoming more truly *present* to us than he could possibly have been as he walked the roads of Palestine! Now free of the limitations of space and time that bind humans, Jesus can be totally with us. He is no longer tied down to one place at one time, talking about one thing to one particular group of people—as was true two thousand years ago. Rather, he is free to be everywhere, with everyone, for all time, loving and caring and calling us to his Father. This is the marvelous reality of the Good News! **9**

For Review

- What human limitation makes it difficult to understand the Ascension?
- What was the main lesson that the scriptural authors wished to teach by describing the Ascension?

9
List at least five implications that the following statement has for the lives of young people: *God is not "out there" but rather "right here."*

Pentecost

The Gift of the Spirit

In the Acts of the Apostles, immediately before the account of the Ascension, the disciples ask Jesus if he is going to restore Israel to its former power as a kingdom. Jesus tells them that only the Father knows what the future holds. Then, he says to them, "'But you will receive power when the Holy Spirit has come upon you; and you will be my witnesses in Jerusalem, in all Judea and Samaria, and to the ends of the earth'" (1:8).

Following Jesus' ascension, another incident occurs—the event of **Pentecost**, when the gift of the Holy Spirit is poured out upon the frightened disciples, suddenly transforming them into courageous witnesses of the Risen Jesus.

When the day of Pentecost had come, [the disciples] were all together in one place. And suddenly from heaven there came a sound like the rush of a violent wind, and it filled the entire house where they were sitting. Divided tongues, as of fire, appeared among them, and a tongue rested on each of them. All of them were filled with the Holy Spirit and began to

Illustration: **After the Ascension and before Pentecost, the disciples and Jesus' mother, Mary, gathered anxiously in an upper room in Jerusalem.**

speak in other languages, as the Spirit gave them ability.

Now there were devout Jews from every nation under heaven living in Jerusalem. And at this sound the crowd gathered and was bewildered, because each one heard [the disciples] speaking in the native language of each. Amazed and astonished, [the people] asked, "Are not all these who are speaking Galileans? And how is it that we hear, each of us, in our own native language? . . ." All were amazed and perplexed, saying to one another, "What does this mean?" But others sneered and said, "They are filled with new wine." (Acts 2:1–13)

The Birthday of the Church

Pentecost is often referred to as "the birthday of the church," because at the first Pentecost, the disciples began a whole new way of living in communion with one another.

The story of the first Pentecost is filled with marvelous imagery—a powerful wind, tongues of fire, people moved to speak in foreign languages, and observers moved to total amazement. The disciples were apparently filled with such joy that people accused them of being drunk! But the message of the story is essentially this: When disheartened and frightened people encounter the spirit of the Risen Jesus, they are transformed by the experience. As the remainder of the Acts of the Apostles powerfully points out, the early believers were so moved by the experience that they went out with joy and courage to share the Good News with others.

Thus, a shattered band of disciples who had followed Jesus during his lifetime was transformed into a community of faith through Jesus' death, resurrection, ascension, and gift of the Spirit. So it was that the church was born, and from that small

but striking beginning some two thousand years ago, the church has grown to a worldwide community numbering nearly two billion people—more than a quarter of the human race.

Jesus Proclaimed as Lord

The gift of the Spirit at Pentecost allowed the early believers to recognize on an even deeper level who Jesus truly was. Jesus' identity as God was of such profound significance that people could only gradually come to any understanding of it. As will be discussed in chapter 13 of this course, it would take several hundred years for the Christian church to come to an "official" explanation of Jesus' identity. But the desire and need to struggle with Jesus' true identity was strong for the earliest believers, and their struggle is reflected in their use of various titles for Jesus. Three titles reflect the core of the early Christian community's post-Resurrection, post-Pentecost understanding of Jesus: *the Christ, the Son of God,* and *Our Lord.*

The church was born at Pentecost because it was then that the disciples were transformed into a community of faith through Jesus' death, resurrection, ascension, and gift of the Spirit.

Photo: **A window in a Catholic church on the Mount of Olives, Jerusalem**

The Christ

Recall from earlier in this course that the title *Christ* is based on the Greek translation of the Hebrew word *messiah*, and it means "anointed one." Because of the roots of *Christ* in Jewish history, it is not surprising that this title was popular among the writers of the Christian Testament. It was initially used as a kind of adjective to describe Jesus after his resurrection, and he was referred to by believers as "Jesus *the* Christ." This wording quickly, and perhaps unfortunately, became shortened to the point that *Christ* became almost a surname, or family name, for Jesus, and he was referred to as "Jesus Christ," a title commonly used for him today.

The Son of God

The title *Son of God* had been used in reference to the kings of the Israelite nation, and it was not unheard of for the Jews to refer to any particularly good man as a son of God. The writers of the Christian Testament, though occasionally using the title in this broad sense, often fundamentally changed the significance of the term by referring to Jesus as *"the* Son of God," indicating his special relationship to the Father. It would be several hundred years, however, before the church would formally proclaim Jesus as one of three divine persons—Father, Son, and Holy Spirit—in the one God. (That proclamation is now known to Christians as the doctrine of the **Trinity**.)

Our Lord

For the early community of believers, no phrase summed up all of Christian faith as fully and beautifully as the proclamation "Jesus is Lord!" The Jewish people avoided speaking the name of God, *Yahweh,* by substituting the word *Lord* and other expressions or words for God's name. Using the word *Lord* for God is common in many parts of the Christian Testament as well. Many times the title is used by Jesus himself in speaking to or about Yahweh, his Father. But rather quickly after Jesus' death and resurrection, believers popularly referred to *Jesus* as "the Lord" or "our Lord."

By giving Jesus this title, the early Christians—particularly the ones who were loyal and faithful Jews—were taking an almost unbelievably radical step. For by calling Jesus "Lord," they were proclaiming a divine identity for Jesus, a unity with Yahweh that was then—and in a real sense, remains—absolutely beyond understanding.

The title *Lord* summed up faith in Jesus so thoroughly that it was used in the closing words of the entire Bible:

> The one who attests these things says: I am indeed coming soon.
>
> Amen; come, Lord Jesus.
>
> May the grace of the Lord Jesus be with you all. Amen. (Revelation 22:20–21, NJB) **10**

For Review

- Why was the first Pentecost a significant happening in the life of the early church? What is the message of the Pentecost story?
- What three titles for Jesus reflect the early Christian community's post-Resurrection, post-Pentecost understanding of him?
- Define the doctrine of the Trinity.
- Why was referring to Jesus as "the Lord" or "our Lord" a radical step for early Christians?

10
List at least five titles or names for Jesus that reflect the meaning he holds for you, or list at least five titles or names for Jesus that might appeal to young people in general.

Insights from Paul's Story

To this point in the course, the focus has been primarily on the Gospel accounts of Jesus' life, death, and resurrection. In those marvelous works of sacred literature, we encounter the Jesus of History recognized by Christians as the Christ of Faith. However, many of the other books of the Christian Testament can offer us insights into the meaning of Jesus and his message. The Acts of the Apostles tells the story of the early church as it begins to proclaim the Good News of Jesus. And in that book we also meet a man whose ideas have powerfully influenced the church's understanding of Jesus throughout history. That man is Saint Paul. Chapter 11 turns to his story.

The early church, spreading out from Jerusalem, proclaimed the Good News of Jesus.
Photo: **A view from Jerusalem**

11

Paul:
Apostle to the Gentiles

MEANWHILE Saul, still breathing threats and murder against the disciples of the Lord, went to the high priest and asked him for letters to the synagogues at Damascus, so that if he found any who belonged to the Way, men or women, he might bring them bound to Jerusalem. Now as he was going along and approaching Damascus, suddenly a light from heaven flashed around him. He fell to the ground and heard a voice saying to him, "Saul, Saul, why do you persecute me?" He asked, "Who are you, Lord?" The reply came, "I am Jesus, whom you are persecuting. But get up and enter the city, and you will be told what you are to do." The men who were traveling with him stood speechless because they heard the voice but saw no one. Saul got up from the ground, and though his eyes were open, he could see nothing; so they led him by the hand and brought him into Damascus. For three days he was without sight, and neither ate nor drank.

Now there was a disciple in Damascus named Ananias. The Lord said to him in a vision, "Ananias." He answered, "Here I am, Lord." The Lord said to him, "Get up and go to the street called Straight, and at the house of Judas look for a man of Tarsus named Saul. At this moment he is praying, and he has seen in a vision a man named Ananias come in and lay his hands on him so that he might regain his sight." . . . So Ananias went and entered the house. He laid his hands on Saul and said, "Brother Saul, the Lord Jesus, who appeared to you on your way here, has sent me so that you may regain your sight and be filled with the Holy Spirit." And immediately something like scales fell from [Saul's] eyes, and his sight was restored. Then he got up and was baptized, and after taking some food, he regained his strength.

For several days he was with the disciples in Damascus, and immediately he began to proclaim Jesus in the synagogues, saying, "He is the Son of God." All who heard him were amazed and said, "Is not this the man who made havoc in Jerusalem among those who invoked [Jesus'] name? And has he not come here for the purpose of bringing them bound before the chief priests?" Saul became increasingly more powerful and confounded the Jews who lived in Damascus by proving that Jesus was the Messiah. (Acts 9:1–22)

A Brief Review

Before going any further, it will be helpful to review what this course has already said about Jesus. After the review, the course will make a major shift in its study of Jesus, his message, and the meaning of both.

From the Jesus of History to the Christ of Faith

The early part of this book focused heavily on the Gospel portrait of the Jesus of History—his cultural and religious background, his preaching and marvelous works, the growing opposition to him by the leaders of his day, and finally, his execution on the cross. The Gospel portrait of Jesus focused more on the impact of his life and ministry in his day than on the historical details surrounding him. That is, the Gospels clearly emerged out of the resurrection faith of the early church—the Christians' conviction that Jesus was Lord. The Gospels were,

---

Paul spread the Gospel message beyond the limits of Judaism and into the Gentile world, in which people worshiped pagan gods.

Photo, facing page: **The ruins of the temple of Apollo, a god of the Greeks and the Romans, in Corinth, Greece, where Paul founded a Christian community**

In Philippi, Paul founded the first Christian congregation on the continent of Europe.
Photo, above: **A stream outside Philippi; Paul may have baptized the first European converts there.**

in part, attempts by the early church to preserve and pass on a portrait of the human Jesus, the first-century Palestinian Jew in whom their God was being fully revealed.

With the discussion of the Resurrection in chapter 10, the focus of this course began to move beyond presenting a portrait of the Jesus of History. The concentration for the remainder of this course will be on the risen Christ of Faith, the Lord. The context for this discussion will be the books of the Christian Testament other than the Gospels, especially the epistles of Paul.

The Resurrection as a Pivotal Event

The event that turns this study from the Jesus of History to the Christ of Faith is the Resurrection. We can see why this is so by tracing the development of the disciples' and the early church's understanding of Jesus' identity.

"Is Not This the Carpenter's Son?"

This course began by focusing on Jesus as an "ordinary" first-century Palestinian Jew, the son of a carpenter, Joseph, and his young wife, Mary. Many of the people of Jesus' day also began their assessment of him with this view. Later, in response to his works and wonders, they would ask, "'Is not this the carpenter's son?'" (Matthew 13:55).

As his ministry grew, Jesus gradually became recognized as a teacher with particular power and insight—so much so that many faithful Jews eventually accepted him as a new prophet sent by Yahweh. Only near the end of Jesus' ministry did some people come to place their hope in him as the Messiah they had been waiting for.

That hope, however, was apparently dashed by Jesus' gruesome execution on the cross. The Jews

Letters in Paul's Day

Letters in Paul's day were quite different from what they are today.

A Different Format

Letters in Paul's day were formal and structured rather than "newsy" and free-flowing like our letters today. Paul's letters followed a consistent pattern:

1. a salutation in three parts—naming the sender (Paul), naming the persons addressed, and then offering a formal greeting
2. a thanksgiving to God for the blessings bestowed upon the receivers of the letter and upon Paul
3. the body of the letter, in which Paul took up various matters related to the Good News, the behavior of the people receiving the letter, and problems in the local church
4. final instructions, at times regarding things unrelated to the body of the letter, such as preparations for an upcoming visit by Paul
5. a closing in two parts—final greetings to various people and a concluding word, often in the form of a prayer

Different Materials and Processes

In Paul's day, letters were ordinarily written on *parchment* (leather prepared for that purpose) or on *papyrus* (thin slices of the papyrus plant glued horizontally onto a backing formed by thin slices placed vertically). A pen was a split reed or a quill, and ink was a composite of materials like carbon and glue or gum. Creating a letter with these materials was such a tedious and lengthy process, and one requiring such skill, that it was normally done by professional scribes or writers.

In the case of his epistles, Paul would first think through what he wanted to convey to his intended audience. Just formulating his complex ideas may have taken weeks of work, especially in the case of a long letter like the one to the Romans. Then his ideas had to be dictated word by word to a scribe or, as was quite common, be expressed in more general terms, with the scribe acting as a kind of editor as well as a secretary.

A scribe could work no more than two or three hours at a

stretch, normally crouched on the ground with a tablet in his left hand and a quill in his right. It took the average scribe about one minute to write just three syllables, which comes to about seventy-two words per hour. (A skilled typist today can type about seventy-two words per *minute*.) The average sheet of papyrus could hold about 140 words. The First Letter of Paul to the Thessalonians, consisting of about 1,500 words, would have required about ten sheets of papyrus and more than twenty hours of work by a scribe. Paul's epistle to the Romans, with over 7,000

words, would have required fifty sheets of papyrus and nearly one hundred hours of writing time!

Weeks, Not Hours

Any one epistle would have taken weeks, not hours, to complete. That fact may partly explain why some of the letters seem choppy, as if written in bits and pieces. The writing process was no doubt interrupted at times, when Paul would gain fresh ideas and insights. And to be sure, no scribe would have been inclined to go back to edit and polish a letter after it was completed!

Letters in Paul's day were sometimes written on parchment, a durable material made from animal skins.
Photo: **Leather stretched on a frame to make parchment**

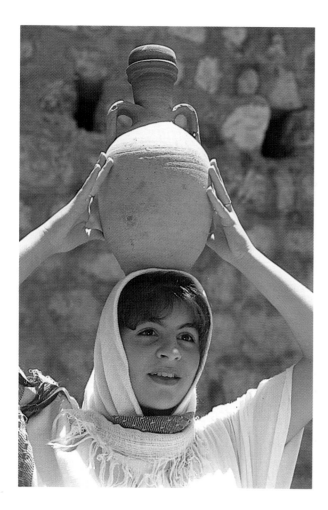

"*the* Son of God," and "Lord"—all titles indicating a profound unity between the Risen Jesus and the people's God, Yahweh. Then, as the church continued to prayerfully reflect on and debate the meaning of Jesus' union with God, it eventually developed the doctrine of the Trinity, which proclaimed Jesus as one of three divine persons in one God.

The development of the church's understanding of Jesus was gradual and occurred in fits and starts rather than in a clearly defined pattern. When summarized in a simplified fashion, the progression of understanding looks like this:

Jesus of Nazareth

↓

Special Teacher

↓

Prophet

↓

Messiah or Christ

↓

Risen Lord

↓

Son of God

↓

Second Person of the Blessed Trinity, equal with God the Father and the Holy Spirit 1

Keeping Things in Perspective

Saint Paul and Others

This chapter and the next will look at the life and missionary work of Saint Paul—one of the most influential figures in Christian history. These two chapters will also briefly examine some of the non-Gospel books of the Christian Testament—

viewed death by crucifixion as a certain sign that the one crucified had been cursed by God. The earthly life and ministry of the Jesus of History appeared to have been a miserable failure.

But Then Came Easter!

With the Resurrection, the followers of Jesus came to the astounding awareness that Jesus was far more than they had ever imagined. They began almost immediately to refer to him as "the Christ,"

Photo: **The early followers of Jesus after the Resurrection were filled with joy.**

Looking at the diagram above, list the understandings of Jesus held by the church, in the order in which those understandings developed. Next, match the following persons with the under-

standing of Jesus they would most likely hold: *a fifth grader, a senior-high student, an atheist, a non-Christian Jew of Jesus' day, the pope, yourself.*

The Acts of the Apostles: "The Gospel of the Holy Spirit"

The Acts of the Apostles is the second part of Luke's two-volume work, the first part being his Gospel.

The First Half of Acts

Acts begins with a description of Jesus' ascension into heaven and moves on to the story of Pentecost. It then describes the early days of the church as the Good News of Jesus spread throughout the Roman Empire. Because Acts always attributes the growth of the church to the workings of the Holy Spirit among the believers, it is often referred to as "the Gospel of the Holy Spirit."

Roughly the first half of the book focuses on the life of the first Christian community living in Jerusalem—the works of various Apostles and disciples there, emerging conflicts between Christians and Jews, and so on—all leading up to the conversion of Paul. (Paul, in the story of his conversion, is referred to by his Jewish name, *Saul*.)

The Second Half of Acts

The second half of Acts is dominated by the personality, preaching, and missionary travels of Paul and his co-workers. The focus shifts from the growth of the church in Jerusalem to Paul's spreading the Gospel message beyond Palestine and to the Gentiles of the Roman world. Acts ends with Paul reaching Rome, which at that time was considered "the ends of the earth." Luke apparently felt that once the Gospel had been preached in Rome, the story was complete.

What Acts Tells Us About Jesus

Beyond the description of Jesus' ascension into heaven, Acts does not tell us anything new about Jesus. What is particularly interesting, however, is that we see how the Apostles began to explain—or better, proclaim—their experience of Jesus to various audiences. Acts includes eighteen discourses, or speeches, by various characters—eight of them by Paul.

Acts is filled with high drama and action-packed, fascinating stories that tell about the spread of the Gospel of Jesus Christ throughout the world.

---

that is, the Acts of the Apostles, the Pauline epistles, the catholic epistles, and the Book of Revelation. The discussion will deal primarily with the writers' treatment of Jesus as the Christ of Faith, even though the prime concern of the writings themselves is more often the growth of the church and the personal spirituality of the early Christians. Remembering the early church's evolving sense of Jesus' identity and the nature of the various writings about him will help keep this discussion in proper perspective.

The Epistles Came First

Because this course began with a Gospel portrait of Jesus, it might seem that the Gospels were the first part of the Christian Testament to be written, followed by the Epistles, which explored the "deeper" issues of Jesus' divinity. But this was not the case. The first Christian writings were letters that Paul wrote to various church communities. In fact, Paul wrote most of his letters about twenty years after the death of Jesus, and that was more than ten years *before* the first Gospel was developed.

Other points about Paul's letters should be noted as well:

A common means of communication: Keep in mind that the Epistles, such as the ones Paul wrote to the churches he established during his missionary work, represent a different kind of writing than the Gospels do. The Gospels were a special literary form that emerged to preserve the story of Jesus and his message, but an **epistle**, or letter, was a common means of communication of the day.

Paul accepted the widespread conviction that the Risen Jesus would soon return in glory "to judge the living and the dead," and that the world as the people knew it would then end. Therefore, Paul would have had no reason to expect his letters to be preserved as part of a treasury of Christian writings. And though the first Christians likely recognized Paul's letters as particularly valuable (because Paul was such a significant figure for their communities), the church would only later recognize his letters as sacred and worthy of the title *Scriptures*.

A focus on Jesus' divinity: In the non-Gospel books of the Christian Testament, the language and images for Jesus that dominate the Gospel portrait are virtually absent. Rather, these books focus on the attempts by the early church to come to terms with the *meaning* of Jesus. This meaning was seen in light of his resurrection and ascension into glory as Lord, as Son of God.

The Epistles (including Paul's letters), for example, offer little about the actual words and actions of Jesus while he walked the roads of Palestine. Also, the Epistles do not retell the story of Jesus, because the writers could *presume* that their readers already knew the story. That is, the writers emphasized Jesus' divinity, confident that their readers were already aware of his humanity.

This difference in the perspective on Jesus is so radical that the unsuspecting reader may believe that the Jesus of History and the Christ of Faith are two different persons. In fact, this misunderstanding was so widespread in the early church that special meetings of church leaders had to be called to clear up all the confusion.

The Church: A Word Now with More to Come

As the early witnesses of the Resurrection gathered to reflect on the meaning of the event and then started to spread the word to others, they gradually formed into communities that are now recognized as the church in its infancy. The final chapter of this course will briefly look at how, over many generations, the church has come to its present understanding of Jesus.

For Review

- How did the ancient Jews view death by crucifixion?
- Which writings of the Christian Testament were produced first?
- In what ways do the Epistles differ from the Gospels?
- Why would Paul not have expected his letters to be preserved?

Getting to Know Paul

Paul is second only to Jesus himself as a central figure in the Christian Testament. Without Paul, early Christianity might have remained little more than a small Jewish sect, and over the course of time, it might well have died away. It was Paul who—through a unique combination of faith, personality, and cultural characteristics—spread the early Gospel proclamation beyond the limits of Judaism and into the Gentile world. The worldwide Christian church that eventually grew from a small seed in first-century Palestine is a lasting monument to Paul's influence and, of course, to the work of God's Spirit in and through Paul. **2**

Sources About Paul

Virtually all that we know of Paul is found in the Christian Testament. The story of his conversion

---

Illustration: **The image we have of Paul from the Christian Testament is of a person unimpressive in physical stature but so on fire with conviction that he could not help but impress people.**

2
Before reading further in this book, read any one of Paul's epistles. Based solely on that epistle, jot down your impressions of who Paul was and what kind of person he was. Then

compare your impressions with what is said about him in this course, briefly noting any similarities and differences.

The Pauline Epistles

Thirteen epistles in the Christian Testament were either written by or attributed to Paul. The practice of claiming an important person as the author of a work, even if that person did not write it, was common in Paul's time. Often the individuals or groups responsible for the writing were disciples of the person named as the author. By attributing the authorship, they showed their respect for that person, and their work gained immediate credibility and stature.

Most scholars agree that Paul wrote seven of the thirteen epistles credited to him:
- Romans
- 1 Corinthians
- 2 Corinthians
- Galatians
- Philippians
- 1 Thessalonians
- Philemon

Three epistles that are credited to Paul were actually written by his followers:
- Colossians
- Ephesians
- 2 Thessalonians

Three other epistles that are attributed to Paul but now believed not to have been written by him are often collectively called the *pastoral epistles*:
- 1 Timothy
- 2 Timothy
- Titus

The word *pastoral* describes the kind of care and guidance that a shepherd might show for a flock. The primary purpose of the pastoral epistles was to offer guidance to two of Paul's co-workers, Timothy and Titus.

(see the quotation at the opening of this chapter) and his career as a missionary is given in the Acts of the Apostles, written by the Evangelist Luke as a continuation of his Gospel. But we learn more about Paul's personality and his understanding of Jesus from Paul's own writings.

At times there are conflicts between what Luke tells us about Paul and what Paul claims about himself. (At this point in the course, such conflicts should no longer be of great surprise or concern.) This chapter is offered as a brief sketch of Paul's distinctive personal and cultural background and relies in part on what Luke tells us about him in the Acts of the Apostles. The next chapter's discussion of Paul's understanding of Jesus is based primarily on what Paul himself wrote.

Both Jew and Roman

Read the description below that Paul gives of himself:

Circumcised on the eighth day, a member of the people of Israel, of the tribe of Benjamin, a Hebrew born of Hebrews; as to the law, a Pharisee; as to zeal, a persecutor of the church; as to righteousness under the law, blameless.

Yet whatever gains I had, these I have come to regard as loss because of Christ. . . . For his sake I have suffered the loss of all things, and I regard them as rubbish, in order that I may gain Christ and be found in him, not having a righteousness of my own that comes from the law, but one that comes through faith in Christ. (Philippians 3:5–9)

Paul of Tarsus

Paul, like Jesus, cannot be understood apart from his roots in Judaism. Paul was born a Jew in Tarsus, the capital city in the Roman region called Cilicia, in Asia Minor, or southern Turkey. Tarsus was a thriving, prosperous city situated at the intersection of major trade routes. Living there, Paul was educated in the philosophies of Greek culture. Although the region he lived in was part of the Roman Empire, Greek culture was still dominant. He learned to speak and write in a style that was familiar to the Greek-speaking people of his time. Paul's family, though devout Jews, had been granted the rare privilege of Roman citizenship. This unique background gave Paul the skills needed to pass on the Gospel message to the Gentile world.

Paul . . . or Saul?

Paul's combination of Jewish faith and Roman citizenship accounts for the fact that he has two names in the Christian Testament. (For example, in the reading at the opening of this chapter, he is referred to not as Paul, but as Saul.) Some have mistakenly claimed that this use of two names is of some religious significance, connected with Paul's conversion experience. The fact is that Paul's Jewish name, the one used within the Jewish community, was *Saul*, while his name in Roman or Greek circles was *Paul*. In the Christian Testament, he is primarily referred to as Paul.

Paul the Jew

Early in this course, some time was devoted to examining the history of the Jews. Later, that historical background became helpful in understanding Jesus. It will come into play now in the attempt to understand Paul.

A Member of the Diaspora

Recall that at the beginning of the Exile in Babylon, about six hundred years before Jesus, many Jews fled the kingdom of Judah to settle in small colonies along the Mediterranean Sea. These people were called the Diaspora, from a word meaning "dispersion." Paul was raised in just such a Jewish colony or neighborhood in Tarsus. In his later missionary work, he would encounter and frequently experience conflicts with colonies of the Diaspora throughout the Roman Empire.

A Pharisee

Paul became an enthusiastic and deeply committed member of the Pharisees, whose sincere but often rigid commitment to the Law made them respected among the common folk but also brought them into serious conflict with Jesus. In Paul's letter to the Philippians, quoted in part on page 218, Paul says that he was such a devout Pharisee that "as to righteousness under the law, [he was] blameless." According to the Acts of the Apostles, Paul had received training in Jewish law and theology under the most respected rabbi in Jerusalem. Paul's writings thoroughly reflect his deep understanding of and commitment to the Jewish Law, as well as his background in Greek philosophy.

A Tent Maker

Despite his impressive educational background, Paul was not a rabbi or a lawyer. He was a tent maker by training, and in that role he probably worked with leather in a variety of ways. (You may remember from the discussion of Jewish daily life in chapter 4 that not all such skills were viewed positively by the people of Paul's day. Tanners of leather, for instance, were looked down upon because they smelled bad.) Even after he began his missionary work—something for which many of the other Apostles were paid—Paul insisted on continuing to earn a living as a tent maker. In part, he did this to avoid the accusation that he was preaching the Gospel message as a way to make money.

A Man on Fire

Virtually nothing is known about what Paul looked like, and some of the hints found in the Christian Testament seem contradictory. In the Acts of the Apostles, for example, Luke suggests that Paul was a captivating speaker. But Paul himself, while acknowledging that his letters may be impressive, suggests a different sense of his speech-making capabilities: "I do not want to seem as though I am trying to frighten you with my letters. For they say, 'His letters are weighty and strong, but his bodily presence is weak, and his speech contemptible'" (2 Corinthians 10:9–10). On other occasions, Paul seems to allude to some illness or physical deformity that afflicts him throughout his ministry. Scholars have suggested that this might be anything from an eye problem to epilepsy. In any case, the basic image we have of Paul is of a person small and unimpressive in physical stature but so on fire with conviction that he cannot help but impress people.

A Man Who Never Knew the Jesus of History

It is important to note that Paul never met the earthly Jesus, the Jesus of History. However, as an educated and devout Pharisee, he may well have heard a great deal about Jesus and his followers and then watched Jesus' popularity grow throughout Palestine. Everything that Paul might have learned about Jesus would have led him to one logical response: despising all that Jesus preached and stood for. Jesus and his message would have been recognized as a direct threat to the Pharisaic Judaism that Paul so deeply treasured.

Paul: Persecutor of Christians

Following the death and resurrection of Jesus, the powerful movement now known as early Christianity started to emerge. Jesus' followers began to proclaim him as the Risen Lord. Conflicts between the Christians and both Jewish and Roman authorities began almost immediately. Not surprisingly, Paul the Pharisee enthusiastically supported any condemnation of the Christians.

At the Feet of Saul

The Acts of the Apostles includes the story of the first Christian to die rather than give up faith in Jesus. He was Stephen, a man who courageously proclaimed his faith when he was brought before

Illustration: **Paul was trained as a tent maker and continued working in that profession throughout his missionary years.**

the Sanhedrin. (For the entire story of Stephen, see Acts 6:8–15; 7:1–60.) The high priest and other members of the Sanhedrin were so enraged at Stephen's testimony that "they dragged him out of the city and began to stone him" (7:58). Stephen confronted his own death with the heroic love first demonstrated by Jesus himself: "While they were stoning Stephen, he prayed, 'Lord Jesus, receive my spirit.' Then he knelt down and cried out in a loud voice, 'Lord, do not hold this sin against them.' When he had said this, he died" (7:59–60).

A chilling detail is noted in the account of Stephen's martyrdom: "The witnesses laid their coats at the feet of a young man named *Saul*" (6:58, emphasis added). Some scholars suggest that Paul may have been attending the execution of Stephen as an official witness and representative of the Sanhedrin. This passage refers to Paul as a young man. Scholars believe that Paul was born in the first decade C.E., perhaps around the year 10. If so, he would have been about twenty years old when Jesus was executed (in about 30 C.E.), slightly older when he watched the stoning of Stephen.

From Persecutor to Apostle

Paul detested the Jewish sect that proclaimed faith in the convicted criminal Jesus. In fact, as revealed in the passage that opens this chapter of the course, Paul was so opposed to the Christian movement that he requested permission from the high priest to arrest any Christians (called followers of "the Way") he might find in Damascus and bring them back to Jerusalem in chains for punishment. It is doubtful, however, that Paul could have been granted such authority by the high priest, who had no authority over Damascus. Luke, who wrote the passage, may have been exaggerating a point to illustrate Paul's deep hatred for Christians. Nevertheless, the fact that such hatred existed in Paul cannot be argued. He was clearly fanatical in his desire to destroy the early church.

Despite the hostility Paul showed toward Jesus' followers, Christians today claim that Paul is one of the most outstanding figures in all of Christian history. He is second only to Jesus in the way he dominates the Christian Testament. What can account for this? The answer lies in the story of what happened to Paul on the road to Damascus.

For Review

- Briefly describe Paul's significance in the development of the Christian church.
- Why would Paul have felt at home among both Jews and Gentiles? Why does he have two names in the Christian Testament?
- What connection can be made between Paul and the Diaspora?
- Describe Paul's initial relationship with the Christian church.

Illustration: **At the stoning of Stephen, the first Christian martyr, "witnesses laid their coats at the feet of a young man named Saul."**

The Damascus Experience

What Happened?

In the passage from the Acts of the Apostles quoted at the beginning of this chapter, Luke tells the dramatic story of Paul's experience on the road to Damascus. In fact, Luke was apparently so impressed by what had happened to Paul that he told the story two more times (see Acts 22:6–16 and 26:12–18), though in those cases Luke portrayed Paul himself as retelling the story. Remember, though, that Luke and Paul do not always agree in their discussions of Paul's life and ministry.

In Paul's Words

Curiously, Paul himself tells us almost nothing about what happened to him on the road to Damascus. The following passage by Paul includes only the briefest mention of the event and then goes on to summarize what he did *after* the event.

When God, who had set me apart before I was born and called me through his grace, was pleased to reveal his Son to me, so that I might proclaim him

among the Gentiles, . . . I went away at once into Arabia, and afterwards I returned to Damascus.

Then after three years I did go up to Jerusalem to visit Cephas [Peter] and stayed with him fifteen days. . . . Then I went into the regions of Syria and Cilicia, and I was still unknown by sight to the churches of Judea that are in Christ; they only heard it said, "The one who formerly was persecuting us is now proclaiming the faith he once tried to destroy." And they glorified God because of me.

Then after fourteen years I went up again to Jerusalem. (Galatians 1:15–24; 2:1) **3**

"Have I Not Seen Jesus?"

Paul offers no further details of his pivotal Damascus experience. Significantly, however, he suggests that he spent years after the experience reflecting on what had happened to him. On some occasions Paul refers very briefly to the event as proof that he deserves full recognition as an Apostle. (To be recognized as an Apostle in the early church, one had to have a personal relationship with Jesus.) In his first letter to the Corinthians, Paul asks, "Have I not seen Jesus our Lord?" (9:1).

What *Truly* Happened?

Scholars have long sought to understand what truly happened to Paul in what is often called "the Damascus event" or "the Damascus experience." Was it strictly an experience in Paul's mind and heart that Luke then expressed through a dramatic story? We cannot say with any certainty. Luke did not write the Acts of the Apostles until approximately fifty years after Paul's experience, so it makes sense to assume that some elaboration of the story took place as it was told over and over again through the years.

Three years after his pivotal Damascus experience, Paul met Peter and the other Apostles in Jerusalem, where Paul had previously persecuted Christians. *Photo:* A street in old Jerusalem

3

In a short paper, compare and contrast Luke's description of Paul's Damascus experience (Acts 9:1–22) with Paul's own description of the event (Galatians 1:15–24; 2:1).

The Catholic Epistles

In addition to the thirteen Pauline epistles (either written by or attributed to Paul) and the Letter to the Hebrews (written by an unknown author), the Christian Testament includes seven writings attributed to Apostles and commonly referred to as letters, or epistles:

- Three are attributed to John.
- Two are attributed to Peter.
- One is attributed to James.
- One is attributed to Jude.

Together, these are referred to as the *catholic epistles*.

For the Whole Church

The word *catholic* means "universal," and it is applied to the writings listed above because they seem intended for the entire, or universal, church rather than for a particular local community. Several of the letters do not have the characteristics of the ordinary letters of the day, and a few of them are so short (see 2 John, 3 John, and Jude) that we may wonder why the church ever decided to include them in the Christian Testament.

In fact, the ancient church was quite reluctant to accept the catholic epistles as part of the Christian Testament. Serious doubts existed about whether they were actually written by the Apostles identified as their authors. Such objections, however, were overcome by the fifth century, and all the letters were accepted as worthy of inclusion in the Bible.

What Do We Learn About Jesus?

For the purposes of this study of Jesus, the catholic epistles are not particularly helpful. A number of them focus on the ethical conduct of believers, warn against false teachers, offer encouragement in light of suffering, and so on. However, the Second Letter of Peter does present a vigorous defense of the belief in the second coming of Jesus, apparently in response to Christians who had become doubtful because of the long delay in Jesus' return. And the letters of John include some beautiful passages in defense of basic teachings about the humanity and divinity of Jesus.

A Profound Encounter with Jesus

We *can* say without question that whatever happened to Paul on the road to Damascus was such a profound encounter with the Risen Christ that it radically changed his life. The experience burned so deeply within him that he spent the next fourteen or more years in prayer, reflection, and study on his own and with other believers, among them the Apostle Peter. Toward the end of this period, Paul began his missionary work, and that ministry ultimately took him to his death in the city of Rome around 62 C.E. There, according to tradition, Paul died the death of a martyr, proclaiming his faith until the end—all in the name of the Risen Jesus, whom he had met on the road to Damascus.

Not an Identity Crisis

Some scholars refer to Paul's Damascus experience as a kind of "identity crisis," bringing to a head a long-standing inner turmoil in which he tried to sort out who he was and what he believed. Many other scholars discount this theory, however, noting that no historical evidence supports it. They observe that if nothing else, Paul seems to have always been *very* sure of himself, whether he was persecuting Christians or recruiting them!

From Conversion to Vocation

Some scholars describe Paul's experience as a conversion. The word *conversion* can be used to describe the point at which someone who had no faith at all comes to believe in God. But if used in this narrow way, the term does not accurately describe what happened to Paul on the road to Damascus. Paul had never doubted Yahweh, and his life reflected a deep and sincere commitment to Judaism. In fact, it was precisely *because* he was so committed to his Jewish faith that he felt compelled to reject Jesus and those who followed Jesus.

The term *conversion* can also be used to describe the experience of someone who has had a radical change in, or deepening of, their attitude toward God and religion. In this sense, Paul certainly experienced a conversion.

Out of this dramatic conversion, Paul discovered his driving sense of vocation. The term *vocation* is based on a Latin word meaning "call." Paul felt himself called by God for a specific and significant purpose—to be a missionary to the Gentile world, to bring the Gospel proclamation of Jesus to all the non-Jews of the Roman Empire.

A Time of Reflection and Growth

As noted earlier, it apparently took Paul a number of years—fourteen or more—to clarify for himself the meaning of Jesus' life, death, and resurrection and to come to a full sense of his own vocation to proclaim the Gospel among the Gentiles. During that time, the many small, scattered communities of the early church were springing up steadily. Paul no doubt spent much time with these communities, learning the story of Jesus and deepening his own convictions about Jesus. It was during those years that the stories and teachings that would eventually become the Gospels were being collected and passed on orally. Paul immersed himself in all of this, thereby growing in the recognition that the message of Jesus was intended for all the world, not just the Jews.

As Paul grew in understanding, he pursued the call from God to be a missionary to the Gentiles. And he did so with deepening passion and a growing sense of urgency. According to Paul, God's final day of judgment was near at hand. There was no time to lose. The decision that people had to make was stunningly clear to Paul: they had to proclaim their faith in the Risen Lord and be saved . . . or reject the Risen Lord and perish.

For Review

- What criterion was required for recognition as an Apostle in the early church? On what grounds did Paul claim to meet that requirement?
- What can be said with certainty regarding Paul's experience on the road to Damascus?
- Define the terms *conversion* and *vocation* and explain their relevance to Paul's Damascus experience.

Many public works projects built under the Roman Empire—such as roads for travel and aqueducts for transporting water—made it possible for Christianity to spread rapidly throughout the empire.

Photo: A Roman aqueduct at Caesarea, which carried water from springs thirteen miles away

Paul's Missionary Work

Paul's story is so rich and exciting that we may want to discuss it at great length. That, however, is not the purpose of this course. What follows is a summary of his missionary work and the writings that emerged from that work. (The map on page 226 will be of help throughout this discussion.) **4**

The Early Years

Paul's experience on the road to Damascus occurred three to five years after the death of Jesus. Shortly after the experience on the road, Paul took up residence in Damascus, where he lived and carried on his ministry for three years. Nothing is known of the effects of his early work there.

From Damascus to Jerusalem to Tarsus

After leaving Damascus, Paul made his way to Jerusalem. This would be the first of three significant trips to the holy city during his ministry. On this trip, he met with Peter (an Apostle and the leader of the whole church) and James (the leader of the Christian community in Jerusalem). This important meeting with Peter and James established that Paul could be recognized as an Apostle along with the founders of the church in Jerusalem. After two weeks, Paul began a mission to Cilicia and Syria, working out of a base in his home city of Tarsus.

On to Antioch, Home of the First "Christians"

At some point Paul arrived in the city of Antioch, the capital of Syria, and worked to help build a Christian community there. In the church of Antioch, the followers of Jesus were first called "Christians." Paul's converts included a large number of Gentiles, and a controversy erupted in connection with this. The Jewish followers of Jesus argued that the Gentiles had to become Jews before they could be baptized into Christianity. Paul and the Gentiles felt strongly that the Gentiles should be baptized *directly* into Christianity. The argument, at times bitter, lasted for several years and became the focus of much of Paul's writing. Paul's strong stand on the side of the Gentiles during this debate was a leading reason that the Christian faith became a worldwide religion rather than remaining a small Jewish sect.

Paul's Missionary Journeys

The Acts of the Apostles describes three main journeys that Paul took in spreading the Gospel message. Known as Paul's "missionary journeys," they spanned more than ten years. The precise details of the journeys are at times unclear. What is very

Paul's missionary travels took him across the Mediterranean Sea.
Photo: **The Mediterranean coast of Galilee**

The Major Cities in Paul's Missionary Work

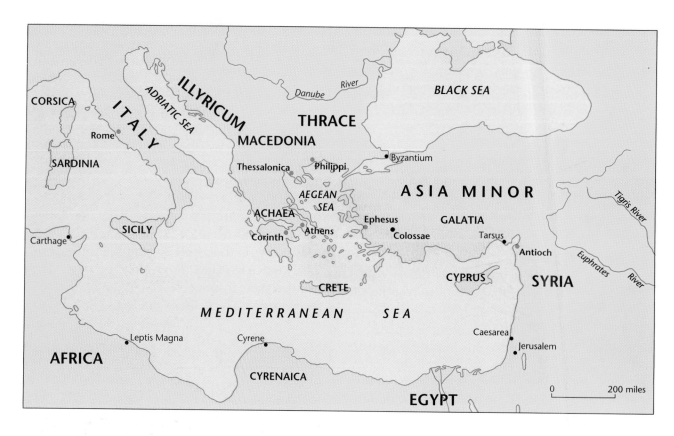

clear, however, is that Paul's travels were anything but easy, as his own description of them illustrates:

Five times I have received from the Jews the forty lashes minus one. Three times I was beaten with rods. Once I received a stoning. Three times I was shipwrecked; for a night and a day I was adrift at sea; on frequent journeys, in danger from rivers, danger from bandits, danger from my own people, danger from Gentiles, danger in the city, danger in the wilderness, danger at sea, danger from false brothers; in toil and hardship, through many a sleepless night, hungry and thirsty, often without food, cold and naked. And, besides other things, I am under daily pressure because of my anxiety for all the churches. (2 Corinthians 11:24–28)

During the following overview of Paul's travels, try to appreciate the lengths to which Paul was willing to go—both in actual miles traveled and in sacrifices endured—to bring the Good News to those who had never met the Lord.

Map: **Antioch**, where Jesus' followers were first called Christians, was the first Christian community to include Gentiles. Paul spent two years at **Ephesus**, a prosperous port city. **Philippi**, on the east-west road of the empire, was the location of the first European Christian community. Paul was well-received by Gentiles in **Thessalonica**, but not by Jews. Rejected by city elders in **Athens**, Paul failed to start a church there. **Corinth**, a major shipping center, was known as a rowdy, vice-ridden city. The capital of the Roman Empire was **Rome**, where Paul was probably beheaded.

The First Journey: To Cyprus and Asia Minor

Paul's first missionary journey took him and his co-workers to the island of Cyprus and then on to several cities in Asia Minor. It is not certain how many of Paul's converts were drawn from Jewish communities and how many came from among the Gentiles. After their stay in Asia Minor, Paul and his co-workers returned to Antioch.

The Jerusalem Council

From Antioch, Paul and two of his co-workers—Barnabas, a Jew by birth, and Titus, a Gentile convert—traveled to Jerusalem to consult with Peter, James, and John. Both groups wanted to make sure that they were all preaching the same Good News. While Paul and his co-workers were in Jerusalem, the controversy over the Gentile converts erupted again when some Jewish converts demanded that Titus be circumcised before being accepted as a "complete" Christian. As the debate continued, a conference was called. It was decided that the mission to the Gentile community could continue *without* demanding that the Gentiles become Jews before being accepted into the church. This conference is known as the *Jerusalem Council.*

A Persistent Tension

Even after the Gentile conversion controversy had been resolved, the tension surrounding it continued for years. At one time it even caused problems regarding the breaking of the bread. Some strict Jewish converts—and at least once, even Peter—refused to share meals with Gentile converts, for fear of breaking the ancient purity laws that bound faithful Jews. As mentioned earlier, this tension surfaces in a number of Paul's epistles.

The Second Journey: Paul's Most Fruitful

On his second—and most significant—missionary journey, Paul founded a number of communities whose names are identified with his letters.

From Galatia to Corinth

Paul was traveling through the region of Galatia when he apparently became ill and had to stop. During his recovery he converted some of his caretakers, and he may have founded the Christian communities to which his letter to the Galatians would later be written. Then he moved on through Asia Minor and into the region of Macedonia, founding churches in the cities of Philippi and Thessalonica. From there he moved on to Athens, Greece, where he failed to found a church, and then on to the city of Corinth, which was also in Greece.

In Corinth

Paul spent about two years in Corinth, and he founded his most famous church there. This was about 51 C.E., roughly twenty years after the death

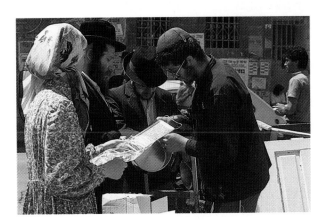

Some strict Jewish converts refused to share meals with Gentile converts for fear of breaking the ancient purity laws that bound faithful Jews.

Photo: In an orthodox part of Jerusalem today, Jews clean their cooking utensils to make sure they are *kosher,* that is, ritually fit for use according to Jewish Law.

The Third Journey: Building upon Past Successes

After a short rest in Antioch, Paul began his third missionary journey. By this time he had already established active communities in Asia Minor, had formed a major center in Corinth, and had begun work in Ephesus. His third journey was intended in part to build upon these past successes.

Most of Paul's third journey focused on further establishing the church in Ephesus, which became the base for his ministry for the next two years. As a meeting place for eastern and western travelers and traders, Ephesus was a significant place for Paul to work from. During this time Paul wrote his important letters to the Corinthians as well as his most famous letter, the one to the church in Rome.

The First Letter to the Corinthians

Paul's first letter to the Corinthians holds strong words for the church there:

It is actually reported that there is sexual immorality among you, and of a kind that is not found even among pagans; for a man is living with his father's wife. And you are arrogant! Should you not rather have mourned, so that he who has done this would have been removed from among you?

For though absent in body, . . . I have already pronounced judgment in the name of the Lord Jesus on the man who has done such a thing. . . . You are to hand this man over to Satan for the destruction of the flesh. (5:1–5)

Paul could be stern when he wanted to be!

Contained in the same letter, however, is Paul's marvelous description of the church as a body in which all members are called to play a vital part (see 12:12–31). (More will be said about this image

of Jesus and fifteen years after Paul's Damascus experience. Paul was probably in Corinth when he wrote the first of his letters that would become part of the Christian Testament—his first letter to the Thessalonians. (This letter is the oldest writing included in the Christian Testament, written some fifteen years before Mark's Gospel.) From Corinth, Paul returned to the city of Antioch with two close friends, Priscilla and Aquila, whose names appear in his letters.

On his journey to Antioch from Corinth, Paul stopped in the important city of Ephesus, on the western coast of Asia Minor, and made some initial contacts there.

Photo: **The ruins of a library in Ephesus, a city known for its grand architecture in Paul's time** in the next chapter of this course.) Also, the letter includes Paul's frequently quoted description of love:

> Love is patient; love is kind; love is not envious or boastful or arrogant or rude. It does not insist on its own way; it is not irritable or resentful; it does not rejoice in wrongdoing, but rejoices in the truth. It bears all things, believes all things, hopes all things, endures all things.
>
> Love never ends. . . . Faith, hope, and love abide, these three; and the greatest of these is love. (13:4–13) **5**

The Second Letter to the Corinthians

Paul later wrote another letter to the community at Corinth. This letter has been lost and is *not* included in the Christian Testament, but apparently it was filled with anguish and anger about the people's behavior. Paul immediately regretted sending it. He feared that the letter was so tough on the Corinthians that he would lose their loyalty to him altogether. Much to his relief, however, the letter met with a positive response in the community.

That letter is sometimes called "the sorrowful letter" or "the letter of tears." We can gain some insight into Paul's tender side from his second letter to the Corinthians, in which he speaks to the people about the sorrowful letter:

> So I made up my mind not to make you another painful visit. For if I cause you pain, who is there to make me glad but the one whom I have pained? And I wrote as I did, so that when I came, I might not suffer pain from those who should have made me rejoice. . . . For I wrote you out of much distress and anguish of heart and with many tears, not to cause you pain, but to let you know the abundant love that I have for you. (2:1–4)

This balance between "tough love" and tenderness is common in Paul's letters.

The Letter to the Church in Rome

Paul eventually returned to Corinth, where he wrote his profound letter to the Christians in Rome. He had not personally founded the church in Rome, but he hoped to visit it and gain the help of those Christians to spread the Gospel message into Spain. Paul's letter to the Romans was the last of his letters to be included in the Christian Testament, although it appears first because it is his longest. It was written, perhaps, in 56 C.E.

The letter to the Romans is considered Paul's masterpiece, and some scholars claim that it is one of the most significant Christian writings. It reflects Paul's lengthy missionary experience, his maturity as an Apostle, and his insightful understanding of the meaning of Christian faith. In this letter, Paul makes his strongest statements regarding the relationship between the Jewish Law and the faith of Christians (a theme explored in the next chapter of this course).

■
Wealthy people had their own private baths for bathing, but common people and travelers like Paul had to go to the public baths.

Photo: **Ruins of the public baths in Corinth**

5
Rewrite Paul's famous description of love (1 Corinthians 13:1–13) in language that would appeal to young people today. Use as few of Paul's original words as possible.

things to come, nor powers, nor height, nor depth, nor anything else in all creation, will be able to separate us from the love of God in Christ Jesus our Lord. (8:31–39)

A Final Trip to Jerusalem

Paul completed his third journey with a trip to Corinth, and from there he went directly to Jerusalem in another effort to demonstrate that Gentiles were full Christians. According to his letter to the Romans (15:30–31), Paul anticipated trouble from the Jews and Jewish Christians in Jerusalem. His fears proved to be justified.

Arrested at the Temple

Upon arriving in Jerusalem, Paul went to the Temple to perform the rites of purification that were expected of Jews. While there, he was mistakenly accused of bringing a Gentile convert into one of the inner courts of the Temple, beyond the barrier that excluded non-Jews. Word of this offense immediately touched off a riot in the city, and Paul was arrested, in part to protect him from the mob. Because of his Roman citizenship, he received good treatment while imprisoned.

An Appeal to Rome

A plot against Paul's life by the Jews was then revealed, and the Romans sent him to the Roman military headquarters in Caesarea to protect him from assassination. The governor kept Paul in prison there for two years to avoid further antagonizing the Jewish authorities. That governor's successor, however, wanted to send Paul back to Jerusalem to face trial. Paul resisted this and, based on his Roman citizenship, appealed to the tribunal of Caesar in Rome.

The letter to the Romans reflects the stunning depth of personal faith that Paul had developed through his life and ministry. Consider these marvelous and energizing words:

If God is for us, who is against us? He who did not withhold his own Son, but gave him up for all of us, will he not with him also give us everything else? . . . Who will separate us from the love of Christ? Will hardship, or distress, or persecution, or famine, or nakedness, or peril, or sword? . . . No, in all these things we are more than conquerors through him who loved us. For I am convinced that neither death, nor life, nor angels, nor rulers, nor things present, nor

Photo: **Paul believed that no misfortune or suffering could separate us from the love of Christ. For Paul, times of suffering were times to become closer to God.**

Rome: The End of the Line

The trip to Rome for the appeal was interrupted by a shipwreck that delayed Paul for three months on the island of Malta. He finally arrived in Rome in 60 C.E., where he was kept under house arrest and awaited trial for two years. It was possibly during this time that a collection of four letters known as the *captivity epistles* were written—the epistles to the Philippians, Philemon, the Colossians, and the Ephesians. Scholars debate which of these letters were actually written from Rome or even by Paul himself.

The Acts of the Apostles ends at this point, with Paul under house arrest in Rome. The concluding lines of Acts serve as a fitting summary of Paul's remarkable career as the Apostle to the Gentiles: "He lived there two whole years at his own expense and welcomed all who came to him, proclaiming the kingdom of God and teaching about the Lord Jesus Christ with all boldness and without hindrance" (28:30–31).

Some early church historians proposed that Paul was then acquitted in Rome and traveled briefly to Spain, only to later be returned to Rome, where he was martyred. Contemporary scholars generally do not accept that claim. It is now commonly held that Paul never left Rome and was eventually executed under the notorious persecutor of the early Christians, the Roman emperor Nero.

As a Roman citizen, he would have been beheaded rather than crucified. The date of Paul's death is widely disputed. Traditional belief is that he died sometime around 67 C.E. A number of scholars, however, suggest a date in the early sixties. Assuming that his birth was around the year 10, Paul would have been in his early to middle fifties when he died.

For Review

- Summarize the controversy regarding the entry of Gentiles into the early church. What decision was made at the Jerusalem Council?
- Why is Paul's letter to the Romans considered his masterpiece? From where was it written? Where does it appear in the Christian Testament and why?
- What false accusation against Paul led to a riot and his arrest in Jerusalem? On what basis did Paul request to be tried in Rome?
- When, where, and how was Paul executed?

Photo, left: **A harbor on the island of Rhodes, where Paul stopped on his last trip to Jerusalem**

Photo, right: **Paul's final destination was Rome, where he lived under house arrest for two years and was eventually martyred.**

The Book of Revelation: Visions of the Ultimate Victory of God in Christ

The Book of Revelation, the last book of the Christian Testament, is without doubt one of the most difficult books to understand in the entire Bible. Traditionally, the authorship of this book has been attributed to John, the writer of the fourth Gospel. He supposedly wrote Revelation while exiled on the island of Patmos, a Roman penal colony. In fact, however, the author of Revelation is never identified, and many characteristics in the writing styles of Revelation and the Gospel of John make it doubtful that the same author wrote both of them. Many scholars today suggest that a disciple of the Evangelist John may have authored Revelation.

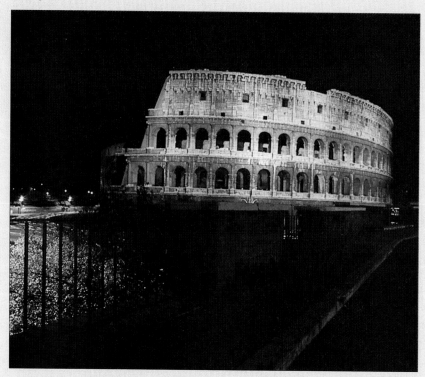

Not to Be Taken Literally

The Book of Revelation is also called the **Apocalypse**, from the Greek word for "revelation." The spiritual visions and strange beasts that fill this book are typical of a kind of writing that was popular at the time the Bible was developing. In our time, some fundamentalist Christian churches tend to interpret Revelation literally. For instance, based on numbers that appear in the book, they may attempt to predict the exact date of the end of the world.

Roman Catholic scholars are unified in the conviction that the Book of Revelation uses mostly symbolic language and cannot, therefore, be interpreted literally. The symbolism is strikingly demonstrated, for instance, when Jesus is portrayed as a lamb with seven horns and seven eyes! Note the meaning behind that image: In the Bible, the number seven signifies perfection. Horns symbolize power, and eyes are a symbol of knowledge. Therefore, this means that the Risen Lord is a being of total power and knowledge. On nearly every page of Revelation we find symbolic numbers, colors, garments, and so on.

The Book of Revelation calls Christians to remain faithful under persecution, trusting that ultimate victory will be accomplished through Jesus.

Photo: The Colosseum in Rome, where early Christians were publicly tortured and executed by Roman authorities

Victory over Satan

Some of the language of the Book of Revelation can seem extremely cruel and brutal. For example, Christian martyrs cry out for revenge against their persecutors, and God is depicted as filled with rage and violent anger against the forces of sin. Scholars suggest that the book may have been written by early Christians as a response to the ruthless persecution of Christians by Roman authorities. It calls Christians to stand firm in the faith and to trust that God will fulfill the promises made in Jesus. Salvation and ultimate victory will finally be accomplished when Jesus comes again in glory at the end of this age and the forces of Satan are destroyed forever.

Ultimately, this message—one of hope, consolation, and courage—continues to make the Book of Revelation valuable for today's believers. Revelation promises that whatever suffering and persecution they may endure, those who dare to believe can be assured that God will be the final victor and they will be saved.

Paul's Epistles in Context

Paul's adventurous, dangerous life—spent in faithfulness to Jesus—gives us a backdrop against which to understand Paul's message. For example:

- Paul, in some of his writings, can seem incredibly harsh and judgmental. We must remember that he may have been writing to an audience that had rejected the Gospel message and had been viciously attacking him.
- Paul often wrote with a sense of urgency and immediacy, demanding that his readers accept Jesus as the Risen Lord *now* or risk eternal damnation. We must remember that the early Christians, and therefore Paul himself, believed that the Risen Jesus was going to return soon to carry out the final judgment of Yahweh.
- And most importantly, Paul focused on Jesus as Lord, Savior, and Son of God, the one whom he had met in a powerful way on the road to Damascus. We must remember that Paul assumed his readers had some knowledge of the Jesus of History. Paul's concern was this: In light of Jesus' death, resurrection, ascension, and exaltation as Lord of the universe, how are believers to understand him?

Chapter 12 turns to Paul's understanding of Jesus as the Christ.

Photo: **A fresco of Saint Paul, from a seventh-century church in Turkey**

12

The Letters of Paul:
Proclaiming Christ Crucified
and Risen

LET the same mind be in you that was in Christ
Jesus,
   who, though he was in the form of God,
      did not regard equality with God
      as something to be exploited,
   but emptied himself,
      taking the form of a slave,
      being born in human likeness.
   And being found in human form,
      he humbled himself,
      and became obedient to the point of death—
      even death on a cross.

   Therefore God also highly exalted him
      and gave him the name
      that is above every name,
   so that at the name of Jesus
      every knee should bend,
      in heaven and on earth and under the earth,
   and every tongue should confess
      that Jesus Christ is Lord,
      to the glory of God the Father.

(Philippians 2:5–11)

An Introductory Overview of Paul's Epistles

- While walking through a shopping mall, Yolanda is approached by a young man who bluntly asks, "Have you been saved? Have you given your life to Jesus?"
- With the remote control in hand, Keith casually clicks from one TV station to another, looking for something worth watching. He comes across a religious program in which a preacher, holding a Bible, challenges members of the audience to come forward and "accept Jesus as your personal

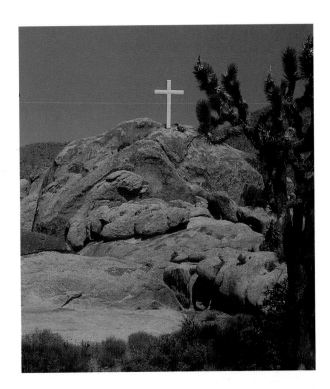

Lord and Savior or suffer eternal damnation!" Keith giggles uncomfortably and quickly changes the channel.

- Jenny is riding in a car with a friend. They pull up behind another car at a stop sign. A bumper sticker on that car reads, "Jesus is the Answer!" Jenny's friend turns to her and jokes, "Okay, but what's the question?"

Scenes like these may be familiar to many of us and may even be a routine part of life. But for many others of us, these situations may be relatively new, and often they can make people uncomfortable.

We could debate whether religious programs should be televised or whether street preachers have the right to impose their views on shoppers. However, more important questions lie behind these Christians' methods: What does it mean to

---

Ephesus, where Paul preached the Gospel and lived for two years, was known for its grand architecture.

Photo, facing page: The ruins of the great amphitheater of Ephesus, which seated 24,000, and the Arcadian street, a magnificent colonnaded avenue

Photo, above: What does it mean to be "saved by Jesus"?

be "saved by Jesus"? In what sense must Christians "accept Jesus as their personal Lord and Savior"? What exactly does Jesus save people from . . . or save them for? **1**

In many of his epistles, Paul attempts to answer these very questions. Biblical scholars admit that for the modern reader, who lives in an extremely different culture than Paul's, the epistles are among the most difficult writings to understand in the entire Bible. This chapter of the course will identify and briefly explore Paul's major themes, the basic ideas that he repeatedly raised in his letters. A general understanding of these themes can make Paul's epistles easier to comprehend and therefore more enjoyable to read.

For Whom? and Why?

One key to understanding Paul's epistles (or any of the Scriptures) is worth repeating: each piece of writing was originally directed to people in a particular place, time, and culture, and was composed in a style suited to the needs of that audience. The more we can understand these factors—audience and purpose—for a given piece of writing, the more accurate will be our understanding.

The Early Christian Communities

Paul, as noted earlier, wrote most of his letters to various small Christian communities that he had founded during his missionary travels. Some of the communities consisted mostly of Gentile believers who were immersed in the Greek worldview and philosophy of their day. Other communities included Jewish converts to Christianity, many of whom were deeply conflicted whenever Paul criticized or even discarded religious beliefs and practices that they had long considered sacred.

Responses to Community Issues

Each of the early Christian communities that Paul wrote to had its own problems, conflicts, and concerns. Several of Paul's epistles were written as *responses* to issues that had emerged within these communities as they grew and developed. In that sense, the epistles are only one side of a two-sided conversation.

Imagine writing a letter to a close friend, offering advice on a tough situation and sharing some of your deepest feelings. Then imagine that a third person, someone who does not know your friend, reads your letter. You will likely feel a great need to further explain yourself, to tell the reader more about your friend so that your letter will make more sense, and so on. We today are in the situation of the third person when reading Paul's letters. We are often forced to read between the lines of the epistles, trying to sort out what was going on in the communities that might have prompted Paul's reactions and insights.

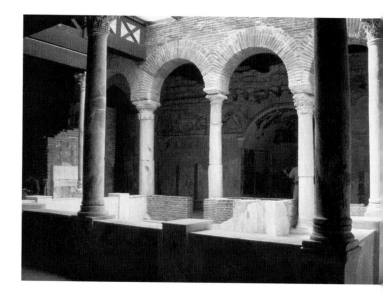

Write a paragraph on what being saved by Jesus means to you, based on your current understanding of Jesus' message.

Photo: **The restored ruins of the interior of a home in Ephesus; Paul might have stayed in a house like this during his time there.**

Paul's Message: Rooted in the Damascus Event

Full of Conviction

To each of his audiences, Paul spoke with a profound passion. It was rooted in his own experience as a faithful Jew who had had his life turned upside down on the road to Damascus. He was on fire with belief in the Risen Jesus—or as Paul often referred to Jesus, "Christ crucified." And Paul's convictions about Jesus did not stop with his belief in Jesus as the Messiah and Lord. Paul was also convinced that Jesus would soon return in glory to conclude the work of salvation and to bring history, as human beings knew it, to an end. For Paul, this was no time to be meek and mild-mannered, no time to mince words.

Showing Deep Faith and Love

Paul knew from personal experience that an encounter with the Risen Jesus could shatter one's past convictions and awaken one to an entirely new way of looking at things. "So if anyone is in Christ," Paul wrote, "there is a new creation: everything old has passed away; see, everything has become new" (2 Corinthians 5:17). He yearned for those who heard and read his words to experience a new way of living. Paul's letters convey the wide range of emotions he experienced in trying to convince people of his message: conviction, anger, impatience, humility, frustration, sorrow, joy. But behind these changing emotions, we see two constant qualities in Paul—a sincere love for the people to whom he preached and an unshakable faith in Jesus Christ.

Paul's Main Themes: Salvation and the Church

Although Paul's writings are generally concerned with conflicts within the communities and with matters involving personal morality and spirituality among the believers, this chapter of the course will focus on Paul's insights into the nature of Jesus and his message. These insights come through in two main themes of Paul's letters:

- Salvation is found in and through Jesus the Christ.
- The church is "the body of Christ."

Paul's experience of the Risen Jesus on the road to Damascus forms the background for these two themes. In that experience, Paul learned profound lessons that greatly influenced his life, ministry, and letters. (For a review of the Damascus event, refer to the passage from the Acts of the Apostles on page 211.)

Justified by Faith

Paul recognized that the God revealed by Jesus always takes the initiative, meets people right where they are, and can change their life on the

---

Photo: **Paul yearned for everyone to experience the new life that he had come to know through his encounter with the Risen Jesus: "There is a new creation: everything old has passed away; see, everything has become new!" (2 Corinthians 5:17)**

spot. According to Paul, it is always God who saves, always God who redeems, always God who reconciles—and God does so through the death and resurrection of Jesus. The following passage from Paul's letter to the Romans makes this point strongly:

> Since we are *justified by faith,* we have peace with God through our Lord Jesus Christ, through whom we have obtained access to this grace in which we stand; and we boast in our hope of sharing the glory of God. . . .
>
> For while we were still weak, at the right time Christ died for the ungodly. Indeed, rarely will anyone die for a righteous person—though perhaps for a good person someone might actually dare to die. But God proves his love for us in that while we still were sinners Christ died for us. Much more surely then, now that we have been *justified by his blood,* will we be *saved through him* from the wrath of God. For if while we were enemies, we were *reconciled to God through the death of his Son,* much more surely, having been *reconciled,* will we be *saved by his life.* (Romans 5:1–10, emphasis added)

In his epistles, Paul uses a number of different expressions for the activity of God in the lives of people—*salvation, redemption, righteousness, justification, reconciliation.* These various terms express slightly different but also closely related concepts. For the sake of simplicity, this course will use *salvation* and *saves* as general terms covering all these concepts from Paul.

Jesus Alive in the Body of Believers

Paul's experience on the way to Damascus would teach him a major lesson about Jesus' presence: The unity between the Risen Jesus and those who believe in him is so strong and so real that persecuting a believer in Jesus automatically means persecuting Jesus. When confronted by the Risen Jesus on the road, Paul asked him, "'Who are you, Lord?'" And the answer shocked Paul: "'I am Jesus, whom you are persecuting'" (Acts 9:5). Over time, Paul grew to realize the incredible implication of that revelation: Jesus is alive *in* the body, or whole group, of believers. Eventually this insight led Paul to his teaching that the church is the body of Christ. With the image of the body of Christ, Paul was saying that the church is the physical presence of the Risen Jesus in the world, just as the human Jesus, in his own day, was the physical presence of Yahweh. **2**

For Review

- In what sense are Paul's letters only one side of a two-sided conversation?
- What issues are most often the main focus of Paul's epistles?
- What are the two main themes of Paul's letters? What experience forms the background for these two themes?
- List the various expressions Paul uses for the activity of God in the lives of people.

The work of missionaries today reminds Christians of Paul's teaching that Jesus is alive in the whole body of believers all over the world.

Photo: A Maryknoll lay missioner, *right,* with villagers in Brazil

2
Paul's writings indicate that a personal encounter with God is possible. In a paragraph, tell about someone—perhaps yourself—who believes he or she has had such an encounter with God.

Focus on John: The Letters of John

The three epistles of John are believed to have been written by the same "school" or community of the Beloved Disciple that was the source of John's Gospel. These letters and that Gospel share a poetic style and a focus on the divinity of Jesus.

The First Letter of John: God Is Love

Perhaps the most well known of John's three epistles is the first one. This letter seems in part to respond to various groups who questioned either the humanity or the divinity of Jesus. It takes the strong stance that Jesus was both God and human.

The letter is most recognized, however, for its striking statement that "God is love" and its powerful claim that people can live out their faith in that God only by loving their brothers and sisters.

Beloved, let us love one another, because love is from God; everyone who loves is born of God and knows God. Whoever does not love does not know God, for God is love. God's love was revealed among us in this way: God sent his only Son into the world so that we might live through him. In this is love, not that we loved God but that he loved us and sent his Son to be the atoning sacrifice for our sins. Beloved, since God loved us so much, we also ought to love one another. No one has ever seen God; if we love one another, God lives in us, and his love is perfected in us. . . .

God is love, and those who abide in love abide in God, and God abides in them. . . . Those who say, "I love God," and hate their brothers or sisters, are liars; for those who do not love a brother or sister whom they have seen, cannot love God whom they have not seen. The commandment we have from him is this: those who love God must love their brothers and sisters also. (4:7–21)

■
Photo: **"God is love, and those who abide in love abide in God, and God abides in them."**

Salvation Through Christ Crucified

Most people in our modern culture, young and old alike, have one of two responses to the question, What does it mean to be saved by Jesus?

- For many people, the notion of being saved means little or nothing, because they have no personal sense of *needing* to be saved from anything or anyone.

- Others respond to the question with an answer based on their past religious training. For example, they might say, "Being saved means having my sins forgiven by God because of Jesus' death on the cross and, therefore, having the chance to make it into heaven when I die." For them, salvation is in the future ("making it into heaven") rather than in their life now, today.

What is most evident from both of these responses is that for many contemporary people, the idea of salvation has no connection with real, everyday life. As will be seen in the following discussion, for Paul, salvation had everything to do with real life.

Salvation and Sin

The concept of sin underlies Paul's notion of salvation and is the key to understanding Paul's writings on salvation. Sin and its effects struck Paul at the core of his identity, both as an individual and as a faithful Jew of his day. For many people of today, though, sin is an old-fashioned notion that is never mentioned in casual conversation and is frequently ignored even in church settings.

For Paul, being saved from sin and its effects was incredibly freeing. For many of us, it seems virtually meaningless. **3**

Sin: Breaking the Rules?

For many Christians today, sin—if it has any meaning at all—is thought of as "breaking the rules," performing an action that in some way makes one a "bad person." In this view, a person commits sins when she or he acts badly, and perhaps she or he is then encouraged to go to confession in order to have those sins forgiven. The impression can be that God is keeping some heavenly tally sheet of people's offenses. Once a person's slate is wiped clean by confession and she or he is "good" again, God finds the person lovable again . . . that is, until she or he commits another sin and the whole process is repeated.

Sin: The Breaking of Relationships

Paul would not have agreed with the notion of sin just described. The entire history of his people, the Jews, centered on an intimate, deeply personal *relationship* with their God, Yahweh.

The story of Adam and Eve: The familiar story of Adam and Eve (see Genesis, chapter 3) was an attempt by the Jews' ancestors to explain how evil entered the world. According to the story, evil had come through the free actions of men and women —represented by Adam and Eve—rather than directly through the will of God. The desire of people to decide for themselves what is right and wrong (to "'be like God, knowing good and evil,'" according to Genesis 3:5) resulted in a break in the relationship between God and the whole human race.

Yahweh's desire for reconciliation: Shortly after the story of Adam and Eve, the focus of the Hebrew Scriptures turns to the relationship between Yahweh and the descendants of Abraham, who shared the human predicament of a broken relationship with the Creator.

3
Without reviewing what was said about sin earlier, write a brief definition of sin as you currently understand it. Then, using your definition of sin, explain what it means to be saved from sin.

All throughout the rest of the Hebrew Scriptures, Yahweh never stops trying to heal that separation, never stops yearning to bring reconciliation to the relationship. At times, Yahweh reaches out to the people through an event in their history—such as through the Exodus or the covenant of Sinai. At other times, Yahweh communicates with the Jews through a particular individual—Abraham, Moses, David, or a prophet. God enters the people's lives very personally, cares about them, and sustains them in their trials.

The gift of the Law: As a guide to help the people remain reconciled with their God, Yahweh provided the Law, the core of which was the Ten Commandments. For the Jews, the Law was not just a cold list of do's and don'ts. Instead, it was a marvelous gift, a sign of Yahweh's abiding love for them. In the good times, the people responded faithfully to Yahweh and carried out both the spirit and the letter of the Law. In the bad times, the people tried to make it on their own, apart from their relationship with Yahweh. They turned their backs on Yahweh and abandoned the Law, Yahweh's gift to them. When they did that, every part of their lives would start to fall apart, relationships would be shattered, and war and other conflicts would threaten their very existence as a people.

All of these events taught the Jews about the essence of sin. Sin was not a breaking of rigid rules. Sin was a *rupturing of relationships,* first between the Jews and Yahweh and then inevitably among themselves as a people. In his teachings about salvation, Paul drew upon his Jewish understanding of sin and reconciliation with God and then went beyond it. With his acceptance of Jesus as the Christ, Paul realized that through Jesus, God is calling all people, not only Jews, into reconciliation.

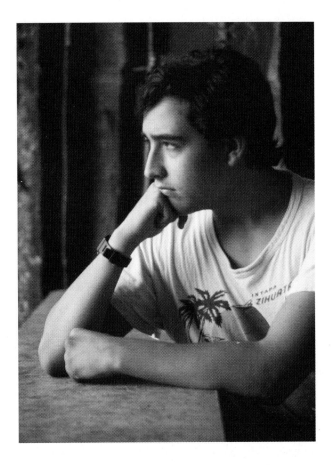

This theme—the need for reconciliation between God and people—dominates Paul's writings. (Paul also writes about Jesus as "the new Adam," who reverses the effects of the first Adam's sin. This chapter will offer more on that later.)

Salvation, the Law, and Love

Trying to Earn God's Favor

Over time, some Jews came to a false understanding of the Law and its role in their relationship with Yahweh. They started to believe that they could win God's favor by following every letter of the Law rigidly. If they just did everything

Photo: **Sin has more to do with rupturing relationships than with breaking rules.**

that the Law dictated (and the Law eventually grew to include over six hundred specific rules!), then Yahweh would *have* to take care of them. A "good person," according to these Jews, was one who kept the Law "perfectly." The trap that such Jews fell into was this: they started to think that a person could *earn* the favor of God, that people were in some way in control of their own salvation.

Such notions about the Law were held especially by the Pharisees, with whom Jesus frequently came into conflict. (Note that not all Jews in Jesus' time held such legalistic attitudes toward the Law. The fact that Jesus' own popularity grew throughout his ministry was a sign that many Jews agreed with him and did not share the legalism of the Pharisees.) As a Pharisee, Paul would likely have shared a rigid view of the Law prior to his experiencing the Risen Jesus. Paul confirms this in his letter to the church in Philippi: "as to righteousness under the law, [I was] blameless" (Philippians 3:6). 4

Paul's New View of the Law

It is easy to lose perspective. Paul's encounter on the road to Damascus changed his rigid view of the Law. In fact, after that encounter, Paul often had strong words for Jews who had allowed the Law to take the place of God in their hearts. In his writings Paul stressed that people could easily lose sight of the proper and healthy role of the Law (that is, the Law as a guide for proper relationships with God and one another). Following the letter of the Law could become an end in itself, rather than a means to an end.

Love, not the Law, is the goal. With the new eyes of faith in Jesus, Paul saw that the Jewish Law, like all other laws, had its limits. Laws can provide order in a society and help to meet the minimum

needs of people, but they cannot meet deeper human needs, such as companionship, purpose, or happiness. Only love can meet such needs, and laws—even good ones—cannot force people to love one another.

The spirit of the Law, as it was given to the Jews by God, had love as its basis. Paul came to see that after individuals had matured enough to perceive the purposes and deeper meaning of the Law, they no longer needed to follow the exact letter of the Law. In other words, they began to live so in tune with God that they achieved the Law's intentions

4
Write a pro or con response to the following statement: *Most people who follow religious laws do so either to win God's favor or to avoid God's anger. That is, they act religiously out of greed or fear.*

Photo: **Only love can meet human needs for companionship, purpose, and happiness. Laws cannot force people to meet those needs.**

without even really thinking about it. (See Galatians 3:23–29 for some of Paul's insight.) This understanding of the Law by Paul reflects Jesus' own teaching that the person who loves fully already fulfills everything written in the Law.

Paul strongly preached that the Law had become a barrier, rather than a bridge, between many Jews and God. Paul knew that only love could be such a bridge, and in the crucified Jesus he recognized such love.

In other words, through the Law I am dead to the Law, so that now I can live for God. I have been crucified with Christ, and I live now not with my own life but with the life of Christ who lives in me. The life I now live in this body I live in faith: faith in the Son of God who loved me and who sacrificed himself for my sake. I cannot bring myself to give up God's gift: if the Law can justify us, there is no point in the death of Christ. (Galatians 2:19–21, JB) **5**

The Effects of Sin Are Everywhere

By the time of Jesus, many Jews were convinced that the people's relationship with Yahweh was in deep trouble, if not totally cut off. They were, after all, a mostly poor people who had been dominated by more powerful nations, first the Greeks and then the Romans. The effects of sin were everywhere—poverty, hatred, conflicts among the Jews themselves, foreign domination, hopelessness. Only people like the Pharisees felt "safe" and therefore believed that they did not need to be saved. The majority of the people yearned to be freed from their condition, and they looked for one who could lead them—the Messiah.

This course has attempted to show how Jesus filled the hungers of many of the Jewish people.

Through his life, actions, and message—and especially through his death and resurrection—Jesus restored hope to those who believed in him, and he gave their life an entirely new sense of meaning and purpose. When taking the perspective of the Jews of that time, we might begin to gain some sense of what it meant for them to be saved by Jesus. And in light of that, we might begin to understand the meaning of Paul's preaching to the people of that time. But what about us? What meaning might salvation have for the people of our time and culture?

For Review

- Define the Jewish understanding of sin and briefly summarize its origins.
- What false understanding of the Law emerged over time among some Jews, and which Jewish group most strongly held this understanding?
- Summarize Paul's new understanding of the Law in light of his faith in Jesus.

5
List the qualities a person needs to possess before she or he can live a good moral life without worrying about laws.

Photo: **The need for salvation is a need to be freed from that which imprisons or oppresses our spirit.**

Salvation Today

Salvation and Contemporary Culture

Today, understanding and appreciating Paul's notion of salvation hinges on examining our own experience of sin. This, in turn, can lead to recognizing a personal and communal need to be freed from sin and its effects.

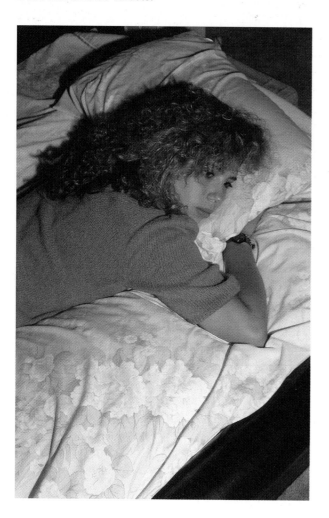

In Search of Meaning

Do the following situations sound familiar to you?

- Nina, a ninth-grade girl, is considered attractive by most people in her school. She has a good figure and can afford all the latest fashions. Many of her friends envy her and tell her so. Yet Nina hates her body, her face, her wardrobe. She jumps from one diet to another, even though she is not overweight. She spends hours working on her makeup, hair, and clothes. She is never satisfied with who she is because she constantly compares herself with magazine models. Nina dreams of someday liking the person she sees in the mirror, but she is haunted by the real possibility that she never will.

- Justin has a terrific sense of humor. He gets good grades, though he has some trouble with algebra. He participates in several sports, and he may well be a starter on the basketball team when he's a senior. But Justin is uncomfortable around girls unless they're "just friends." Sometimes he wonders if he's gay, and the thought terrifies him. Though he seems to have a lot going for him, he spends a lot of his private time worrying.

- Geralyn is a loner. Her family life is a mess. She's extremely shy, and she has no friends. Some people do feel sorry for her and try to be friendly, but she is so unsure of herself and so awkward with others that she's hard to be around or talk to.

- Chad's life looks like it is headed toward disaster. Since the breakup of his parents' marriage when he was in the seventh grade, he has been confused and trying to find a group of friends he can feel at home with. A year ago he started to hang around with kids who are into drugs, and he began to use crack. His entire life now seems

Photo: **What will fill our hearts with peace when we are all alone with our thoughts, our fears, our dreams?**

caught up in getting crack and smoking it. A school counselor tried to confront Chad about this, but Chad just denied that he has a problem. The situation looks hopeless.

Looking for Something More

You may know young people like Nina, Justin, Geralyn, and Chad. You may even see yourself in them. What will make them truly happy with who they are? What will fill their heart with peace when they are all alone with their thoughts, their fears, and their dreams? They are looking for a deeper sense of meaning. They are looking for something—or someone—who can save them from the pain in their life. 6

Imagine what Nina, Justin, Geralyn, and Chad will be like when they become adults. They may be like many of the adults you know now. They may be successful by every common standard of our society—earn a good income, own a nice home, have a happy family—yet they may still be anxious, lonely, frustrated, even depressed. Or they may live on the edges of society . . . or not really live at all. Why? Because they may still be looking for something deeper in life, something that can make sense of who they are in the world, something that can bring them a feeling of peace and satisfaction, something to sustain them when they are alone with their thoughts and their dreams. They may be looking for meaning. They may be looking to be saved from the pain in their life.

A World in Need of Salvation

The world sometimes seems dominated by obvious evil and the clear effects of sin—war, poverty, sexism, racism. When we allow ourselves to see

---

Photo: **Contemporary society offers "salvation in a shopping mall." But true salvation answers life's deeper questions about meaning and purpose, and it cannot be purchased.**

6
List the names of the four young people just described. Next to each name, put a check mark for every person you can think of who has a similar difficulty.

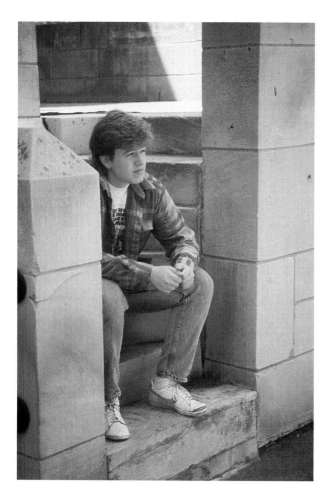

redemption the way Paul understood it. On a personal or private level, we often experience the effects of sin as deep loneliness, a lack of hope, or a desperate yearning for meaning. Such feelings are not necessarily caused by our own sin, though at times, of course, that may be the case. **7**

Now Is the Time

The Christian conviction is that Jesus and his message can speak to the part of our heart that we often hide from others, even our closest friends. Sometimes we even hide that part of our heart from ourselves—by filling our life with sounds and activities and relationships, even with studies! Yet when we are all alone in bed at night, when the radio has been turned off and darkness fills the room, we find ourselves wondering: What does it all mean? How do I fit in? Will anyone ever love me enough to fill the hole in my heart? When we ask such questions, we are dealing with the guts of life and with the central questions of faith. When we have the courage to ask such questions, we are ready to listen to Paul's words about Jesus.

Jesus According to Paul: "The New Adam"

Paul tells the readers of his letters that Jesus shattered the limitations of the Law and brought true reconciliation between humanity and God. According to Paul, Jesus accomplished this by offering his own life in an act of total and selfless love.

The Jewish story of the fall of Adam and Eve was mentioned earlier. Paul explains the role of Jesus in terms of that ancient story. Just as sin had corrupted humanity through the actions of Adam and Eve, so God's saving grace was released through

and acknowledge such evil, we begin to realize that truly, the world is as much in need of salvation today as it was at the time of Jesus.

We experience the effects of sin simply by living in this world as social beings who are affected by the actions of others. However, without dismissing the need to understand the social nature of sin, we must look at the personal level of sin in our life if we are to understand the meaning of salvation and

---

Photo: **By living in this world as social beings, we are affected by the sinful actions of others. We may experience deep loneliness, a lack of hope, or a desperate yearning for meaning.**

7
Write a pro or con response to this statement: *If it were not for the bad influences of society and culture, most people would naturally do what is right and good for themselves and others.*

Jesus' life, death, and resurrection. Therefore, Paul characterizes Jesus as "the new Adam."

The One Who Made Things Right Again

According to Paul, Jesus—as the new Adam—was the one in whom human history would have a new beginning.

If, because of the one man's [Adam's] trespass, death exercised dominion through that one, much more surely will those who receive the abundance of grace and the free gift of righteousness exercise dominion in life through the one man, Jesus Christ.

Therefore just as one man's trespass led to condemnation for all, so one man's act of righteousness leads to justification and life for all. For just as by the one man's disobedience the many were made sinners, so by the one man's obedience the many will be made righteous. (Romans 5:17–19)

Jesus had made things right again with God. Paul preached often about this "righteousness"—this being right with God—that had been restored by the death and resurrection of Jesus.

The One Who Was Perfectly Obedient

The opening reading for this chapter of the course, which is from chapter 2 of Paul's letter to the Philippians, reflects Paul's theme of Jesus as the new Adam. Verses 6–11 of the passage are part of a hymn that was likely used in worship services by the early Christians. In the hymn, Jesus is referred to as the one "who, though he was in the form of God," was willing to give up his equality with God

Photo: **Paul preached that "righteousness" had been restored by the death and resurrection of Jesus so humanity could experience the joy of once again "being right with God."**

Fools for Christ

Paul realized that his message of how Jesus fulfills God's plan for saving humanity would not make sense to nonbelievers. In fact, the meaning of the cross—that life can spring from suffering and death—could be appreciated only by those who had already experienced the power of God in Jesus.

The message about the cross is foolishness to those who are perishing, but to us who are being saved it is the power of God. . . . For Jews demand signs and Greeks desire wisdom, but we proclaim Christ crucified, a stumbling block to Jews and foolishness to Gentiles, but to those who are the called, both Jews and Greeks, Christ the power of God and the wisdom of God. For God's foolishness is wiser than human wisdom, and God's weakness is stronger than human strength. (1 Corinthians 1:18–25) **8**

Saved from Sin, Freed to Be Fully Human

The preceding quotation, from Paul's first letter to the Corinthians, gives us a clue as to what salvation in Jesus can mean for Christians today. In his life, death, and resurrection, Jesus saves us from all the false values and misleading messages of contemporary society. Jesus saves us from society's distorted claims about what it means to be fully human, and he frees us to be fully human in the way God intends us to be—as persons who have God at the center of our life and who love our neighbors as we love ourselves.

The culture of our time tries to sell us a particular vision of what human happiness requires—a sexy body, expensive possessions, freedom from commitment, power over others. When we see all of these things through the eyes of Jesus, we recognize how shallow they are, how little happiness

to become one with humanity, humbling himself even to the point of death on the cross.

In the Genesis story of the Fall, the attitude held by Adam and Eve is the exact opposite of the attitude held by Jesus. The serpent in the garden tempts Adam and Eve by saying that at the moment they eat the fruit of the forbidden tree, "'[their] eyes will be opened, and [they] will be *like God,* knowing good and evil'" (Genesis 3:5, emphasis added). Adam and Eve yearn to be like God, whereas Jesus freely takes on the burdens of being human. Because of their sin, Adam and Eve are banished from the garden, whereas because of Jesus' perfect obedience,

> God . . . highly exalted [Jesus]
> and gave him the name
> that is above every name,
>
> . . . .
>
> and every tongue should confess
> that Jesus Christ is Lord.
>
> (Philippians 2:9–11)

Phony values

Illustration: **Paul cautioned his followers that the meaning of the cross—that life can come from suffering and death—is considered "foolishness" according to the standards of human wisdom.**

8
Jot down your reflections on Paul's message to the Corinthians about the foolishness of the cross.

they really bring to those who have them. In this way, salvation is as much about freeing us for life as it is about saving us from sin. **9**

Asking the Right Questions

To live fully, we need to ask the right questions, because the questions we ask automatically dictate where we go in search of answers. Recall from the beginning of this chapter, the example of the bumper sticker "Jesus is the Answer!" and the response it evoked: "Okay, but what's the question?" Both the bumper sticker and the response miss the point of what Jesus and his message are all about. The fact is, Jesus is the Questioner.

When people look at the life and message of Jesus, they must confront the questions on which happiness in life truly hinges. And the questions Jesus asks are drastically different from those posed by popular culture.

- Popular culture asks, How can I acquire a lot of wealth? Jesus asks, How can I share what I have with others?
- Popular culture asks, How can I become popular? Jesus asks, How can I love others, even my enemies?
- Popular culture asks, How can I gain power over others? Jesus asks, How can I serve those in need?

The questions asked by Jesus lead us to drastically different answers than do the questions posed by our culture. And, as Christians believe, Jesus' questions lead us to the right answers—that is, to truth.

■ *Photos, left and right:* **Jesus prompts us to ask the question, How can I share my time or talents with others?**

9
In a paragraph, explain the meaning of this statement: *Salvation is as much about being freed for life as it is about being saved from sin.*

We Cannot Do It on Our Own

Confronting the questions posed by Jesus is an awesome experience. Clearly, living according to Jesus' values and principles means living contrary to many of the values of modern society. We may be inclined to think that there is no way we can handle that challenge, and Paul would respond, quite bluntly, "You're right. You cannot handle it on your own. But all things are possible with God."

Salvation Is God's Work

Paul constantly reminded the people of his time—and reminds contemporary Christians as well—that people cannot save themselves. The idea of being able to save oneself was what Paul recognized as the primary danger of blind adherence to the Law. People of his time who followed the letter of the Law were tempted to believe that they were earning salvation, that *they* were the source of righteousness. Many modern Christians seem to have the same misunderstanding. They think that if they fulfill their religious obligations, like regularly attending Mass and even giving to charity, then they have paid their religious dues, are assured of going to heaven (being saved), and can get on with "more important things" in their life.

Paul's message is that salvation is a gift from God—that is, an act of grace. Grace is the total and unconditional love of God that is always offered to people regardless of anything they do or fail to do. People cannot turn the flow of God's love on and off as if they control some magical faucet. People are not in charge; God is. All people can do is recognize when grace is offered, accept it as a gift and thank God for it, and celebrate the gift with others. In other words, salvation is God's

work and a gift of God's grace, not the result of human effort. This is what Paul means by the expression *justification* (being saved) *by faith.*

Loving Actions Are the Fruits of a New Heart

If salvation is a gift, then some people might say that our religious observances and loving actions are meaningless, without value, or not necessary. They might ask, Why pray and serve others if these actions do not necessarily bring about salvation? Such people would be missing the point of Paul's—and Jesus'—message. Paul, as noted in the last chapter of this course, spoke eloquently about the value and power of love. But he did not say that

---

Illustration: **Salvation is an act of God's grace, freely given by God and not something we can earn. We cannot turn the flow of God's love on and off by our actions.**

Christians should love others as a way of earning God's love in return. Rather, loving action is the response that flows from accepting God's gift of grace. When people experience the overwhelming and gracious love of God for them, they are given a "new heart," a new power to reach out to others in care and concern. If a person accepts the gift of God's love, she or he inevitably will act differently, more lovingly, toward others.

Loving actions, then, are an essential part of God's work of salvation. If people do not love one another as Jesus commanded, this is a sign that they have not truly accepted the gift of grace and allowed it to transform the way they live. Salvation is not magic. It requires a personal response.

The Christian Is "a New Creation"

When people recognize their dependence upon God through faith in Jesus, says Paul, they discover the power to live in accordance with the Dream and values of Jesus. The source of their power is not themselves but, rather, the spirit of the Risen Jesus working within them. As Paul puts it, "I live now not with my own life but with the life of Christ who lives in me. . . . I live in faith: faith in the Son of God who loved me and who sacrificed himself for my sake" (Galatians 2:20, JB). According to Paul's thinking, the Christian is "a new creation" (2 Corinthians 5:17), guided by the right questions in search of the right answers. And the answers we find in Jesus are as freeing and full of life today as they were two thousand years ago.

Faith as More than "Me and God"

Paul had another major insight into the way faith in Jesus the Christ gets lived out in the life of the Christian: If salvation consisted only of turning one's life over to God through a personal commitment to Jesus, a person could do that in total isolation from others. But Paul understood that the Christian's salvation in Christ is intimately connected to his or her relationship with the community of believers—the church. The connection is so real, in fact, that Paul could call the church "the body of Christ."

For Review

- List some ways in which we experience the effects of sin, both on a social and on a personal level.
- What is the basic meaning of the term *righteousness*?
- What does Jesus save us from? What does he save us for? How is salvation an act of grace?
- In what sense is loving action a response?
- What is the source of the power to love in accordance with Jesus' Dream?

Photo: **All people can experience the overwhelming and gracious love of God and thereby be given a "new heart."**

The Church as the Body of Christ

Earlier in this course, the point was made that people are bound by their experience to think in terms of time and space. When discussing the ascension of Jesus, for example, people tend to think of Jesus as going "up there" to heaven, somewhere in space, removed from us. Paul might have had the same temptation were it not for his encounter with the Risen Jesus on the road to Damascus.

When Jesus identified himself with those Christians whom Paul had been persecuting, Paul's old way of looking at reality was shattered. With startling clarity, Paul saw that Jesus was alive in the midst of Paul's own experience. Through the image of the church as the body of Christ, Paul has challenged Christians throughout the ages to live out this vision.

Building upon Jesus' Own Words

A central theme of Jesus' preaching was that people live out the Gospel message not just by accepting Jesus but by living as he lived. In a familiar passage describing the final judgment (see Matthew 25:31–46), Jesus tells his followers that "'just as you did [a compassionate deed for] one of the least of these who are members of my family, you did it [for] me'" (verse 40). In other words, Jesus saw a direct connection between faith in him and the commitment to serve the needs of others.

When Paul speaks of the church as the body of Christ, however, he seems to be describing an even more intimate connection between the Risen Jesus and the believing community. The church is now called to be the concrete, visible presence of the

Risen Jesus in the world, just as Jesus, when he himself walked the earth, was the visible manifestation of God. The role of Christians has been expressed this way:

We are the hands of Christ.
　Where we work, he works.
We are the feet of Christ.
　Where we go, he goes.
We are the heart of Christ.
　When we love, he loves.
Where we are, Christ is.

Each Member Vital to the Whole

At times Paul takes the image of the body to an almost humorous extreme to demonstrate the value of each individual member in the church:

The body does not consist of one member but of many. If the foot would say, "Because I am not a hand, I do not belong to the body," that would not

Photo: **We are the hands of Christ. Where we work, he works.**

make it any less a part of the body. . . . If the whole body were an eye, where would the hearing be? If the whole body were hearing, where would the sense of smell be? But as it is, God arranged the members in the body, each one of them, as he chose. . . .

Now you are the body of Christ and individually members of it. (1 Corinthians 12:14–27)

In a similar way, Paul writes of the unique contributions that each member can make to the life of the body as a whole:

Now there are varieties of gifts, but the same Spirit; and there are varieties of services, but the same Lord; and there are varieties of activities, but it is the same God who activates all of them in everyone. To each is given the manifestation of the Spirit for the common good. . . . All these are activated by one and the same Spirit, who allots to each one individually just as the Spirit chooses. (1 Corinthians 12:4–11)

Though Paul briefly mentions the notion of the body of Christ in several epistles, his longest reflections on the theme appear in his first letter to the Corinthians (particularly chapter 12 of that letter). Recall that the Corinthians were a community

with many problems, including a great deal of bickering and divisiveness between individuals and groups. Paul's preaching on the church as the one body of Christ would have held particular importance for such a community. **10**

Jesus: The Head of the Body

Paul distinctly says that although the church is the body of Christ in the world, it does not function apart from God. Paul emphasizes that Jesus is the "head" of the body (Ephesians 5:23), the one "in charge," the one whose vision and message must guide the workings of the body.

Paul's vision of the unity of Christians as the body of Christ, with Jesus as the head, is beautifully summarized in his letter to the Ephesians:

I . . . the prisoner in the Lord, beg you to lead a life worthy of the calling to which you have been called, with all humility and gentleness, with patience, bearing with one another in love, making every effort to maintain the unity of the Spirit in the bond of peace. There is one body and one Spirit, . . . one Lord, one faith, one baptism, one God and Father of all, who is above all and through all and in all.

. . . The gifts [Christ] gave were that some would be apostles, some prophets, some evangelists, some pastors and teachers, to equip the saints for the work of ministry, for building up the body of Christ. . . . We must no longer be children, tossed to and fro and blown about by every wind of doctrine, by people's trickery. . . . But speaking the truth in love, we must grow up in every way into him who is the head, into Christ, from whom the whole body, joined and knit together by every ligament with which it is equipped, as each part is working properly, promotes the body's growth in building itself up in love. (4:1–16)

■

Photo: **Paul taught that all people have their own unique gifts, or talents, but that all of these gifts can build up the body of Christ as a whole.**

10
List other images that express the same reality about the church that Paul's image of the human body does. Pick your favorite image from your list and expand on why you think it works.

Guidelines for a Healthy Body

Paul often spoke of community problems and moral issues out of his strong sense of the church as the body of Christ. Whenever members of a community were in conflict with one another, Paul saw the body of Christ in pain. Whenever members of a community worked and prayed together as one, the body was healthy and strong and able to carry on its mission.

Paul's understanding of Christian morality rests on the following basic principle: Christians live out their relationship with Jesus by living well in community with one another. In Paul's letter to the Romans, Paul describes in perhaps idealistic but uplifting terms what behaviors and attitudes are required if Christians are to live out the Dream of Jesus:

Let love be genuine; hate what is evil, hold fast to what is good; love one another with mutual affection; outdo one another in showing honor. Do not lag in zeal, be ardent in spirit, serve the Lord. Rejoice in hope, be patient in suffering, persevere in prayer. Contribute to the needs of the saints; extend hospitality to strangers.

Bless those who persecute you; bless and do not curse them. Rejoice with those who rejoice, weep with those who weep. Live in harmony with one another; do not be haughty, but associate with the

Illustration: **As members of the body of Christ, we are connected with people on every continent of the earth.**

lowly; do not claim to be wiser than you are. Do not repay anyone evil for evil, but take thought for what is noble in the sight of all. If it is possible, so far as it depends on you, live peaceably with all. Beloved, never avenge yourselves. . . . No, "if your enemies are hungry, feed them; if they are thirsty, give them something to drink. . . ." Do not be overcome by evil, but overcome evil with good. (12:9–21) **11**

The Contributions of Paul: A Second Look

Chapter 11 of this course made several claims about Paul's importance in the history of Christianity:

- that he "is second only to Jesus himself as a central figure in the Christian Testament"
- that he "is one of the most outstanding figures in all of Christian history"
- that "without Paul, early Christianity may have remained little more than a small Jewish sect, and over the course of time, it might well have died out"
- that "it was Paul who—through a unique combination of faith, personality, and cultural characteristics—spread the early Gospel proclamation beyond the limits of Judaism"
- and finally, that "the worldwide Christian church that eventually grew from a small seed in first-century Palestine is a lasting monument to Paul's influence and, of course, to the work of God's Spirit in and through him"

At first, these statements may have seemed to be exaggerations, an attempt to paint an impressive portrait of Paul. Hopefully, the discussion in the previous chapter and this chapter has shown the truthfulness of the claims and confirmed the uniqueness of Paul and his influence in Christian history. But in many ways, Paul's influence is a great testimony to the workings of the Spirit in the church. Only the Spirit could transform someone like Paul, who initially hated Christians so much that he hunted them down for persecution, into such a powerful example of Christian faith and hope.

For Review

- Complete this sentence: *Just as Jesus on earth was the visible manifestation of God, so the church is* _____.
- With what imagery does Paul explain the value of each member of the church? Illustrate your answer with an example.
- What does Paul mean when he describes Jesus as the head of the body?
- What is the basic principle behind Paul's understanding of Christian morality?

11
Paul's letter to the Romans describes several requirements for Christians. Select the ten behaviors or attitudes that you feel are most important. In a short essay, explain your selections, using language that your friends could relate to.

Photo: In Paul's understanding of morality, Christians live out their relationship with Jesus by living well in community with one another.

Throughout history, various interpretations of Paul's notion of the church as the body of Christ have become popular. Here are two interpretations:

The Perfect Body

Quite commonly, the church has been understood as "the perfect body." With this image, the church is seen as a kind of idealized society in which all the members know, accept, and fulfill their various roles; God's will is always followed; and peace reigns. In other words, the church is seen as the reflection of the resurrected body of Jesus, which has been cleansed of all human imperfection. This interpretation would suggest that if the church suffers at any time, it is because the world beyond the church has been corrupted by evil and sin.

The image of the church as the perfect body was in part the product of the classical Greek culture. The Greeks idealized the human body, almost worshiped it, and this attitude was reflected in much of their art, particularly their sculpture. Not surprisingly, therefore, the converted Greeks applied the

ideal of the perfect body to the church as the body of Christ.

The image of the perfect body has as much appeal today as it did in the early church. We still tend to idealize that which is strong and healthy and reject that which is weak and sickly.

The Broken Body of Jesus

In recent years, some theologians and biblical scholars have suggested that the idealized image of the church as a perfect body is misleading. Personal experience, first of all,

teaches us that the church—whether our local parishes or the worldwide community of faith—is hardly perfect. It is a community of people who frequently make mistakes, who are subject to all human weaknesses, and who are in constant need of forgiveness and healing. The church is not subject only to the sin of people outside the community. Rather, the church itself is a community of sinners in constant need of reconciliation.

The church has come to recognize that humanity is in a constant struggle for survival in the midst of often horrifying pain. In this century alone, tens of millions of people have suffered and died as victims of war, disease, racism, poverty, and starvation. Theologians and biblical scholars suggest that if Jesus is to be seen in the world today, he will be recognized in his brokenness, his pain, his suffering. It is not the glorified Risen Jesus we see reflected in the world; rather, it is the face of the crucified Jesus we see in the newspaper headlines and TV news.

The church, too, is more properly understood as the

Photo: **Jesus is seen in the world today in pain and suffering as well as in joy and happiness.**

broken body of Jesus than as the perfect one. This does not mean that the church is powerless to help its own members or to bring healing to the world. On the contrary, Paul would tell us, it is precisely in acknowledging our weakness and turning to God that we find a power beyond comprehension. If we believe in our own invincibility, our own power, we will arrogantly believe we do not need God. It is in confronting our own weakness that we are forced to turn to the Source of all power and healing. Here is how Paul expressed it:

> Three times I appealed to the Lord [to relieve me of my pain], but he said to me, "My grace is sufficient for you, for power is made perfect in weakness." So, I will boast all the more gladly of my weaknesses, so that the power of Christ may dwell with me. Therefore I am content with weaknesses, insults, hardships, persecutions, and calamities, for the sake of Christ; for whenever I am weak, then I am strong. (2 Corinthians 12:8–10)

The History of the Church's Teachings About Jesus

With the conclusion of this course drawing near, it is time to reflect on how the church through its history has carried on the mission begun by Paul and the other Apostles. The primary concern of chapter 13 will be the way in which the church's understanding of Jesus has been passed on from one generation of Christians to the next.

Throughout the discussion of Jesus in this course, the words, teachings, and issues that are commonly associated with Jesus in contemporary religious education have rarely been mentioned. For example, little has been said regarding the doctrines, or official church teachings, about Jesus: teachings about the **Incarnation** (that God became flesh in Jesus), Jesus' relationship to God the Father and the Holy Spirit in the Trinity, the fact that Christians claim Jesus to be "true God from true God, . . . one in Being with the Father," and so on.

The reason that a full discussion of these matters has been delayed is that they can be reasonably presented and understood only in the context of the church and its history. These matters could not be effectively discussed within a study of the Christian Testament, simply because they do not even appear in those sacred writings—at least not in the same sense and with the terminology they have today. The official teachings of the church have developed over hundreds of years of reflection on Jesus' life, death, and resurrection. Chapter 13 offers a brief discussion of that development.

Photo: **The Via Egnatia, near Philippi, the principal road connecting the Roman Empire; Paul would have traveled this road in his tireless effort to proclaim Christ crucified and risen.**

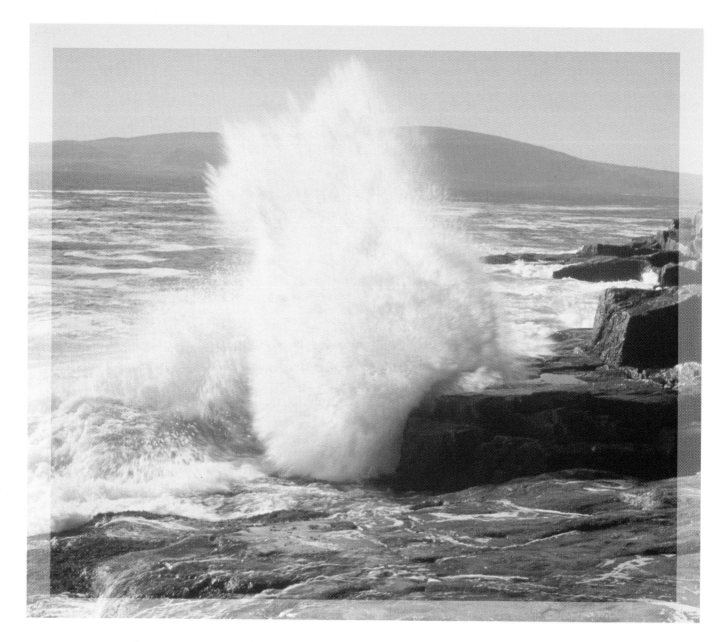

13

Good News from Age to Age:
The Church's Understanding
of Jesus Christ

THEY [the members of the early church] devoted themselves to the apostles' teaching and fellowship, to the breaking of bread and the prayers.

Awe came upon everyone, because many wonders and signs were being done by the apostles. All who believed were together and had all things in common; they would sell their possessions and goods and distribute the proceeds to all, as any had need. Day by day, as they spent much time together in the temple, they broke bread at home and ate their food with glad and generous hearts, praising God and having the goodwill of all the people. And day by day the Lord added to their number those who were being saved. (Acts 2:42–47)

The Church's History

The above passage from the Acts of the Apostles tells us a number of important things about what the Christian church, in essence, is all about. First, we learn that the **church** is a *community of persons who have come to some personal recognition of the Risen Jesus in their life.* That is, they have experienced the transforming power of Jesus' message about a God whose love is never-ending and unconditional. The church as a *community of believers* forms when these individuals, moved and transformed by their experience of Jesus, gather with others to share and celebrate and deepen their awareness of Jesus' message. We learn from Acts how they express themselves as a community:

- by recalling their past experiences of Jesus and the Apostles' teachings about him
- by committing themselves to care for one another so that everyone's needs are met
- by celebrating Jesus' risen and living presence among them through signs and symbols such as

the "breaking of the bread," known as the Eucharist
- by going out as a renewed people to share the Good News with others

These experiences in the first Christian communities set the stage for the gradual development of the church's understanding of Jesus Christ. This chapter will pick up where the Christian Testament leaves off and trace the development, in very general strokes, of the church's long and complex journey throughout history.

A Difficult Journey

One cannot adequately understand the history of the church's thinking and teaching about Jesus without at least some sense of the history of the church itself. Just as the early community of faith gradually grew in its understanding of Jesus following his death and resurrection, so too has the church gone through constant change, growth, and development from its early days until now.

Moving Out into the World

What was initially a small, loose sect of Jews in Palestine gradually spread out into the world. This meant coming in contact with, and being affected by, diverse cultures and peoples, some of them quite different from what Jesus and the Apostles were accustomed to. The difficulties encountered by Paul as he went about spreading the Good News were but a preview of what the church would encounter as it moved into the second century. The early Christians soon felt the need to ensure some sense of integrity, cohesiveness, and stability as a community of believers in the midst of all this diversity. For that reason, the church gradually placed more and more emphasis upon maintaining

Photo, facing page: **The church's understanding of Jesus has developed with the challenges of each age, like a coastline gradually transformed over time.**

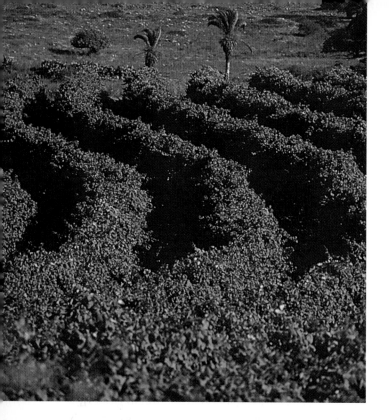

certain traditions, preserving right teachings, evolving lines of authority, developing various roles for church leaders, and so on. All of this was necessary if the church was to survive in a world that was, especially in the first three centuries of the church's existence, very hostile toward it. **1**

Under the Guidance of the Spirit

Any review of the church's understanding of Jesus through history must constantly affirm a central conviction about the church held by Christians. That is, Christians believe that their history as a church has been guided by the presence of God's Spirit, who Jesus promised would lead them to all truth (John 16:7–15). As discussed in the previous chapter, Paul expressed this reality by calling the church the "body of Christ," or the visible manifestation of the Risen Jesus in the world today. Therefore, while the church is made up of free people capable of making many mistakes, it is also

a community that is profoundly graced and loved by God.

Over its long history, some leaders and other members of the church occasionally—though perhaps unavoidably—seemed to lose touch with the church's central mission and purpose. There have, no doubt, been times when Christians have lived contrary to the Gospel of Jesus, when their faith has been deeply affected by superstition, misunderstanding, or poor leadership. But through it all the church has survived. It has done so primarily because of the deep and constant faith of so many of its members—people influenced, guided, and supported by the ever-present Spirit of God.

It's Not Over Yet

The development of the church as well as the development of its understanding of Jesus, continues to this day. For instance, the church must still struggle with balancing the need for unity while respecting a healthy diversity. This is one sure sign that the church's development is not over yet. In fact, struggling for such a balance may be more necessary today than ever before in the church's history. For instance, the experiences of the world's oppressed peoples are a growing influence on church teachings. When such developments affect the church's understanding of Jesus and his message, they often radically affect nearly every facet of the church's life as a community of faith. They do so because the church's understanding of Jesus is always at the center of its identity.

The effect of a new insight into Jesus and his message on the church is similar to that of throwing a stone into a calm pool of water. A new insight will strike with various degrees of intensity, but it will always result in a ripple effect of steadily

Going out into the world to spread the Good News reminded the early Christians of going into a vineyard to reap a plentiful harvest.
Photo: **A vineyard in Israel**

1
Respond in writing to this opinion: *Belonging to the church was important when Christians were threatened by their society. But today Christians can stay faithful to Jesus even without the church.*

expanding changes. For example, a new insight may change the ways in which the community of faith expresses its beliefs or the manner in which it celebrates its sacramental life as a community. Christians might also learn new ways of bringing the healing touch of Jesus and his message into a wounded world, such as by participating in the efforts of human rights organizations like Amnesty International or Habitat for Humanity.

In the midst of change, the constant challenge for members of the church is to more fully attune

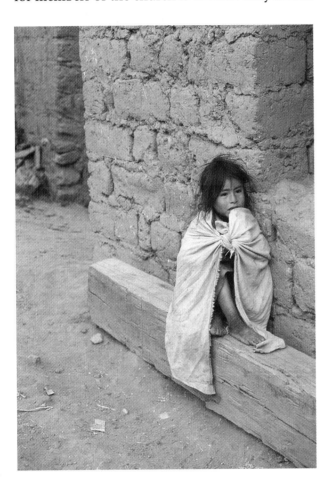

themselves to the Jesus of the Gospels, who is the compass and the foundation for understanding their identity as Christians and as the church.

Did Jesus Intend to Found a Church?

Before moving into a discussion of the church's evolving understanding of Jesus throughout history, an important question must first be addressed: Did Jesus ever intend to form a community of faith at all, much less one like the church as we know it today?

What If He Did?

If Jesus did intend to found a church, then it would seem that he wanted his followers to discover him and preserve his teaching in union with one another. This would imply a need for believers to gather with other Christians or, to use more familiar language, to "join a church."

If Jesus did not intend to found a church, then it would seem that individuals have a perfect right to "do their own thing" regarding how or whether they respond to Jesus. In other words, an individual's response would not need to be determined, governed, or subject to evaluation by a broader community of people.

What Do the Scriptures Tell Us?

The question of Jesus' intentions regarding the establishment of a church is a complex one, and a lengthy discussion of various arguments regarding that question is beyond the scope of this course. The Scriptures shed some light on the issue:

• If Jesus ever directly preached or implied the concept of a "church," he would likely not have had in mind the kind of structured institution

Increasingly, the experiences of today's oppressed peoples influence church teachings and understandings about Jesus.

Photo: **A child in a city in Peru, where poverty and hunger are a way of life for many people** that is a part of Christians' understanding and experience of the church today, because *his* experience just did not include that structure.

- Nevertheless, many of the Gospel images imply that Jesus' followers shared some kind of communal experience. Parables like those of the shepherd and his flock (John 10:11–18) and the vine and the branches (John 15:1–10) reinforce the imagery of a community nurtured by Jesus. The Gospels' many sayings about the Kingdom convey a similar picture.
- The moral or ethical teachings of Jesus also show a real concern for the communal nature of our actions (Matthew 5:23; 7:3–5).
- Jesus' relationship with and training of the Apostles seems to indicate an ongoing role for them as the foundation of some sort of gathering for those who believed in and followed Jesus.

In the Hands of Jesus' Followers

From most indications, then, it seems that Jesus did intend for some kind of community of believers to continue following his death—though perhaps he did not plan for an organized religious community like the church in its current form. (In fact, many scholars believe that Jesus intended only to renew and revitalize the *Jewish* community, not to create or develop an entirely new community.) It was up to the early followers of Jesus themselves, always under the guidance of the spirit of Jesus, to give the initial community its form and direction. As noted earlier, the church's structure and the way it presents its message about Jesus are inevitably affected by the cultures and times in which the church finds itself. Each generation of Christians has been faced with the challenge of building upon the foundation set by the early church and finding the best ways to convey the

message of Christ, given the circumstances and needs of the current time and place.

The question of whether Jesus intended to found a church goes beyond the scope of this course. Perhaps the most important point to remember here is that Jesus did send the Spirit to be with his followers in the midst of their struggle to live out and proclaim the Good News.

Two Persistent Tensions in the Church's Thinking

To comprehend the historical developments in the church's understanding of Jesus, we also need an awareness of two persistent and related tensions in the church's thinking throughout its history:

Illustration: **In this parable, Jesus alludes to a community nurtured by himself: "I am the vine, you are the branches. Those who abide in me and I in them bear much fruit." (John 15:5)**

Balancing Jesus' Humanity and Divinity

The church has struggled to find some balance in its treatment of the Jesus of History (the historical figure of first-century Palestine) and the Christ of Faith (the Risen Lord). The danger always exists that in emphasizing one dimension of Jesus over the other, an accurate understanding of Jesus can get confused. In a brief review of church history, this tension of overemphasizing either Jesus' humanity or his divinity will be recognized again and again.

Balancing the Intellectual and the Emotional

A related tension exists between an intellectual, academic approach to understanding Jesus and a more emotional approach, which is often reflected in popular piety. Again, the challenge here is to find proper balance, not choosing one perspective at the expense of the other. The church's understanding of Jesus can and should respond to both the emotional and the intellectual needs of the believer.

The tension between emphasizing either the Jesus of History or the Christ of Faith and the tension between emphasizing either the intellectual or the emotional dimensions of Christian faith are both understandable and even healthy realities in the church. Perhaps one of the surest signs of the working Spirit within the community of faith is that anytime the church seems to be losing its sense of balance in these matters, something happens—the rise of a religious movement or the emergence of a great Christian thinker, for example—to restore a proper perspective.

Throughout the following discussion occasional reference is made to these twin tensions and to the ways in which the Spirit keeps bringing the church back into balance. **2**

For Review

- Briefly, how did the early church form?
- What do Christians believe has been the guiding force behind the church's journey through history?
- What importance does the question of whether Jesus intended to found a church have for individual Christians? Briefly summarize the evidence supporting the claim that Jesus intended to found some kind of continuing community.
- Name the persistent tensions in the church's historical struggle to understand Jesus and his message.

2
In a paragraph, describe some area of your life in which you have had to struggle for balance—for instance, in working out the tension between your schoolwork and your involvement in other activities. What helped you find the right balance?

Photo: Jesus sent the Holy Spirit to be with his followers in the midst of their struggle to live out and proclaim the Good News.

Understanding Jesus in the Early Centuries

In the Beginning: What Was Going On?

A number of significant things were happening in the early church as it began its search for a full understanding of Jesus. It is particularly important to remember the following points:

The early Christians believed the Risen Jesus would come again soon. Following the death, resurrection, and ascension of Jesus, and the gift of the Spirit at Pentecost, Paul began to interpret for the church the significance of the Jesus of History as the Christ of Faith. At the time of Paul's ministry, Christians believed that the Risen Jesus would return soon, certainly in their lifetime, to complete the work of his Father.

The four Gospels were written to preserve and pass on the story and message of Jesus. Only when it became evident that Jesus was not returning soon did the early Christians realize the need for preserving the life and message of Jesus in some written form. It was out of that need that the four Gospels emerged.

Tensions increased between Christians and Jews. As the proclamation about Jesus took root in small Christian communities throughout the Roman Empire, tension steadily deepened between Christians and Jews. The Gospel was first proclaimed to Jews, and the Jerusalem Council's decision that Gentile converts to Christianity did not have to first convert to Judaism represented a major turning point, even a breaking point, in the relationship between Christians and Jews. Around the year 70 C.E., the Romans destroyed the Jewish Temple and the Jews were then forced to use the synagogues as their central gathering places. As tensions between Christians and Jews increased, Jewish Christians were banned from the synagogues, and the break between Christianity and Judaism was virtually complete.

The canon of the Hebrew Scriptures was set. In a related development, around the year 90 C.E., Jewish leaders made a final decision about the canon, that is, which books were to be officially recognized as the Hebrew Scriptures, the Jewish Bible. This was done partly to ensure that the writings then emerging in the Christian community—that is, the letters of Paul and others, as well as the Gospels—could not be included in the Jewish Bible. From that point until this day, Judaism survived largely because of its faithful commitment to the Hebrew Scriptures and to synagogue worship. Christianity, after its initial break from Judaism, began its own fascinating journey through history.

From Proclamation to Explanation

As the church moved into the second century, and away from the influence of Judaism, one of the most significant steps in the development of its understanding of Jesus took place. This was the switch from the joyous *proclaiming* of the Good News that is typical of the Epistles and the Gospels to an *explaining* of Jesus and his message.

A New Way of Thinking

By the end of the second century, theologians trained in Greek philosophy of the time dominated the church's thinking. These theologians tried to translate the experiences of the Apostles and earliest Christian communities into a language and mind-set that made sense to themselves and suited their audiences. These men—today referred to as the *Fathers of the church*—tried to re-evaluate the Christian Testament in terms of their own way of thinking about and understanding the world.

This move toward a Greek philosophical approach seems to have been a reasonable, even a necessary, step to take if people from various cultures were to understand Jesus at all. Some church historians suggest that it is *only* because of this development that the church was able to survive as it spread beyond its birthplace in Palestine. At the same time, other historians feel that this development often conflicted with, if not totally contradicted, authentic Christianity and that, if taken to an extreme, it represented a departure from the true message and meaning of Jesus.

From the Concrete to the Abstract

What eventually resulted from the influence of Greek thought was that many Christians stopped talking about the basic but moving Gospel proclamation of "Jesus is Lord!" and began talking about Jesus in more technical and complex terms. Words like *God-man, substance, person, nature,* and hotly debated definitions of each word entered into discussions about Jesus and his identity. These were Greek philosophical terms of the time, and their use amounted to a major shift in the church's way of thinking about Jesus—a shift from a concrete, tangible, and somewhat simple approach to a more abstract, complex, and technical approach. For many people, Jesus and his message became a mystery to be explained rather than a relationship and vision to be lived. In addition to the joyous proclamation of the Gospels, a whole new language began to develop; for example, the church began to

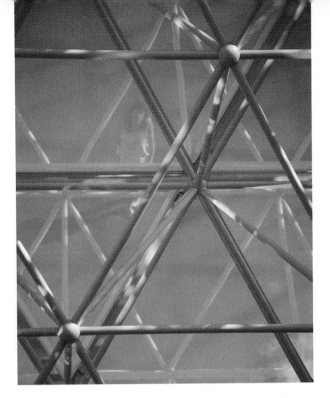

try to explain more than proclaim Jesus, describing him as "one person with two natures sharing one substance." **3**

The Great Christological Heresies and Councils

The shift in the church's way of viewing, understanding, and discussing Jesus invited all kinds of problems and arguments. Three major *heresies,* or false teachings, arose out of the debates. Each one of these heresies resulted in the calling of a church *council,* or official gathering of church leaders, to try to respond to the false teachings and clarify the church's statement of who Jesus is.

Jesus:
More than Human, Less than Divine?

About the year 300 C.E., a priest named Arius made a daring pronouncement. Arius taught that Jesus was not one with God, as the early church

---

Photo: Influenced by Greek thought, the church underwent a shift in its approach to understanding Jesus. It moved from a concrete, tangible, and somewhat simple approach to one that was more abstract, complex, and technical.

3
List what you think are the dangers or implications of viewing Jesus and his message as a mystery to be explained rather than as a relationship and vision to be lived.

claimed him to be. Rather, Arius saw Jesus as a special creature of God, a being of a very high order created by God at a particular point in time. In other words, he viewed Jesus as more than human but less than divine. This teaching led to the calling of the first *ecumenical,* or worldwide, council of the church: the First Council of Nicaea, in the year 325. This council solemnly declared that in Jesus, God had truly appeared on earth in the person of God's own Son.

The **Nicene Creed,** the profession of faith that is commonly recited in eucharistic celebrations, was first drawn up by this council. This creed, on page 267, articulates the church's belief about Jesus.

The Jesus of History and the Christ of Faith: Two Different Beings?

About the year 400 C.E., a theory was proposed that the divine person who was acknowledged as "one in being with the Father" and the man Jesus of Nazareth, who had walked the face of the earth, were in fact two different persons rather than one and the same. This was an attempt by some to

Illustration: **The bishops who debated the Arian heresy at the Council of Nicaea in 325 C.E. came from a variety of cultures and regions of the spreading Christian world.**

The Nicene Creed

Out of the debates about Jesus at the First Council of Nicaea evolved one of the great creeds of the church. A *creed* is an official statement of belief issued by the church, which attempts to find words to express realities that are truly beyond words. The Nicene Creed was initially drawn up by the First Council of Nicaea in the year 325 C.E. and then later reaffirmed by a council convened in Constantinople in 381. Since the seventh century it has been officially known as the *Nicene-Constantinopolitan Creed,* but this is often shortened in common usage to simply the *Nicene Creed.*

This creed is often recited by the community of faith—both Roman and Eastern Orthodox Catholics and members of all the major Protestant denominations—during liturgies. Unfortunately, this central statement of belief is often said too quickly and without much thought by many worshipers. Here you are asked to read the creed slowly, reflectively, even prayerfully. As you do so, recall the hundreds of years of church history, the numerous arguments and discussions by devout Christians, and the profound expressions of faith and prayer that led to its development. Recall as well not only the historical situation that gave birth to this statement of the faith but also the portrait of Jesus that has been presented in this course. In doing so, you will recognize in this creed the basic Gospel proclamation of Jesus and also the effects of the history of the church as it tried to come to terms with the man and his message.

We believe in one God,
the Father, the Almighty,
maker of heaven and earth,
of all that is seen and unseen.

We believe in one Lord, Jesus Christ,
the only Son of God,
eternally begotten of the Father,
God from God, Light from Light,
true God from true God,
begotten, not made, one in Being with the Father.
Through him all things were made.
For us men and for our salvation
he came down from heaven:
by the power of the Holy Spirit
he was born of the Virgin Mary, and became man.

For our sake he was crucified under Pontius Pilate;
he suffered, died, and was buried.
On the third day he rose again
in fulfillment of the Scriptures;
he ascended into heaven
and is seated at the right hand of the Father.
He will come again in glory to judge the living and the dead,
and his kingdom will have no end.

We believe in the Holy Spirit, the Lord, the giver of life,
who proceeds from the Father and the Son.
With the Father and the Son he is worshiped and glorified.
He has spoken through the Prophets.
We believe in one holy catholic and apostolic Church.
We acknowledge one baptism for the forgiveness of sins.
We look for the resurrection of the dead,
and the life of the world to come. Amen.

uphold a false and unbiblical notion of God's "purity." That is, they wanted to establish a complete separation between divinity and humanity. Their notion of God's purity was threatened by an understanding of Jesus as both human and divine.

At this time, a debate also flared up about the mother of Jesus, Mary, and her role in God's plan of salvation. One side argued that Mary could not be given the title "Mother of God" because, among other reasons, a human mother could not be said to give birth to a divine being who already existed from eternity. The other side argued that if Jesus were truly to be recognized as both God and human and yet one person, then Mary could rightly be called "Mother of God," because she gave birth to the Jesus of History.

In response to these disagreements, the Council of Ephesus was convened in 431. This council proclaimed that despite the differences between his divine and human natures, there is but one person in Jesus. The council also formally and officially gave Mary the title "Mother of God," though this title was more of an attempt to make a statement about Jesus than an attempt to describe the nature of Mary herself.

Jesus: Only Pretending to Be Human?

At about the same time, another group of devout people proposed that Jesus possessed a divine nature only, and that despite all the apparent indications of his humanity while on earth, he was not truly a human person. Jesus, according to this belief, only played the role of a human person; he only acted human for our benefit. In the year 451, the Council of Chalcedon was called to deal with this heresy. This council solemnly declared that Jesus was not only divine but also fully human. 4

A Decisive Time for the Church

In many ways, the first five to six centuries of the church's history were some of its toughest and most exciting. It was during this early period that critical decisions had to be made about what Christians believed and did not believe about Jesus. Though other church councils have dealt with the identity of Jesus, the three councils of Nicaea, Ephesus, and Chalcedon—often referred to as "the Great Christological Councils"—were by far the most formative.

- The Council of Nicaea defended Jesus' divinity as the Christ.
- The Council of Ephesus defended his unity as both God and man.
- The Council of Chalcedon defended his full humanity.

These conclusions about Jesus literally laid the foundation of the church's understanding of Jesus. In effect, these conclusions set the parameters for nearly all future discussions of Jesus by Christians, making the later discussions more like elaborations upon these earlier teachings rather than whole new teachings about Jesus.

For Review

- What significant things were happening in the early church about the time it began searching for a full understanding of Jesus?
- What role did the Fathers of the church play?
- Identify the three Great Christological Councils and briefly explain what each council decided about Jesus' identity.
- Why did the church officially name Mary as "Mother of God"?

4
Which, if any, of the three christological heresies dealt with by the early church do you think might still exist today? Write a comment expressing your thoughts.

Understanding Jesus in the Middle Ages

The Rise of Scholasticism

The influence of Greek philosophy on the church's understanding of Jesus continued through the centuries and reached its peak in the Middle Ages with the rise of **Scholasticism.** This was a form of philosophy based heavily on the concepts of the Greek philosopher Aristotle, and it relied to a great extent on order and logic. As a philosophy, or way of understanding reality, it has endured to this day. Its primary advocate in the church was Saint Thomas Aquinas (1224–1274), almost without question the greatest and most influential theologian in the entire history of the church.

An Emphasis on Order

Scholastic philosophy, as applied to Christian faith by Thomas and others, became the basis for the thinking and teaching employed by the church for nearly seven hundred years. It was the approach used in the religious education of many of today's adult Catholics, especially those who were formally taught in either Catholic schools or parish religious education programs before the 1970s.

The Scholastic approach involves an extremely ordered and organized approach to reality. Just as the adoption of Greek ways of thinking early in the church's history may have saved the church from disappearing altogether, so Scholastic theology broadened and therefore strengthened the church's understanding of Jesus. As the foundation of Catholic teaching for centuries, particularly in seminaries and universities, this approach has no doubt strengthened the faith of many millions of Christians.

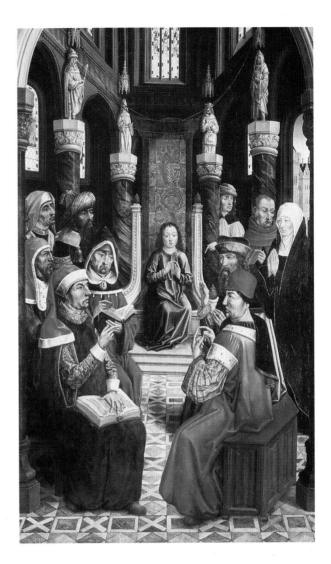

A Limitation of Scholasticism

A problem with a Scholastic approach to understanding Jesus—at least when it is taken to an extreme—is that Jesus and his message can seem like cold and impersonal realities, more like logical problems to be solved than the Good News of a loving God. People can become so bound up with

---

The understanding of Jesus in the Middle Ages was affected by the orderly, logical approach of Scholastic philosophy.

Photo: **A fifteenth-century painting, "Christ Among the Doctors," depicts the story of Jesus as a child in the Temple.**

learning and remembering philosophical arguments in defense of church teachings about Jesus that they can lose a clear sense of his humanness. Such an emphasis on an intellectual response to Jesus can come at the expense of a more personal, emotional response. As a result, it can seem like a person's holiness is somehow determined by his or her level of intelligence. The challenge facing the church, as was noted in the introduction to this chapter, is always one of achieving balance in our understanding of the mysteries of Christian faith.

Rediscovering the Common Touch

Earlier in this chapter, it was stated that whenever the church begins to lose its bearings, the Spirit of God leads it back to a balanced view of Jesus. During the Middle Ages, the Spirit worked through a strong reaction by "the common folk" against the image of Jesus presented by theologians who relied heavily on Greek philosophy in their teachings about Jesus. For example, people like Saint Francis of Assisi (1181–1226) recognized the need for a more personal and human understanding of Jesus, and they started a popular movement based on imitating the Jesus of the Gospels and performing other acts of piety.

A New Problem

Despite the great benefits of the popular movement, however, a new problem gradually evolved: the danger shifted from overcomplicating to *oversimplifying* the person of Jesus and his message. When the approach to understanding Jesus becomes governed by a need for emotional experiences or when people seek artificial experiences of the sacred or mysterious dimensions in life, they can become open to superstition, distortion, and

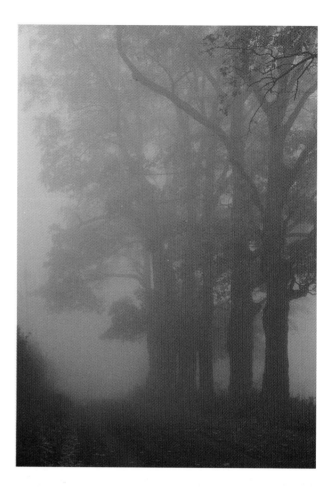

even magical understandings of Jesus. This happened in the Middle Ages as legends about Jesus began to develop, art forms began to reflect false notions about him, and people initiated popular practices that were out of touch with the Jesus of the Gospels.

The Struggle for Balance Continues

Of course, nonscriptural notions about Jesus have not been confined to the church of the Middle Ages (500 to 1500 C.E.). This recurring tension

Photo: **During the Middle Ages, popular piety sometimes distorted or clouded the understanding of Jesus.**

in the church is reflected in its celebrations of major liturgical feasts. For example, Christmas as a celebration of the birth of Jesus emerged as a major Christian feast only in the fourth century. Before that time, Easter, the celebration of Jesus' resurrection from the dead, was recognized as the central Christian feast. Christmas became the major focus of popular devotion during the medieval period, when many of the traditions that surround the Christmas season today originated.

In recent years, the Catholic church has attempted to recover the sense of Easter as the central Christian feast. Unfortunately, some Christians try to emphasize Easter by criticizing the cultural celebration of Christmas. Certainly, much of the commercialism and materialism associated with Christmas seems to conflict with the message of Jesus. But perhaps the chief lesson of this tension is that the struggle to find balance in the church's understanding of Jesus continues to this day. **5**

The Reformation

Rooted in a Desire for Renewal

Toward the end of the Middle Ages, the kind of philosophical analysis and discussion of Jesus that had characterized the church for centuries began to fade somewhat. The church became increasingly concerned about itself, its own identity, purpose, and role in the world. New teachings and ideas challenged the church's accepted traditions, and scandalous behavior among the clergy became commonplace.

These factors, combined with a rise in an awareness of the Scriptures and a heightened personal spirituality among some members of the church, led many people to yearn for a renewal of the church. Out of this climate of great tension and

desire for change, the **Reformation** was born in the sixteenth century, and *Protestant churches* (the name given those who "protested" against the Roman church) gradually formed.

Conflicts over the Church, Not Jesus

During the Reformation, ideas and teachings about Jesus were discussed more in the context of disagreement about the nature of the church than

---

5
Ask an adult Catholic fifty years old or older to describe her or his religious education. Write a report on your interview and note any connections with the material discussed on pages 271–277.

Illustration: **Many of the traditions that surround the Christmas season today—such as the Christmas crèche or manger scene—originated in the Middle Ages.**

as points of contention about Jesus. Martin Luther (1483–1546), for example, revolted not against the church's teachings about Jesus but against the Roman understanding of the church, the papacy, and the questionable practices by some leaders in the church.

For the next three centuries, Catholics and Protestants were caught up in debates about who was right and who was wrong in the church, about proper forms of church government, about the number and nature of the sacraments, and so on. Jesus and the God he revealed were no longer the focal points of the church and its members. The church was dangerously close to losing touch with the Jesus of the Gospels. 6

For Review

- Define *Scholasticism*. What can happen to the discussion of Jesus and his message when the Scholastic approach is taken to an extreme?
- What popular response did the extreme use of Scholasticism evoke during the Middle Ages? What were the dangers of the new movement?
- What factors led Catholics such as Martin Luther to yearn for a renewal of the church?
- What was the central conflict of the Reformation? What was in danger of being lost because of the conflict?

6
Using an encyclopedia or other sources, write a brief report on one of the following leaders of the Reformation: Martin Luther, Huldrych Zwingli, John Calvin. Include a discussion of the main denomination and its major characteristics that grew out of the efforts of the person you choose.

Photo: **A painting showing the interior of Saint Peter's Basilica in Rome in about 1750 during the Age of Enlightenment**

Understanding Jesus in the Modern Age

An Antireligious Cultural Climate

Though the study of science and technology as we know it today had its start in the sixteenth century, the scientific approach exploded during the eighteenth and nineteenth centuries. This period is often referred to as the *Age of Enlightenment.* With this explosion came a completely new set of problems for the church. Chief among these problems was the fact that religious beliefs and practices began to be looked down upon as "unenlightened" and obsolete. **7**

Explaining Away Jesus and God

During the Age of Enlightenment, some people tried to prove that Jesus had never even existed or, more commonly, that he had just been an ordinary person with no special relationship to the Divine. The Apostles' belief in and reaction to the Resurrection were explained away by some people as symptoms of psychological disorders. From this perspective, human beings were increasingly seen as self-sufficient, and God was explained as a "projection of people's minds," a kind of psychological "father figure" created by people through the years to explain the mysteries of the world. *Atheism,* or the rejection of a belief in any God, was proposed as a philosophical position. **8**

Defending the Faith

The Catholic church was already in a defensive posture from its experience with the Reformation. The increasingly scientific mentality of the modern age, with all the doubts and questions it raised, only strengthened the church's commitment to defend the faith against all attacks. Christian education, for example, became recognized as the process of preparing Catholics to become "soldiers of Christ," ready to stand in defense of the faith. For that role, students were expected to memorize answers to basic questions about Catholic belief.

For many Catholics, the approach of knowing correct answers intellectually did not easily lend itself to developing a love relationship with God in and through Jesus. This approach was predominant until just the last few decades in the church, but it is clearly not so today. What happened to change things so much?

The Contemporary Church

The Catholic church of today, particularly since the Second Vatican Council in the early 1960s, has

---

7
Over the ages, the church has withstood periods of severe attack and ridicule. Today, many people simply ignore the church. Which do you think is the greater threat to the church and why?

8
Write down your reflections on this statement: *Some young people my age claim they do not believe in God. But I think their problem is with religion, not God.*

■
Photo: **Roman Catholic bishops of the world at Saint Peter's Basilica during the Second Vatican Council; this council made significant changes that affected the church's understanding of Jesus.**

responded to its long history in a variety of ways, many of them dramatic, and nearly all of them touching upon its understanding of Jesus. **9**

What's New in the Church Today

Just a few of the more significant changes that have had the greatest impact on current Catholic understandings about Jesus are outlined below. These changes have taken place within the Catholic church, in large part, as a result of the Second Vatican Council.

A return to the Scriptures: For many years, lay Catholics were not encouraged to read the Scriptures as part of their private devotions, at least not nearly to the extent that Protestants were. As a result of the Second Vatican Council, however, a tremendous renewal has taken place in the church's interest in and study of the Scriptures. Today, many more Catholics are reading and studying the Gospels. The result is that more and more Catholics are getting a better sense of the Jesus of the Gospels.

A different understanding of church: A different perception of the church itself has emerged—a movement away from the sense of it as a defensive protector of the faith and toward an image of a faith-filled "People of God." With this new image has come the desire to get in touch with Christianity's roots in the early church of the Christian Testament. The idea that the church is on a journey guided by the Spirit toward the Kingdom of God is emphasized as well.

A decreased tension between religion and science: Finally, the modern faith community has experienced a new awareness of the relationship between science and religion and a decrease in

tension between the two. To a great extent, the breaking down of the division has made a renewed understanding of the Scriptures possible by opening us to the real contributions that can be made by the sciences. For example, without the help of archaeology, it would be difficult to know much about the world in which Jesus lived.

With the Impact of a Boulder

With these new developments in the church's understanding of both Jesus and itself, Catholic Christians have witnessed a dramatic change in all their expressions of faith—in their sacramental worship, in their discussions of theology and the meaning of Jesus, and in their relationships with Christians in other churches and denominations.

Recall the analogy made earlier in this chapter between the effects of changes in the church's life and understanding of Jesus and a stone being thrown into a pool of calm water. The Second Vatican Council, and the increase in biblical scholarship that was so much a part of it, struck the deceptively calm and controlled body of water that was the church of the eighteenth, nineteenth, and early twentieth centuries with the impact of a huge boulder. The resulting waves of change have

---

9
Using resources suggested by your school librarian and teacher, write a report on the Second Vatican Council. Why was it convened? In what ways did it change life in the church? What impact does it have on the church today?

■
Photo: **Today, Catholics read and study the Scriptures more, sometimes in Bible study groups, to gain a better sense of the Jesus of the Gospels.**

amounted to a tidal wave for some adult Catholics, at times completely shaking them from their roots in the past. But for many others, the effects of this monumental period in the church have only served to cleanse and purify the community of faith, thrusting them not into chaos but back to their deepest roots in the Gospel proclamation of the early community of faith.

A Shift in Starting Points

A significant change brought about by all this recent history is a shift in the starting point of the Catholic church's understandings and teachings about Jesus. As indicated by the title of this text, there are basically two choices of where to begin the understanding of Jesus: as the Jesus of History or as the Christ of Faith.

"Jesus from Above"

One choice is to start with the Risen Jesus, the Christ of Faith, and move toward the Jesus of History, an approach known as a "Christology from above." (**Christology** is the branch of theology that studies the person, role, nature, and message of Jesus.) In approaching Jesus from above, Christians *begin* their discussion and understanding of Jesus with a recognition of his special eternal relationship with God. This approach rightly affirms Jesus as the divine Son of God, sent by God to take on our humanity in order to save us from our sins and lead us to salvation. By starting from this point of view, great weight is logically given to the *Incarnation* (the formal term for the teaching that the Son of God took on human nature in Jesus). Jesus is seen as freely accepting death as a perfect offering to his Father, thereby satisfying our debts to God and opening the gates of heaven to us once

again. For the most part, this understanding of Jesus from above has been the dominant emphasis in the church's teachings about Jesus throughout its history.

A Christology from above greatly stresses Jesus' divinity. If it is not balanced with an appreciation of Jesus' humanity, however, it can give the sense that the Jesus of the Gospels is more a superman of sorts than human like us. He can seem removed from our human experience and not truly in touch with life as we experience it.

"Jesus from Below"

Today many Christian scholars and teachers increasingly refer to an understanding of Jesus that starts at the other end, so to speak—a "Christology from below." A renewed interest in the Scriptures

---

The approach of understanding Jesus "from above" begins with a recognition of Jesus' special eternal relationship with God— his divine sonship.

Photo: A fifteenth-century painting, "Madonna of Humility," by Fra Angelico and the Jesus presented in the Gospels came about in the latter half of this century. That interest is largely behind the shift from one Christology to the other. In this approach to understanding Jesus, Christians begin not with his divinity but with his humanity—his historical life as a faith-filled Jewish preacher of first-century Palestine. Primarily through studying and reflecting upon the Gospels, Christians gradually come to terms with Jesus' message about the Kingdom of God and its profound implications for their understanding of both God and Jesus.

Following the disciples' lead: Many contemporary Christians now consider how the disciples only slowly grew to a full awareness of the identity of Jesus. Then they reflect upon how they, as Christians of today, can follow the disciples' lead. Such Christians see Jesus not as a superman, but as a marvelous person who, while being divine, also truly shared in their humanity, with all its fear, loneliness, confusion, and pain; and they discover deep consolation in that knowledge. In this view of Jesus, everything about him comes together and makes sense, not just in his death on the cross but even more so in the event that followed it—the resurrection of Jesus by God.

A different path to the same truths: Many adult Catholics have been greatly freed and even relieved by this Christology from below. Their reaction is not necessarily caused by a discovery of

The approach of understanding Jesus "from below" begins with a recognition of Jesus' humanity and his historical life as a Jew born and raised in Palestine.

Photo: A twentieth-century "madonna and child" in Lebanon

"new" truths. On the contrary, what an understanding of Jesus that begins with his humanity can offer is another path to precisely the same essential truths the church has always professed.

The strength of this approach is that it follows the common journey of human persons more closely. Therefore, what were before perhaps only mysterious teachings to be memorized and accepted as truths now become far more understandable realities that can touch the hearts of believers as well as their minds. And so the Gospel of Jesus Christ can be more fully realized as the wonderful reality the church has always proclaimed it to be—the Good News that can bring joy, peace, and love to the lives of those who believe.

One Without the Other Doesn't Work

An idea expressed previously in this chapter can be repeated here: the church must constantly strive for *balance* as it searches for a sound and truthful understanding of Jesus. In other words, neither a Christology from above nor one from below is particularly helpful when taken to an extreme or followed exclusively.

An understanding of Jesus that emphasizes his divinity and ignores his humanity results in a viewpoint that can seem so "spiritual" that it is disconnected from the daily life experience of believers. Likewise, an approach that emphasizes Jesus' humanity and ignores his divinity can lead to an image of the church as a kind of "self-help group," with an image of Jesus as just a particularly good man who was its founder and model.

In the centuries preceding the Second Vatican Council, the church was in danger of losing touch with Jesus' humanity. Some have cautioned that in the decades since the Second Vatican Council, the church has overreacted to its past and is in danger of losing touch with Jesus' divinity as Lord. The constant attempt in this course has been to strive for a healthy balance in its portrait of Jesus, but one clearly rooted in an understanding of Jesus from below. **10**

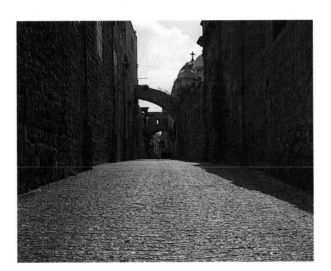

For Review

- Define *Age of Enlightenment* and describe its attitude toward religion. How did the church respond to the Age of Enlightenment?
- In the early part of the twentieth century, how did many average Catholics view Jesus?
- Name three significant changes resulting from the Second Vatican Council that have had great impact on current Catholic understandings about Jesus.
- Briefly compare the major characteristics of an approach to Jesus "from above" with an approach "from below"—including the benefits and limitations of both.

■
Jesus' disciples saw his obvious humanity first and then gradually came to recognize his divinity, in light of his death and resurrection.

Photo: The Via Dolorosa, the route believed to have been taken by Jesus on the way to his crucifixion

10
Respond in writing to this statement: *"Christology from above" and "Christology from below" are simply two different paths to the same truth.*

A Word of Encouragement to Young Catholics

Young Catholic Christians sometimes express confusion, even alienation, over what seems to be disagreement and anger among adult Catholics regarding some of the issues about Jesus discussed in this chapter and throughout this course.

For example, in a homily during Mass, the priest may interpret a scriptural passage in a way that conflicts with what a parent may have previously believed, and that becomes a topic for conversation on the car ride home. Or some adult Catholics may appear to disagree with the church leaders on an issue. Naturally, young people exposed to such conflict might begin to wonder who they should listen to in the church—or whether they should care enough to listen at all.

Those who find themselves in such circumstances might find some consolation in the following two points:

First, young Catholics today, especially those who have the opportunity to take religion courses like this one, may well be better informed and have access to more information than any previous generation of Catholics.

Second, the church today is experiencing tremendous growth in its understanding of many dimensions of Christian faith—not only Christology but also the understanding of sacraments, prayer, and spirituality. While times such as these can be quite frustrating and confusing for almost everyone, they can also be times of great excitement. The times that Catholic Christians are currently experiencing give witness to the richness of the message of Jesus as well as the depth of insight gained through the church's history. Understood in this way, times of growth and change can be seen as opportunities to make one's faith come alive.

The Journey of Faith in Jesus

Heir to a Rich History

As a young person born into the Christian community, you are heir to a profoundly rich history of some two thousand years of struggle by Christians to come to terms with the historical Jesus, whom they recognize as the Christ, their Lord and Savior.

The Decision Is Yours

The invitation and the challenge to come to your own recognition of Jesus—offered to you by the larger community and in this course—is an intensely personal one. The intent of this invitation is not to compel you to accept faith in Jesus. What can and must be asked of you, however, is that you take the person and message of Jesus seriously and recognize the questions he posed about the meaning of life as central to your own struggle to become a mature person. *What* you ultimately decide about him is for you to determine with honesty, openness, and integrity. *That* you must decide is a reality that can be postponed but not permanently avoided.

In the Company of Others

The history of the church has demonstrated that one's personal search for a response to Jesus seems to take place best in communion with other believers. The question presented in the Gospels almost two thousand years ago is put to each of us today: "Who do you say that I am?" As you search out your own answer to this question posed by Jesus, you are urged to do so in the company of others who can share that search with you—in a faith community.

A Concluding Prayer

The prayer of Paul for the Christian community at Ephesus is also meant for you as you contemplate embarking on the marvelous journey of a life lived with faith in the God revealed by Jesus:

For this reason I bow my knees before the Father, from whom every family in heaven and on earth takes its name. I pray that, according to the riches of his glory, he may grant that you may be strengthened in your inner being with power through his Spirit, and that Christ may dwell in your hearts through faith, as you are being rooted and grounded in love. I pray that you may have the power to comprehend, with all the saints, what is the breadth and length and height and depth, and to know the love of Christ that surpasses knowledge, so that you may be filled with all the fullness of God.

Now to him who by the power at work within us is able to accomplish abundantly far more than all we can ask or imagine, to him be glory in the church and in Christ Jesus to all generations, forever and ever. Amen. (Ephesians 3:14–21) **11**

For Review

- Why is it important for a person to be in community with other believers as he or she seeks to make a personal decision about Jesus?

■
Photo: **Others can share with you in the journey of searching for your own response to Jesus.**

11
Write an honest evaluation of this course and your experience of it. What were its strengths and weaknesses? What would you change about the course? What would you tell another student who is about to begin taking the course?

Glossary

Abba. An Aramaic word used by Jesus to address God. It is an affectionate and intimate term for "Father," equivalent to our *Dad* or *Daddy.*

Acts of the Apostles. A book of the Christian Testament written by Luke as a continuation of his Gospel. It is concerned with the early Christian communities after Jesus' resurrection and ascension, recording the church's development under the leadership of Saint Peter and the spread of the Good News throughout the Roman Empire by Saint Paul. Acts is sometimes referred to as "the Gospel of the Holy Spirit."

Age of Enlightenment. The historical era when the study of science and technology that had begun in the sixteenth century exploded in the eighteenth century, bringing about an emphasis on reasoning as the dominant way of viewing reality. One result of this period was that the church came to be viewed as "unenlightened" and obsolete.

"Amen" statements. A way of speaking that was unique to Jesus in his time. He used *amen* at the beginning of statements to confirm or give weight to what he was saying. The word *amen* is a Hebrew word meaning "truly" or "it is true."

Apocalypse, the. *See* **Book of Revelation.**

Apostles, the. In the Christian Testament, primarily the twelve men chosen by Jesus to be his closest followers and to play a central role during his ministry and in the future. The title *Apostle* is also applied to Saint Paul, who never met the historical Jesus.

Ascension, the. After the Resurrection, the event in which Jesus passed totally into the presence of his Father.

Babylonian Exile. The period from 598 to 539 B.C.E., when citizens of the kingdom of Judah were held captive in Babylon. This period of captivity tested the faith of the Jews, and while many lost faith in Yahweh, others (the remnant) began to live with a much deeper faith and trust in Yahweh. *See also* **Remnant, the.**

Baptism. In many religious traditions, the act of bathing in water as a sign of spiritual purification. Jesus was baptized (by John the Baptist) at the beginning of his public life. In the Christian tradition, baptism is a sacrament that celebrates a person's joining the church on its journey toward the Kingdom.

Beatitudes, the. A series of statements found in Matthew's Sermon on the Mount and in Luke's Sermon on the Plain. The Beatitudes summarize the attitudes of people whose lives are grounded in and focused on Jesus' vision of the Kingdom of God. These statements are among the most familiar and popular passages of the Christian Scriptures.

Body of Christ. Saint Paul's favorite image of the church, one that suggests an intimate connection between the Risen Jesus and the believing community. The church is understood as the visible manifestation of the Risen Jesus on earth.

Book of Revelation. The concluding book of the Christian Testament, dealing with the expectation among Christians that Jesus will return again in glory at the end of time to fulfill God's work on earth. Characterized by symbolic language and imagery, it was probably written to encourage continued faithfulness in the late-first-century Christians, who were suffering persecution for their beliefs. The Book of Revelation is often called "the Apocalypse," from the Greek word for "revelation."

Canon. The authoritative list of sacred writings accepted officially as the scriptures for a religion. The word *canon* is based on a Latin word for "rule" or "standard." The church organized and approved the canon of the Christian Testament—that is, the twenty-seven books now contained in the Christian Testament—at the end of the fourth century.

Catholic epistles. In the Christian Testament, a collection of seven letters attributed to James (one letter), Peter (two letters), John (three letters), and Jude (one letter). These letters are called "catholic" (meaning "universal") or "general" because they are addressed to believing Christians as a general audience rather than to specific individuals or communities.

Christ, the. The title that the early Christians used for Jesus in order to confess their belief that he was the Messiah, "the One sent from God," who would save them from all oppression. The word *Christ* is based on the Greek word *Christos,* meaning "the anointed one." *See also Christ of Faith; Messiah, the.*

Christianity. The movement based on Jesus' life and teachings.

Christian Scriptures. The entire Christian Bible, composed of both the Hebrew Scriptures and the Christian Testament.

Christian Testament. The section of the Christian Scriptures pertaining specifically to Christian faith and containing the Gospels; the Acts of the Apostles; various epistles, or letters; and the Book of Revelation. The Christian Testament has commonly been referred to as "the New Testament."

Christ of Faith. A title for Jesus that recognizes the tremendous Christian conviction that he was in fact raised from the dead by God and that he truly was and is forever Lord and Savior. *See also Christ, the; Jesus of History; Messiah, the.*

Christology. The branch of theology that studies the person, role, nature, and message of Jesus.

Christology from above. An understanding of Jesus that begins with the recognition of his special eternal relationship with God. A Christology from above first emphasizes Jesus' divinity and then moves toward an understanding of his humanity.

Christology from below. An understanding of Jesus that starts with an attempt to grasp his humanity and his historical roots in first-century Palestine, and then moves toward a comprehension of his divinity.

Church, the. The gathering of people who profess faith in the Risen Jesus and his message and who, through the power of the Spirit, live in loving service to all people.

Conversion. The point at which someone who has had no faith at all comes to believe in God, or the experience of someone who has had a radical change in, or deepening of, their attitude toward God and religion.

Covenant. A special agreement between two parties, either as individuals or as communities. In Jewish history, such a special relationship between the Jews and their God, Yahweh, was established during an encounter between Yahweh and Moses on Mount Sinai. There, Yahweh promised to be the caring God of the Jews, and they in turn promised to follow the dictates of the Law—in particular, the Ten Commandments. This event came to be known as the Sinai covenant. Christians believe that a "new covenant" between God and people was established through the life, death, and resurrection of Jesus.

Cross. A symbol based on the wooden structure on which Jesus was executed. The cross has taken on profound and complex significance for Christians, representing both sacrifice and victory.

Crucifixion. At the time of Jesus, a method of execution reserved for non-Roman citizens and slaves. The person being executed was nailed to or hung on a wooden cross and eventually died from bleeding, choking, the inability to breathe, or attacks by wild animals.

Damascus event. Paul's profound encounter with the Risen Jesus on the road to Damascus, which radically changed Paul's life. This event is described in the Acts of the Apostles 9:1–22.

Day of Atonement. A major, solemn Jewish feast when the Jews repent of their sins. This day involves ceremonies, fasting, prayer, and ritual bathings.

Diaspora, the. The Jews who settled in regions outside of Palestine during or after the Babylonian Exile. The word *Diaspora* is derived from a word meaning "dispersion" or "those who have been dispersed."

Disciple. In the Christian Testament, any follower of Jesus' teaching. The word *disciple* is derived from a Latin word meaning "pupil" or "follower."

Discipleship. Common among the ancient Jews, a style of teaching and learning in which a rabbi would attract disciples who would then study his teachings through lengthy discussion, memorization, and so on. In contrast, Jesus called his disciples to a personal, lasting relationship of love with the Father, and Jesus then sent his followers out to share in his mission of proclaiming the Kingdom.

Ecumenical council. A worldwide official gathering of church leaders. The first was the First Council of Nicaea, in 325 C.E., and the last was the Second Vatican Council, in the early 1960s.

Epistle. The common method of written communication in the time of Paul. The word *epistle* means "letter." *See also* **Catholic epistles; Pauline epistles.**

Essenes. A faction of ancient Jews who withdrew from Jewish society in order to observe strict religious traditions.

Eucharist, the. The sacrament in which Christians recall and enter into the mystery of Jesus' life, death, and resurrection through a sacred meal, sharing Jesus' body and blood under the signs of bread and wine. The Mass is a celebration of the Eucharist. The word *Eucharist* is based on a Greek word meaning "to give thanks."

Evangelists. A title given to the authors of the Gospels—Matthew, Mark, Luke, and John. The word *evangelist* is derived from the Greek word *evangelion,* meaning "the proclamation or announcement of good news."

Exile, the. *See* **Babylonian Exile.**

Exorcism. The act by which an "evil spirit" is driven out of a "possessed" person.

Faith sources. Documents, such as the Christian Scriptures, that came forth from believing communities as a testimony of their belief and that serve as a starting point for later believers.

Fathers of the church. Theologians trained in Greek philosophy who, at the end of the second century, tried to translate the experiences of the Apostles and earliest Christian communities into a language and mind-set that made sense to themselves and suited their audiences. This development by the Fathers of the church had profound effects on the church and its teachings.

General epistles. *See* **Catholic epistles.**

Gentile. Any person who is not a Jew.

Gospels, the. The major sources of information about Jesus, contained in the Christian Testament and attributed to Matthew, Mark, Luke, and John. The word *gospel* is derived from the very old English word *godspell,* meaning "good news."

Grace. God's unconditional and unmerited love for people.

Great Sanhedrin. The official governing body of the ancient Jews, recognized as such by the Romans. It consisted of representatives of the priestly families, the scribes and doctors of the Law, the elders (outstanding Jewish laymen), the Pharisees, and the Sadducees. In the trial of Jesus, the Great Sanhedrin acted like a kind of supreme court.

Hebrews. A collective group of ancient tribes that made up the earliest ancestors of the Jewish people. Abraham, Isaac, Jacob, and their families were Hebrews.

Hebrew Scriptures. The first part of the Christian Scriptures, containing the books of the Jewish canon. The Hebrew Scriptures have commonly been called "the Old Testament."

Heresies. False teachings about matters of faith, officially rejected by the church.

High priest. At the time of Jesus, the influential head of the priestly caste and, often, president of the Great Sanhedrin. He held a special kind of authority, like that of a king, and was appointed by the political masters of the country. During the trial of Jesus, Caiaphas was the high priest.

"I am" sayings. A distinctive literary feature of John's Gospel, in which Jesus expresses his identity and role by comparing himself to another reality. For example, "I am the living water."

Incarnation, the. The official church teaching that God took on our human nature in Jesus.

Infancy narratives. Stories about the birth of Jesus and his early life. These are found in the Gospels of Matthew (1:1–25; 2:1–23) and Luke (1:5–80; 2:1–52).

Israel. Any one of the following: (1) the political and religious group of people with whom Yahweh made the Sinai covenant, that is, those descended from the twelve tribes named for the twelve sons of the patriarch Jacob, who was called "Israel" by God; (2) after the death of Solomon, the northern kingdom, consisting of the ten northern tribes, which split off from the two southern tribes of Judah to form a separate nation and would later be destroyed by the Assyrians; and (3) more generally, the People of God, regardless of what land they occupy or what their national or political status is.

The modern state of Israel is seen by many Jews around the world as the political and national descendant of the ancient people of Israel. *See also* **Judah.**

Israelites. The descendants of Jacob, the patriarch who was given the name *Israel* by God. Later they would be known as Jews.

Jerusalem Council. An important meeting of Paul and his co-workers with Peter, James, and John in Jerusalem. Its purpose was to ensure that all the church leaders were preaching the same Good News. The meeting resulted in the decision that the mission to the Gentiles could continue *without* demanding that the Gentiles become Jews before being accepted into the church.

Jesus. A popular Jewish name of Jesus' day. It meant "Yahweh saves" or "Yahweh is salvation."

Jesus of History. A term for the historical figure Jesus of Nazareth, whose existence can be verified even by nonbiblical and non-Christian writers. The term is often used to distinguish a historical understanding of Jesus from that of him as the Christ of Faith, a conviction held only by Christians. *See also* **Christ of Faith.**

Jew. A follower of Judaism.

Jewish Law, the. A statement of the Israelites' responsibility in their covenant with Yahweh, the cornerstone of which was the Ten Commandments, given to Moses by Yahweh on Mount Sinai. More broadly, the Law is the first five books of the Hebrew Scriptures, or the Torah.

Judaea. At the time of Jesus, the region of central Palestine formerly known as Judah. It had been dominated in succession by the Persians, the Greeks, and the Romans.

Judah. The southern kingdom of the Jews (the northern one was Israel), formed by two of the original twelve tribes of Israel. This kingdom was eventually destroyed by the Babylonians, and its citizens were exiled. But a remnant, or group of the exiles, survived and returned to resettle the area under foreign domination. *See also* **Israel** (2).

Judaism. The religion based upon the remnant, who survived the destruction of the southern kingdom of Judah and later returned to rebuild it. *Judaism* is the word from which the term *Jew* is derived.

Kingdom of God. Jesus' description of the rule, or reign, of God over the hearts of people. The Kingdom is an ideal future but also a present reality that is communal in nature and implies a new relationship between God and people and between people themselves. It therefore implies the development of a new social order based on unconditional love.

Lamb of God. An image of Jesus that links him with the paschal lambs, which were slaughtered and sacrificed by the ancient Jews during Passover. This image is used in John's Gospel and in the Book of Revelation.

Last Supper. A supper during Passover that was the last meal Jesus shared with his disciples before being handed over for crucifixion. It is remembered by Christians as the occasion of the first Eucharist and commemorated by them on Holy Thursday.

Law, the. *See* **Jewish Law, the.**

Legalism. An overemphasis on minute rules and regulations. In the Jewish society of Jesus' time, it tended to dominate almost every aspect of life.

Letter to the Hebrews. A book in the Christian Testament that is a kind of extended sermon to a group of Christians who are in danger of falling away from their belief in Jesus. This book is often attributed to Paul, but scholars generally believe it was written by an unknown author.

Lord. A title commonly used in the Hebrew Scriptures as a substitute for God's name. Jews believed that calling God by name was sacrilegious, because doing so implied that people had control over God. Often the word is presented in all capital letters in the Hebrew Scriptures.

In the Christian Testament, the title is applied to Jesus in two ways: (1) as an Aramaic form of address comparable to "Sir" and (2) after the Resurrection, as a way of acknowledging that Jesus is divine and one with God. *See also* **Yahweh.**

Magi. Non-Jewish members of the priestly caste of the Persians, serving as chaplains to and representatives of the royalty. The Magi were known for their understanding of astrology and the occult. They appear in Matthew's infancy narrative.

Matriarchs, the. Women who played key roles throughout Jewish history. In the era termed "the patriarchal period," *matriarchs* refers to Sarah, Rebekah, and Rachel—the women who, with the patriarchs, founded the religion we now know as Judaism. The word *matriarch* literally means "mother." *See also* **Patriarchs, the.**

Messiah, the. The title given to the saving leader who was hoped for by the Jews. Later the title was applied to Jesus, who Christians believe fulfilled the hope of the Jews. The word *Messiah* is based on a Hebrew word meaning "anointed." *See also* **Christ, the; Christ of Faith.**

Miracles. Works of wonder or extraordinary occurrences revealing divine intervention. As performed by Jesus and written about in the synoptic Gospels, miracles were intended to show God's power over all creation and, in a special way, over the forces of sin and evil.

Nationalism. Allegiance to a nation. In Jesus' society, an excessive sense of nationalism led some Jews to believe that "love your neighbor" referred to Jewish neighbors only.

Nicene Creed. The profession of faith commonly recited in eucharistic celebrations, declaring the church's beliefs about Jesus. It was written at the First Council of Nicaea, in 325 C.E., as an official statement of the faith that was handed down by the Apostles.

Oral tradition. The sharing of carefully selected and highly polished recollections primarily by word of mouth. The early Christians' oral recollections of Jesus became the basis for the Gospels.

Palestine. A former country on the eastern shore of the Mediterranean Sea. Jesus was born and lived in Palestine, which was part of the Roman Empire at the time.

Papyrus. The material on which letters were written in Paul's day. It consisted of thin slices of the papyrus plant glued horizontally onto a backing formed by thin slices of the plant placed vertically.

Parables. A special form of storytelling, used by Jesus in the synoptic Gospels. A parable usually builds from a simile (where two very different things are compared to each other) in order to illustrate a point. The word *parable* comes from a Greek word meaning "comparison."

Paschal lambs. In Jewish history, the lambs sacrificed in the Temple during the feast of Passover, as part of the ritual of a special meal recalling the one eaten by Moses and the Israelites before the Exodus. The word *paschal* is derived from a Hebrew word meaning "to pass over." Jesus is often referred to as "the new paschal lamb" because of his sacrificial death on the cross.

Paschal mystery. The ways in which Jesus' death and resurrection constitute "a new Passover," or salvation, for history and for those who believe in him. *Paschal mystery* refers to the Christian belief that death ultimately leads to life.

Passion. The arrest, trial, and crucifixion of Jesus, recorded in all four Gospels in a detailed and generally consistent way.

Passover. The holiest and most celebrated Jewish feast, memorializing the miraculous liberation of the Israelites from Egypt, or the Exodus. In Jesus' time, Passover lasted for a week and included the ritual sacrifice of lambs in the Temple. This feast played a central role in the events surrounding the Last Supper and the crucifixion of Jesus.

Patriarchs, the. The key historical men upon whom the religion that we now know as Judaism was founded. The word *patriarch* literally means "father and leader of a family or a people." It is commonly used to identify three special Hebrew leaders—Abraham, Isaac, and Jacob. *See also* **Matriarchs, the.**

Pauline epistles. In the Christian Testament, thirteen letters either written by or attributed to Saint Paul. These were intended to support and further educate individual Christians or small communities who had been brought to belief in Jesus through the missionary work of Paul and others.

Pentecost (Christian). The event in which the gift of the Holy Spirit was poured out on the disciples, transforming them into courageous witnesses to the Risen Jesus. This is described in the Acts of the Apostles (2:1–13).

Pentecost (Jewish). The Jewish celebration of the giving of the Law to Moses. It is also called "the Feast of Weeks." The word *Pentecost* is derived from the Greek word for "fiftieth" and reflects the belief that it was fifty days after leaving Egypt before Moses received the Law on Mount Sinai. Historically, this feast also celebrated the Jews' harvesttime, a time for experiencing the wonderful gifts of Yahweh and expressing gratitude for them.

Pharisees. An influential and respected group within ancient Judaism. The Pharisees were conservative in politics in that they refused to compromise their strict faithfulness to the covenant in order to gain political power. They were liberal in matters of religion in that they accepted new developments in Jewish thought. They also accepted the elders' oral traditions regarding the Jewish Law, and this often added significantly to what was required by the written Law. The Pharisees' tendency toward legalism put them in conflict with Jesus. Their chief political and religious rivals were the Sadducees. *See also* **Sadducees.**

Priests. A group of leaders within the ancient Jewish community who were responsible for offering sacrifices in the Temple.

Pronouncement stories. A form of storytelling used in the Gospels. Stories act as setups for punch lines containing the main lessons Jesus wanted to get across.

Prophets. The special figures in Jewish history who continually challenged the people to live in accordance with their covenant with Yahweh. The word *prophet* literally means "one who speaks out."

Rabbi. In the time of Jesus, a scribe who taught in a synagogue. The word *rabbi* means "master" or "teacher."

Reformation, the. The movement that was begun in the sixteenth century by Martin Luther, protesting the Roman Catholic understanding of the church, the papacy, and questionable practices by some leaders in the church.

Reign of God. *See* **Kingdom of God.**

Religious truth. The deeper meaning that God intends to reveal to people through historical events.

Remnant, the. The group of faithful Jews from the southern kingdom of Judah who survived the destruction of Jerusalem and exile in Babylon and later returned to rebuild Jerusalem and the Temple.

Resurrection, the. The event in which Jesus was raised from the dead by God.

Revelation, Book of. *See* **Book of Revelation.**

Sabbath. A weekly day of rest and prayer, based on the Creation story in the Book of Genesis. The Jewish Sabbath lasts from Friday evening to Saturday evening. The Christian practice of Sunday worship has its origins in the Jewish Sabbath.

Sadducees. The priestly aristocracy within ancient Judaism. The Sadducees were willing to compromise with the Romans in politics, but they were conservative in religious matters (that is, they were not open to new developments in Jewish thought or to the oral traditions of the elders). The Sadducees' chief political and religious rivals were the Pharisees. *See also* **Pharisees.**

Salvation. God's work that frees humanity from the evils of sin. Salvation is a gift from God and not something achievable by human effort. Paul used the term *salvation* somewhat synonymously with the terms *redemption, righteousness, justification,* and *reconciliation.*

Sanhedrin. *See* **Great Sanhedrin.**

Scholasticism. A form of philosophy based heavily on the concepts of the Greek philosopher Aristotle and relying to a great extent on order and logic.

Scribes. Within the ancient Jewish community, leaders and scholars who were responsible for teaching the Law of Moses. They were given the title *Rabbi*. In the Gospels, scribes are often portrayed in conflict with Jesus, because they imposed such heavy burdens on people by their righteous interpretations of the Law. Most of the scribes were Pharisees.

Second Vatican Council. An official worldwide gathering of leaders of the Roman Catholic church in the early 1960s. Its teachings brought about tremendous changes in the Catholic church, including a return to the Scriptures, a different understanding of church, a decreased tension between religion and science, and a renewal of the liturgy, especially the eucharistic celebration.

Signs. *See* **Miracles.**

Sin. Most commonly thought of as a personal, freely chosen action that has negative effects on the sinner as an individual and on his or her relationships with others and with God. Sin can also be understood as a social evil that affects all people simply because we live in community with one another.

Son of God. A term used by Israelites to refer to the kings of their nation, or any particularly good man. Later the term's use was fundamentally changed in the Christian Testament to signify Jesus' special relationship with God.

Synagogues. In communities outside of ancient Jerusalem, Jewish centers where worship and the study of the Hebrew Scriptures were conducted. After the Romans destroyed the Temple and Jerusalem in 70 C.E., these institutions became the principal places of Jewish religious activity.

Synoptic Gospels. The Gospels of Matthew, Mark, and Luke. They are called "synoptic" because their authors often seem to have used the same sources or one another's work while writing. The word *synoptic* means "to see together."

Tax collectors. Jewish agents hired by the Romans to attain a quota of taxes from the Jewish people. After reaching their quota, the tax collectors could keep whatever "extra" money they managed to collect. They were clearly a despised group of men.

Temple, the. The magnificent "house of Yahweh" built by Solomon in Jerusalem. It became the center of Jewish life and worship. In 587 B.C.E., the Temple was destroyed by the Babylonians, but decades later it was rebuilt by the Jews returning from exile in Babylon. A new, much more grand Temple was built by Herod the Great before the birth of Jesus, but it was destroyed by the Romans in 70 C.E.

Ten Commandments. The cornerstone of the elaborate system of Jewish Law given to Moses by Yahweh on Mount Sinai and contained in the Hebrew Scriptures. The Commandments are followed by Jews and Christians alike, guiding ethical conduct in everyday life.

Testimonies of faith. *See* **Faith sources.**

Torah. The written version of the Jewish Law contained in the Hebrew Scriptures. Also, *Torah* is the name given to the first five books of the Hebrew Scriptures.

Tradition. Among Christians, the teachings believed to have been handed down by Jesus and the Apostles; among Roman Catholics, the essential teachings and practices that have emerged from the ongoing, lived faith of the Christian community. Roman Catholic Tradition includes the official decrees of church councils and popes that are considered true and authoritative.

Trinity. The belief and official church teaching that three divine persons—Father, Son, and Holy Spirit—exist in the one God.

Vocation. The call from God for a person to fulfill a specific and significant purpose. The word *vocation* is based on a Latin word meaning "call."

Yahweh. The Hebrew name for God, translated as "I am who am" or "I am the One who is present." The Jews of Jesus' time held this name in such reverence that they refused to pronounce it, even when reading their Scriptures. *See also **Lord.***

Zealots. In the time of the Christian Testament, a Jewish faction dedicated to achieving Jewish independence from the Roman Empire through a military overthrow of the Romans.

Index

Italic numbers are references to photos.

A

Abba, 124, 138, 139, 281
Abraham (patriarch), 47, 48, 56, 97, 103, 241
Acts of the Apostles, 19, 37, 215, 281
Adam (first man), 103
Adam and Eve, 131, 240, 246–248
Age of Enlightenment, 273, 281
agriculture, 77, 81
Alexander the Great, 58, 66
allegories, 147, 158–159
"amen" statements, 139, 281
animals, 51–52, 76, 180, 200
Antioch, Syria, 38, 225
anti-Semitism, 94
Antonia Fortress, *184*
Apocalypse, 20, 232–233, 281
Apostles, twelve, 13, 115, 116–117, 195, 225, 273, 281. *See also* disciples
Arius (heretic), 265–266
ark of the covenant, 53
Ascension, 203, 205, 281
Asia Minor, 227
Assyrians, 56
atheism, 273
Athens, *60*
authority of Jesus, 137, 176

B

Babylonian Exile, 54, 56–57, 64, 281
Babylonians, 56
baptism, 187, 281; of Jesus, 97, 109–111
B.C.E. (before the common era), 15
Beatitudes, 143, 281
Bethany, 7
Bethlehem, 7, *24, 28, 28, 102,* 103, *104, 117*
betrothal. *See* marriage
Bible. *See* Christian Scriptures
biblical scholarship, 13, 26, 274
blasphemy, 184
body and blood. *See* bread; Eucharist
body of Christ, 237–238, 251, 252–257, 260, 281
bread: in Emmaus story, 196; importance of wine and, in Jesus' time, 74, 76, 77, 78; and Last Supper, 178–179, 201; meaning of, in Lord's Prayer, 145

C

Caesarea, *32, 224*
Caiaphas (high priest), 93, 184
Cana, 7, *162*
Canaan. *See* Palestine
canon, Christian, 19, 282. *See also* Christian Testament
Capernaum, 7, *140, 161*
carpentry, 7, 28, 107
casting out demons, 157, 164, 170
catholic epistles, 19–20, 223, 282
Catholicism: effect of religious heritage on members of, 90; and Eucharist, 179; and Kingdom of God, 130; Peter's importance to, 115; and Tradition, 27; view of sin in, 132
C.E. (common era), 15
Chalcedon, Council of, 268
children: and first Passover, 51–52; and Slaughter of the Innocents, 66, 99; view of, in ancient Jewish society, 84
Christian education: effect of Scholasticism on, 269; since Second Vatican Council, 274–275; and "soldiers of Christ," 273; and young people, 278, 279
Christianity: based on Gospel teachings, 14; defined, 17, 282; Jesus' death and resurrection at heart of, 177, 183, 193, 194–195, 198; and Jesus' Dream, 119, 120, 130, 134, 254–255; and miracles, 168; Paul's importance to, 217, 255; relationship of, to Judaism, 17, 33, 38, 40

Acknowledgments

The scriptural quotations in chapters 1–5 are from the New American Bible with Revised New Testament. Copyright © 1986 by the Confraternity of Christian Doctrine, Washington, D.C. Used with permission. All rights reserved.

Unless otherwise noted, the scriptural quotations in chapters 6–13 are from the New Revised Standard Version of the Bible. Copyright © 1989 by the Division of Christian Education of the National Council of the Churches of Christ in the United States of America. Used with permission.

The scriptural quotation on page 199 is from the Jerusalem Bible. Copyright © 1966 by Darton, Longman & Todd, of London, and Doubleday & Company, of New York.

The scriptural quotation on page 208 is from the New Jerusalem Bible. Copyright © 1985 by Darton, Longman & Todd, of London, and Doubleday, a division of Bantam, Doubleday, Dell Publishing Group, of New York.

The quotation of Josephus, on page 16, is from *Jerusalem and Rome: The Writings of Josephus,* selected and introduced by Nahum N. Glatzer (New York: Meridian Books, 1960), page 145. Copyright © 1960 by Meridian Books.

The excerpts from an account by Tacitus, on pages 16–17, are quoted in *The Jesus Event and Our Response,* by Martin R. Tripole, SJ (New York: Alba House, 1980), page 42. Copyright © 1980 by the Society of Saint Paul.

The quotation of Suetonius, on page 17, is quoted in *The New Encyclopaedia Britannica,* Macropaedia, 15th edition, under "Jesus."

The excerpt on pages 42–43 is adapted from *How to Read the New Testament,* John Bowden's translation of Etienne Charpentier's *Pour lire le Nouveau Testament* (New York: Crossroad, 1982), page 19. English translation copyright © 1981 by John Bowden. Adapted with permission from the Crossroad Publishing Company.

The quotation on pages 73–74 is from *Daily Life in the Time of Jesus,* Patrick O'Brian's translation of Henri Daniel-Rops's *La vie quotidienne en Palestine au temps de Jesus* (New York: Hawthorn Books, 1962), page 15. Copyright © 1962 by Hawthorn Books.

The information on page 77 is adapted from *Harper's Introduction to the Bible,* by Gerald Hughes and Stephen Travis (New York: Harper & Row, 1981), page 104. Copyright © 1981 by Lion Publishing, Oxford, England. Used with permission from Lion Publishing.

The modern parable on page 149 is from *Fables for God's People,* by John R. Aurelio (New York: Crossroad, 1988), page 7. Copyright © 1988 by John R. Aurelio.

The excerpt on page 171 is from *Jesus: A Gospel Portrait,* by Donald Senior (Dayton, OH: Pflaum Publishing, 1975), page 131. Copyright © 1975 by Donald Senior.

The illustration on page 204 is reprinted with permission from Saint Joseph New American Bible (New York: Catholic Book Publishing Company, 1987). Copyright © 1987 by Catholic Book Publishing Company, New York, N.Y. All rights reserved.

The creed on page 267 is the English translation of the Nicene Creed by the International Consultation on English Texts.

Photo Credits

Large cover photo and front cover, inset photo: Erich Lessing

Back cover, inset photo: Z. Radovan, Jerusalem

The Adoration of the Magi; Fra Angelico and Fra Filippo Lippi; National Gallery of Art, Washington, D.C.; Samuel H. Kress Collection: page 99

D. L. Baldwin, ProFiles West: page 124

The Bettmann Archive: pages 27, 37, 176

F. H. C. Birch, Sonia Halliday Photographs: pages 234, 257

Daniel Blatt: pages 21, 22, 40, 73 (inset), 76, 78, 95, 106, 155, 184, 191, 192, 197, 209, 225, 260, 277

The photo on page 43 is reproduced from *The Faces of Jesus,* by Frederick Buechner, with photographs by Lee Boltin, published by Harper & Row, with permission from Stearn Publishers, Ltd.

Paul Buddle Photography: page 241

Ernesto Cardenal: page 101

Mike Carr, ProFiles West: page 261

Catholic News Service: page 273

Christ Among the Doctors; Master of the Catholic Kings; National Gallery of Art, Washington, D.C.; Samuel H. Kress Collection: page 269

Christ in Majesty; Maria Antoinette Evans Fund; courtesy of Museum of Fine Arts, Boston: page 203

CLEO Freelance Photography: pages 119, 134, 159, 246, 252, 265

Gail Denham: pages 12, 13, 141, 145, 200, 243, 247, 249 (right), 251, 253, 278 (left)

Editorial Development Associates: pages 11, 60, 190 (right), 211, 228, 231 (right), 233, 236, 263

Sonia Halliday Photographs: pages 28, 29, 232

Tim Haske, ProFiles West: page 125

Jack Hoehn, Jr., ProFiles West: page 135

Michael Holford: page 58

Interior of Saint Peter's, Rome (between 1746 and 1754); Giovanni Paolo Pannini; National Gallery of Art, Washington, D.C.; Alisa Mellon Bruce Fund: page 272

Phil Lauro, ProFiles West: page 245

Jean-Claude Lejeune: pages 255, 270, 278 (right)

Erich Lessing: pages 2, 44, 53, 68, 104, 113, 136, 156, 157, 164, 175, 177, 229

Patricia Barry Levy, ProFiles West: page 144

The Madonna of Humility; Fra Angelico, workshop of; National Gallery of Art, Washington, D.C.; Andrew W. Mellon Collection: page 275

Maryknoll: page 238

Mary Messenger: pages 120, 149, 235, 242

National Aeronautics and Space Administration (NASA): page 98

Tom Nebbia: pages 14, 26, 30, 31, 85, 102, 105, 107, 112, 152, 207, 276

Richard Nowitz: pages 6, 19, 24, 39, 47, 62, 71, 89, 96, 117, 118, 122, 140, 153, 158, 173, 174, 183, 214, 227, 231 (left)

Paul Pavlik: pages 146, 190 (left), 230, 244

Z. Radovan, Jerusalem: pages 32, 46, 61, 70, 73 (large), 80, 87, 91, 108 (left and right), 139, 148, 150, 210, 213

Lorraine O. Schultz: pages 17, 84, 127, 161, 162, 196, 224

Alfons Senfter: pages 69, 81, 116, 222

Shaffer Photography: pages 133, 189, 201, 256

Vernon Sigl: pages 237, 258

Skjold Photography: pages 25, 38, 41, 121, 239, 249 (left), 274

Jane Taylor, Sonia Halliday Photographs: page 181

Wheater, Maryknoll: page 131

Bob Winsett, ProFiles West: page 279